Painted and Engraved by J.T. Smith, Engraver of the Antiquities of London & Environs.

IOHN CRANCH,

Born at Kingsbridge in Devonshire, 12.th of Oct.r 1751 Aged 44;

*Fellow of the American Society of Arts & Sciences, Painter of an unique Picture of
the Death of Chatterton; & Author of the Oeconomy of Testaments; &c.
Engrav'd from a Picture, which, with the Death of Chatterton, is in the possession of
Sir James Winter Lake, Bar.t F.S.A.*

* Vide. Langworthy's attempt to promote the Commercial Interests of Great Britain.

Publish'd Oct.r 20. 1793, by N. Smith, Rembrandt's Head, May's Buildings, St Martins Lane.

John Cranch

Uncommon Genius

The Life and Achievements of a Self-Taught
Polymath, Artist and Wit from Devonshire

by

John W. Lamble

The Wolborough Press
Cambridge

First published in Great Britain in 2019 by

The Wolborough Press
Cambridge

A division of Wolborough Publishing
www.wolboroughpublishing.com

ISBN 978-1-9161445-0-7

A catalogue reference for this publication is available from the British Library

Printed in England

Dedicated to the Memory of

Cranch William Lamble

1977-2014

Nothing is more common than for persons who have not genius to mistake it for something else in those who have.

John Cranch

CONTENTS

ILLUSTRATIONS

Introduction

John Cranch (1751-1821) who is the subject of this biography was an autodidact, lawyer, writer, artist and antiquarian of considerable accomplishment as well as being a witty fellow. One fact of importance in his life was that his uncle Richard Cranch was the brother-in-law and great friend of John Adams, second President of the United States and, as a result, John Cranch had considerable interaction with America before and after it acquired independence and he was elected to two of its learned societies which still exist today.

From this point onward the subject of this biography will be referred to as JC.

JC clearly had admirers of his learning and other achievements during his lifetime and copies of the portrait engraving of him by J.T. Smith, which forms the frontispiece of this volume, were quite widely distributed. He is also the subject of an entry in the British *Dictionary of National Biography*, modest, outdated and inaccurate as it is. But he has been largely forgotten? Why? When his paintings appeared at auction during the 20th Century, several were acquired by important collections in the UK and abroad because, belatedly, the importance of his art was appreciated. As a painter he often depicted domestic life of ordinary people and tradesmen, popular themes of Dutch art of the period but not widely fashionable in England during JC's lifetime or for some time afterwards. JC's role as mentor to the young John Constable is acknowledged nowadays but Constable too suffered a long delay before appreciation of naturalistic paintings developed in England. During the relative eclipse of interest in JC, several of his most notable paintings seem to have been lost. However, his works still occasionally surface at auction for the first time, having been in private hands for the intervening two centuries. What should also be a claim to fame was his pioneering antiquarian work but despite the importance attached to preservation of ancient things in Britain nowadays this does not extend to the pioneers who sought to alert the world to the destruction of ancient things and attempted to preserve what they could.

Individual owners of paintings and other artefacts associated with JC whom the author has encountered during the writing of this biography have expressed high regard for him but they have often known little of the man or other work he did apart from their own possessions.

Another reason for his relative obscurity is that he never married and had children who might have better preserved the record of his life. This was not the result of reluctance to marry or distaste for family life on his part and records exist of several close relationships he had with women. More than once he thought marriage was close but it never happened. His attitude to the opposite sex seems quite modern, for example, he knew personally and appreciated the work of the bluestocking author Hannah More.

A further reason was the fact that he was a polymath and individuals who knew of his achievements in one field either knew nothing of his talents in others or failed to appreciate them. In fact, his near abandonment of his legal practice, which bored him, attracted some *post mortem* criticism from a few provincial philistines who knew him little or even not at all. This biography will not dignify them by giving them much attention.

Also, he moved around the country to a degree unusual for the period. There were actually prolonged periods of his long life which were centred on Kingsbridge and Axminster in Devonshire, London and finally Bath in Somersetshire but friends and acquaintances in one place often knew little of his activities elsewhere. Even within London JC had multiple changes of address because he usually lived in lodgings which changed from time to time. Indeed, only modern means of disseminating information such as the internet have made practical the collection of some of the widely scattered information which has made this biography possible, albeit still leaving many gaps in his life story.

Finally, there was the factor of snobbery in England during JC's life and after. The inability to give credit to an autodidact from the provinces by individuals who were gentlemen and little else probably accounts for some of JC's undeserved lack of posthumous fame. For example, JC's eager antiquarian activity in Bath, which would nowadays be called 'rescue archaeology', resulted in his discoveries of Roman remains which formed the founding collection of the first museum there dedicated to this important era in its history. There was some acknowledgement of this work in his lifetime and for a while afterwards but there is no recognition today of his role in preserving many historic artefacts which would undoubtedly otherwise have been destroyed.

It is to be hoped that this biography will dispel to some degree the obscurity into which this gifted and, above all, very civilised man has fallen. The author was brought up knowing of JC's existence from an early age and during the years it has taken to research and write about his life, admiration and affection for the man has developed considerably. If this effort has been a success the reader may come to share those feelings.

The uneven availability of information has determined the structure of this biography. There are chapters which chart what has been discovered of JC's life and activity in the four towns where he spent most of his life. However, more information is available about some aspects of his life than others and so additional chapters have been dedicated to his career as a painter, his relationships with women and his interaction with Americans.

It seems important here to mention one extraordinary coincidence. In the 18th century the Cranch family produced not just one formidable autodidact who lived in the small town of Kingsbridge, Devonshire and was called John, but two who were distant cousins and rough contemporaries. This 'other' John Cranch (1785-1816) of his own volition studied marine organisms and in consequence was befriended by the well-known zoologist Dr William Elford Leach of the British Museum who recommended him as naturalist to an expedition to explore the River Congo, where he died of a fever. A number of marine organisms are named after him. There is no record to say the paths of JC and this cousin ever crossed although both came from branches of the family traditionally engaged in cloth production and they would certainly have been aware of each other's existence.

Editorial policies

Although it has often been possible directly to quote the words of JC and others, this volume is not the sort of formal 'life and letters' where every dot and comma of punctuation is faithfully reproduced. Use of English words among educated people has changed remarkably little in two centuries and the quotations are faithful transcriptions of the texts but to improve readability, spelling and punctuation have been silently edited to more current British usage. On the rare occasions when an additional or replacement word has been necessary for sense, it is enclosed in square brackets. Often only extracts from documents have been quoted and ellipses at the beginning of each quotation indicate where this has been done. Correspondents' retained drafts or copies of letters are not distinguished from those known for certain to have been posted and received. When crossed-out text is still legible, and seems of sufficient interest to be quoted, it is incorporated in italics. Dates have all been expressed in the current British form of day, month, year.

A familiar problem to any biographer is that of distinguishing family members with the same given names and to cite life-dates every time an individual is mentioned is clumsy. As mentioned above, the subject of this biography is uniquely identified here solely by his initials but four other John Cranches are also discussed in the text although their relationship to JC has been made as clear as possible. In the index, a numbering system is adopted where individuals with the same name need to be distinguished. Another problem worth mentioning here is the great prevalence of the name *Elizabeth* among JC's relations and acquaintances. Contractions of the name, e.g. Eliza or Betsy, were in common use at the time and where it is known which was generally applied to an individual it is used in the text.

Sources and References

In general, references to printed or handwritten documents have been preferred. Occasionally the internet has been the only source of the information discovered but, in the experience of the author, websites can be more ephemeral than books. A high proportion of JC's surviving correspondence is to be found in the Rare Books Department of Boston Public Library (BPL) in Massachusetts, U.S.A. This material has been catalogued but, in several instances, bundles of letters on connected subjects have been given the same identifying code. It will thus become apparent to the reader that different letters written on a variety of dates sometimes have the same catalogue reference.

Acknowledgements

I thank my Wife, Andrea, for help with numerous aspects of this project, notably for transcribing many handwritten documents by authors of whom few wrote as legibly as JC himself. I am also grateful to Robert D. Mussey Jr who allowed me to benefit from his numerous transcriptions of the Cranch documents housed in Boston Public Library and gave support in other ways. David Knapman kindly guided me around Axminster and gave me the benefit of his considerable local knowledge. Mark Trewin and Rachel Ponting of the Devon Heritage Centre have assisted, as have Suz Massen of the Frick Art Reference Library, David H. Solkin of the Courtauld Institute, Sophia Dahab of the Grolier Club, Martin Maw of Oxford University Press, Abbie Weinberg of the Folger Shakespeare Library, Nicholas Rogers of Sidney Sussex College, Katharyn White of the Peabody Essex Museum, Kimberly Reynolds of Boston Public Library, Gwen Fries of the Massachusetts Historical Society, Ann Lidstone of Kingsbridge History Society, Anne Buchanan of Bath Local Studies Library and Ashley Cataldo of the American Antiquarian Society. Thanks are also due to Roy Sims, Arnold and Alexandra Wilson, Peter Seddon, Kathleen Menendez, Lisa Coombes, Caroline Gardner, John Harris, Lowell Libson and John Cunningham.

Chapter 1

Kingsbridge and Axminster

The Cranch Family

A longstanding oral tradition was that the family was descended from an immigrant to Devonshire called Krantz. However, the oldest surviving written records only take the name back to the 1600s and then only with the 'Cranch' spelling. By the time of John Cranch's (JC) generation the Cranches were quite widespread in Devonshire with tendrils extending elsewhere, even as far as America. There was considerable pride of family and this extended down to the author's great grandmother, born Clara Cranch, who bestowed Krantz on her younger son (the author's grand-father) as his second given name. Certainly, whilst making no claim to social rank, the Cranches were generally successful in avoiding the lower forms of employment such as agricultural labourer. JC's branch of the family were skilled tradesmen in wool-processing and leather-working and acquired education well beyond the average for their time and material circumstances. Not the least consequence of this was that many of the Cranch womenfolk could read and write well at a time when that was not a given in either the English provinces or America.

JC, known as Jack to his family and friends, was born on the 12th October 1751 in Kingsbridge, Devonshire, the seventh of nine children[1]. His father, Joseph, who was married to Elizabeth Lidstone from Buckland, Devonshire, was a saddler and farmer. Little information about Joseph has been found but judging by the tone and content of JC's surviving letters to him he must have been an amiable man, quite well educated and posses-sed of a sense of humour. Little seems to be known about JC's mother and it appears that she had already died by the time JC went to live in Axminster in his early twenties. A letter from JC to his father in 1774[2] indicates that he loved and admired both his parents:

"…No doubt it ever was, and will yet be, a great pleasure to our excellent father to instruct his children in the ways of virtue, and to imprint himself (as it were) on their hearts, if yet susceptible of so noble an impression. Therefore, I earnestly require, that you will add, in writing, to that

1

previous testimony which I received of my late mother's affection to her children."

JC's uncle Richard (1724-1812) was Joseph Cranch's youngest brother who emigrated to America in 1746. He became an important figure in JC's life although the two can never have met. Joseph and Richard were part of a family of seven children, the eldest of whom, John, acquired a scholarship to train for the non-conformist ministry[3] but died before JC was born. Richard and Joseph were brought up to trades, in Richard's case initially related to the wool processing business. A final important member of JC's parents' generation was his aunt Mary who married Joseph Palmer while still in Devonshire and emigrated with him to America on the same ship as Richard[4]. Chapter 2 is devoted to JC's interactions with his American relations and acquaintances.

Of his own generation JC's self-declared favourite sibling was his brother William (1754-1820), who succeeded in their father's business as a saddler in Kingsbridge but who shared some of JC's enthusiasm for antiquarian research[5]. Of great importance to the survival of the written record of the family is his eldest sister Mary, born in 1742, who married James Willcocks who was a friend of JC. James died in 1808 but she and her sons (the eldest of whom was also called James) remained in close touch with JC towards the end of his life and their correspondence is an important source of information for this biography. She ultimately survived JC by three years.

Another sister of JC who also should be noted is Elizabeth (b.1744) who married James Elworthy and moved to London where he opened a chandlery business at 1 Broad Street. Their household became something of a hub for family affairs involving both London and America, serving for quite a while as a family post office. They also had rooms to let and JC made their house his base when he first moved to London. She died in 1794 not very long after JC went to live in London. JC's sister Hannah (b.1746) married William Bond, a goldsmith turned clockmaker who emigrated to America. Their son (JC's nephew), William Cranch Bond, married his English cousin, Selina Cranch of Kingsbridge, and remained in close touch with his English relatives including JC.

To complete the list of JC's siblings, the first child baptised Joseph (b.1741) died of smallpox at 2 months but a younger brother born in 1748 was also named Joseph and lived a normal span in Kingsbridge. He was the direct ancestor of the author of this biography. JC's sister Ebbett (b.1750) also went to America and lived there with the Bond family but died in her 40s without marrying. The lastborn child, Frances, (b.1758) also died in infancy.

Early Life and Education

JC writing in middle age described his 18-year old self as having been 'self-lettered'[6] from which we can assume that he had little formal education beyond learning to read and write[a]. As a child he appears to have learned no Latin which would have been a *sine qua non* of secondary education at the time. However, his earliest surviving letters indicate that by early adulthood he was widely-read and had learned to write English well with exceptionally neat handwriting and an excellent vocabulary. One must deduce from this that individuals in Kingsbridge who were wealthy enough to own books viewed the intelligent youth sympathetically and allowed him to read through their libraries. For non-business purposes JC early on adopted a droll, ironic style of writing which still amuses two centuries later.

Not a great deal is known of JC's early childhood but at the age of 10 or 11 he started an apprenticeship of ten years' duration with a Kingsbridge lawyer called Knowling Hawkins, whom he later described as "a very honest gentleman"[6]. There is no evidence to suggest that any specific training was provided for him and no formal indenture has been found. It is fair to surmise that JC was a messenger-boy who might also have done lowly clerking jobs such as copying documents. He later described this period of his life as 'unprofitable' by which he would have meant there was neither monetary reward nor any route to advance his career nor opportunity to develop his wider cultural interests. It is apparent though that his lifelong love of reading and wide-ranging intellectual curiosity arose during this period.

---

[a] There was a grammar school in Kingsbridge originally endowed in 1670 by one Thomas Crispin (the building is now the Cookworthy Museum) and while the record of its functioning during the 18th century is patchy, dated carvings in its woodwork by schoolboys, including one Alfred Cranch in 1763, indicates some sort of ongoing activity at the relevant period. However, as indicated above, JC will never have attended the school but is said to have set about learning Latin in early adult life.

Chapter 1

The Hawkins family were prominent in Kingsbridge during the 18th and 19th centuries. Knowling Hawkins (b.1719) who employed JC was descended from the famous Admiral Sir John Hawkins who with his relation Sir Frances Drake was instrumental in repelling the Spanish Armada. In Polwhele's *History of Devonshire* John Hawkins was recorded as "the first Englishman that engaged in the slave trade" and, in a marginal handwritten note in his copy, JC added, "Would to God that he had been the last[6]". Knowling's nephew, Abraham Hawkins, was the author of a book about early-19th century Kingsbridge[7]. He was a captain of militia, Deputy Lieutenant of Devonshire, Latin scholar and Justice of the Peace who according to the family historian, Mary Hawkins, was "the terror of Kingsbridge[8]". However, he obviously had a soft spot for the two clever Cranch cousins born in Kingsbridge, the marine biologist and JC of whom he said in his book:

> "…He was born at Kingsbridge on the 12th day of October 1751 and is at present resident at Bath but practised some years at Axminster as a respectable attorney. He is a man of real abilities and has displayed taste, talents, application and discrimination, in various ways and on numerous occasions; is particularly partial to antiquarian researches and does great honour to his native place."

Not much is known about JC's religious upbringing but later he was to demonstrate knowledge of even obscure parts of the Bible. Throughout his life he made friends with Church of England priests although possibly more because of shared intellectual interests than spiritual matters. When he died, his funeral was in the local Anglican church and it is therefore fair to assume that he never adopted the non-conformism of his Cranch forebears. In a letter of 1783 he described[9] Edmund Rack, the prominent Quaker, as "his very particular friend" and in 1786 had an invitation to visit him in Bath[10]. But however congenial they found each other's company it would again probably have been shared intellectual interests which brought them together and there is no reason to believe that JC ever considered becoming a Quaker. He would certainly have taken for granted certain basic Christian beliefs, for example, he and his relatives frequently mentioned their hopes for an agreeable life after death in their surviving letters, but no record has been found to suggest that he discussed his own religious convictions in detail with anyone. It would not be surprising if he was a Deist since that belief system was quite prevalent among cultured people of the time.

One aspect of provincial life for an ambitious youth in England of those times was the process of unlearning the local dialect. Cranch certainly knew local usages but apart from a surviving letter intentionally written in local idiom[11] he didn't use it himself. In fact, later, he was to admonish his lifelong friend the lawyer John Andrews of Modbury in Devonshire about this[12]:

> "...But to the point, I cannot but agree with those who object that your pronunciation of many common words is barbarously provincial and contrary to general or national usage. For instance, you are the only gentleman and, indeed, now almost the only man I know who *kaalth* what other gentlemen...only *call*. Yet surely those who so object cannot but be aware that your habits of speech are now too strongly fixed to be altered...I luckily found myself in many of these errors several years ago and still more luckily made up my mind to forsake them, which I resolutely did."

It can be deduced from this that they must have been *very* good friends although they were later to have a falling out over politics.

A list of local Devonshire dialect words can be found in an 1874 book about Kingsbridge[13] and many of these were in local oral use well into the 20th century. But JC's writing seems very modern in its use of language with almost all his words still in general use today with identical meanings.

When he was eighteen years old JC wrote what must be his earliest surviving work of art, a prose poem of thirty stanzas (Fig. 1) on the subject of Buckfast Abbey[b] in Devonshire which was then a romantic ruin, not to be replaced by the current architectural pastiche until the 20th century. What survives is a copy he retained until middle age and then pasted into his copy of Polwhele's *History of Devonshire*[6]. Whilst he apparently had slightly modified the poem it was not sufficient to prevent him from still writing notes quite critical of his youthful effort. These are interesting because in them he recognized his youthful borrowings from Addison, Milton and Shakespeare, a sign of the extent of his youthful reading. JC had intended to dedicate the poem to a local worthy, William Ilbert of Bowringsleigh, West Alvington, which is close to Kingsbridge. Ilbert was

---

[b] When he wrote his poem, JC named the Abbey 'Buckfest' although it became more commonly known as 'Buckfast' during his lifetime. However, when he later worked for Lord Petre's estate JC was able to confirm from old documents that the original name of the abbey had been Buckfestre.

Sheriff of Devonshire in 1768 and described by JC as an 'accomplished gentleman'. JC's diffidence meant that the work was never presented to Ilbert although it seems likely that he had hoped by so doing to impress a dignitary who might have been able to advance his career. In the event it was another member of the gentry who provided employment which, if it was not much of a promotion, at least took him away from home and later gave him opportunities to develop.

Axminster

From the late 16th century until 1793 the Manor of Kingsbridge belonged to the noble Petre family[7]. Thus it is not too surprising that a bright young man of the town who had worked for a lawyer and possessed excellent handwriting might come to the attention of Lord Petre's agent, John Knight, and get offered a job as clerk in Axminster at £10 or £15 per annum (depending on which source you believe).

JC wrote to his father on 29th December, 1771 to describe his journey to Axminster and the start of his employment[14]. This letter is worth quoting from extensively because it gives an idea of travel conditions in Devonshire then as well as an introduction to the nature of JC's employment. On modern roads the distances described are as follows: Kingsbridge to Newton Abbott 21.5 miles, Newton Abbott to Exeter 17.1 miles and Exeter to Axminster 32.7 miles. One assumes that JC got a lift to Newton Abbott and had hoped to join the stage coach there which would have carried him all the way to Axminster but was "disappointed" which presumably means he could not get a seat. So, evidently, he decided to walk to Exeter:

> "...[I stayed at] Newton [Abbot] on Saturday night and setting out for Exon [Exeter] from thence on Sunday morning 3 o'clock I had a very pleasant walk, met nothing worth mentioning besides a spring of good water in going up Haldon [Hill] and Dr. Adams's two sons in going down. I walked very leisurely and before 12, got to the 7 Stars[c] where I dined and having viewed the New Bridge works changed my stockings and got my shoes polished and I rebetook myself to my staff and bundle. I found

---

[c] The Seven Stars Inn in JC's time was in Okehampton Street, Exeter. It continued to function as a public house until WWII when it was bombed. It has been replaced by a modern pub nearby of the same name.

myself before one at the Bear[d] in Southgate Street enquiring after my box and the master of the waggon to whose own proper person I resolved to apply on account of the preceding day's mishap, the consequence of which now ached in my leg bones. This monarch of the highway being deeply engaged on business (that is to say) with a rump of beef and fowls in the parlour I waited half an hour before I could get an audience and as we had settled the necessary preliminaries I sat down by the fire and called for some beer in company with the waggoner and a drowsy council of Hackney coachmen and deputy bootcatchers.

Dick and Jack Burnell went with me to the waggon warehouse and, with some difficulty, got my box admitted to be fixed outside the waggon, for on the inside there was but tolerable room left for the persons of myself and the other two passengers; a woman and a boy, both blacks and natives of Jamaica going to London. The regard which the people in Exeter (who were acquainted with the woman) had for her and partly (you may suppose) the novelty of such a group of figures brought us together a mob of about 30 people so that upon the whole I thought my case had more resemblance to the apparatus of an execution than of a transportation and had actually put my mouth out of the waggon and told one of the boys to cry up the Last Dying Speeches before my prudence overtook my fancy.

It was exceeding dark and near an hour and half before we had jolted as far as Heavitree [Exeter's gallows] which I began to be apprehensive would be the place of my execution, either by squeezing or suffocation: for here the rascal of a waggoner had appointed to take up 4 travellers more…all remonstrances were [in] vain.

The company when we started from this horrid place consisted of the following particulars: Nancy Yaya and Blackey Jacky (the Creolians) a mango parrot, a tabby cat and 2 canary birds, a Sergeant of Marines and his trull and a great bouncing country lass under the protection of a little prinking Macaroni tailor of a yard high who (notwithstanding his deficiency in point of measure) had found means to cabbage the girl's good graces. This animalcula (being tired when we arrived about 4 miles the other side of the gallows) resigned what little room he was allowed to occupy to a squat brawny fellow from Cornwood who had very little to say during the expedition and took up more room than attention. Our outside passengers, whom I should by rights have considered first, were of too high a quality for the inside of a waggon, the one a Scotch drummer who seemed in a fair way to have the command of a regiment early in the next warm weather season [i.e. he was lousy] and the other being one of his Majesty's sea-subjects travelling 50 miles beyond London by virtue of

---

[d] Through the 17th and 18th Century, the Bear Inn was an important Exeter hostelry used as a terminus for carrier services around Devonshire and beyond. It was noted for the number of packhorses it could accommodate, before the waggon took over as the turnpikes improved. It ceased to be an inn in the 1850s and was demolished to make way for a church in the 1880s.

and under the Statute of Rogue and Vagabond with vermin enough to colonise a French Navy.

Nearly 13 hours was I dragged along without having the least glimpse of house, hedge or sky and under the most melancholy waking apprehension in regard for my box which all the while hung tottering like a precipice over the front of the waggon the motion of which with the sounds of 6 & 30 bells of different sizes tied about the horses' necks made such dismal and disconsolate noise as served only to increase my vexation. About half after 7 o'clock I got out on a large open down called Shute Hill 2 miles from Axminster at which latter place to my great satisfaction I got safe with my baggage at half past 8 having took a final leave of waggons and bid adieu to the poor souls who were going forwards.

I met with a middling reception at Mr Knight's who brought me into his Clerk's Office and with great dexterity counted about 50 skins of parchment of which together with a room, a fireless fireplace in it and half a set of tools, he made me by way of introduction. I got some breakfasting and about noon went to bed where I lay 'till 9 o'clock this morning.

I have but just seen my Mrs. She is more than 6 foot high and looks pleasant. They have a son 2 years old, a daughter of 6 and another of 4 at home who are all become my playfellows. The eldest son of 11 years is at a boarding school in France. Axminster is a miserable looking place in itself. It lies on the side of a hill and consists of near 20 little dirty lanes which they call streets, with here and there a pretty house. Very pleasant country lies round it and upon several small elevations you can see 40 villages at once.

Mr Knight's is a fine spacious house out of town in the middle of a large square champagne of 4 or 5 acres. We are 4 miles from Lyme [now Lyme Regis] which is our nearest sea.

Hark! The bell strikes one.

We take no note of time but from its loss.

Good night and a Merry Christmas,

John Cranch"

There is plenty of evidence that JC was a great walker as the following (probably somewhat exaggerated) description confirms[15]:

"...Mr Cranch, who is very fond of walking and thinks twenty or thirty miles a day necessary for a sedentary life and who talks of ten miles as a morning or evening airing, invited us to take a walk around the town [Axminster] and upon some of the eminences which command extensive prospects."

It is scarcely surprising that there are several mentions of accidents affecting his legs in JC's correspondence during the course of his life although none seems to have permanently disabled him. There is also evidence that he rode horses for longer journeys, on occasion, as might be expected of the son and brother of saddlers, but none that he ever owned a horse.

JC's opinion of Axminster as a town never improved. Writing in middle age[6] he noted that: "Axminster stands on a naturally very beautiful situation but as a town (I lived in it 15 years) it always appeared to me to have been constructed merely by divine permission – without the least symptom of human taste, prudence or common sense". The dwelling where JC now found himself was Hilary House[16] in Chard Street, which had been built in 1761 for one Amos Callard, who was steward of Lord Petre's estate. He sold it in 1763 to John Knight, Callard's successor as steward to the Petre estate and JC's immediate superior.

Knight was a Roman Catholic as was the Petre family and added a chapel to his house and brought a Roman Catholic priest, William Sutton, to live with him. Sutton is said to have helped JC with his continuing studies, *inter alia* teaching him Latin[17]. Now followed two tedious years for JC. Almost immediately he must have sought an escape because on the 17th December 1773 in a letter to his father[18] he thanked his parent for applying on his behalf to a Mr Westlake for alternative employment and went on to write:

> "…You approve of my leaving Mr K[night] – I rejoice at it – and on the other hand dread running the least risk of subjecting myself again to tyranny and an ungenerous and unmanly temper. I don't mention nor support any such qualities in Mr. Westlake – but another consideration is that if I have any talent it is high time to set about improving it for my own advantage, and that cannot be done in a state of servitude either like this I am going out of or that which I am invited to go into; the employments of both being mere drudgery from which I can receive no improvement; and an employment in which one can't improve that willingly would, is certainty very unprofitable and disagreeable. If therefore you approve of my declining to accept Mr W.'s offer, I desire you will forward the enclosed letter to him immediately. I will consult with you in what course to steer next when I see you. I am rather easy about that matter, since according to the old saying, 'there are but few difficulties to a willing mind'… Though I gave K[night] 2 months' notice of quitting his service he insists on my staying till 28 January and, as the consequence of a non-compliance might in all likelihood be no small pecuniary loss to me, I submit."

Drudge JC may have been but clearly Knight trusted him and recognized his ability because further on in the same letter he writes:

> "…Our eldest son and heir [Knight's eldest son William] is just arrived from the English School at Bruges in the French Netherlands where he has been upwards of 2 years – but upon the late annihilation of the Jesuitical Society (of which most of his tutors were members) he was sent for to come home. The essentials of his education have been apparently neglected for, though he has some aptitude and is of an amiable disposition, he can neither write nor read English. He is now under my management of which I am not a little proud but, however, I shall take care to bring him to walk well upon his foot, before I put him on horseback."

JC next found employment as a clerk with Simon Bunter, a well-off local attorney, who lived in Oak House (Fig. 2) a little further downhill on Chard Street towards the centre of Axminster.

Unusually for that part of the world the splendid Oak House was constructed mainly of brick and was to be described later by Pevsner as "the best house in Axminster". It has had subsequent 'lives' as a school and boarding house and is, at the time this is being written, a care home and visibly in need of some maintenance. Whether JC ever lived there we do not know but he will certainly have worked there. Simon Bunter's wife, Meloria, died in 1774, the same year as JC became his apprentice. Clearly Bunter had taken a shine to JC who must have been a bright, organised and diligent employee.

The opulent memorial[e] to Bunter's wife can still be seen in Axminster church and by his later account JC was entrusted with writing its inscription. According to one source[19] JC had great interest in epitaphs and collected them, although his collection has not been found.

As relevant extracts from a letter[20] to his father from JC dated 9th December 1774 make clear, Bunter set about persuading JC to train as an attorney:

> "…I arrived here from London with Mr Bunter this day about one o'clock, since which we've heard nothing but ringing and congratulation. Our

---

[e] Meloria's brother, Nathaniel Gundry, is recorded on her memorial as being a Justice of the Court of Common Pleas. Polwhele, in his History of Devonshire, describes him as Lord Chief Justice and in a marginal note in his copy JC wrote, "I do not think Gundry was ever Chief Justice: if he was then I have put a wrong inscription on Mrs Bunter's monument."

principal business in town was the disposal of a large estate in this neighbourhood. As I was honoured with no inconsiderable share in the transaction, one of the parties (very opportunely!) presented me with a handsome watch. My worthy patron Mr Bunter plies me daily with the most forcible eloquence, to be – a Lawyer! If I remember rightly I have said somewhat to you on this subject already, and I would now gladly have your advice thereon, in order to which it may not be unnecessary for you to be informed touching Mr B.'s proposals and my own inclinations respecting the matter. In the first place I must promise that Mr B. is a gentleman of great good sense, valuable connections, affluent fortune and unbounded generosity. I am rivetted in the opinion that his regard for me is not the common one of the master to his servant and I have depended much too far on my discernment and observation, if there is not something friendly or even paternal in it. His eldest nephew (who it is expected will be his executor) he has not a great regard for, though perhaps as much as the young man's sullenness and extravagance deserve. He is now Clerk to an Attorney at Beaminster and it is said will soon set up his business in this town. The vicar of our parish has offered one of his sons [as Bunter's employee] to fill the station now offered to me with the additional circumstance in his favour of being a relation. A gentleman of the neighbourhood of Totnes made a like offer last week. Even a nephew of Lady North's has been proposed and notwithstanding all this, an unworthy son of yours – a poor stranger – is preferred! Mr B. offers to enter into Articles immediately, to instruct me in the profession of an Attorney of the court of K[ings]. B[ench]. and to find me all necessaries [for] 5 years in consideration only of my faithful attachment to him during that term.

For my part I have weighed and weighed the matter 'till I have almost worn out the scales and after setting the precariousness of the present times with the advantages which I may in future derive from being regularly brought to the profession under a gentleman of Mr B's character, fortune, situation and connections. I say after setting these and some other circumstances (obviously favourable) – against the appropriating 5 years of the prime of my life to no immediate profit, after having served 11 or 12 to no profit at all, I must confess that I think the balance breaks in favour of the proposal. I purpose to read your answer to Mr B. and shall earnestly expect it per second post."

Evidently the advice he received was encouraging because on 31st December 1774 JC was indentured for five years to Attorney Bunter (Fig. 3.) and embarked on formally qualifying as what he described in a gossipy 1783 letter[21] to an American acquaintance as, "a poor country retailer of law".

To round out what else is known of JC's father, he lived a further 7 years although any further correspondence with him seems to be lost. Indeed in JC's letter[22] on 1st December 1774 he complains to his father of a long silence. In his later years Cranch senior had suffered from what was then called "gout" which was a crippling and debilitating condition[22,23]. It can't be certain that this affliction coincided exactly with the modern definition which is painful accumulation of urea crystals in the joints, although that may have contributed to the symptoms. Perhaps other forms of rheumatism also fell under the same name in the 18th century. Contemporary letters portray it as a fairly common, severe and even fatal disorder which was thus generally dreaded[24]. Correspondingly, any remission was greeted with rejoicing. Although at various points in his surviving correspondence JC discusses his health problems he himself never seems to have suffered from gout.

The Country Lawyer

According to an Act of Parliament in 1729 admission to the profession of attorney required a five-year apprenticeship as clerk to an enrolled attorney and, subject to examination by a judge who would assess his fitness at the end of that period, the clerk would then be sworn in as an attorney. Within these loose parameters clerks might be little more than general servants or be intensively and correctly trained in their future role. Judges might nod candidates through on the say-so of their masters or genuinely test their knowledge. One factor that was almost unvarying, however, was that the clerk paid a premium to his master before being indentured although the amount of this covered a huge range between a few pounds and hundreds[25]. However, it is hard to believe that JC paid a penny given the lack of resources of the Cranch family. If this is true it contributes to the idea that Simon Bunter regarded JC almost as a surrogate son and nothing that occurred later would really dispel that impression although, like many actual sons, JC became impatient with Bunter's foibles. Clearly JC was correctly trained and duly qualified as an attorney and functioned as such for the nine years he remained in Axminster and probably to some extent afterwards. However, while that profession conferred respectability, in a small country town it was no path to riches.

Then, as now, most work of a provincial lawyer would have been concerned with property. The less well-off citizens often rented their cottages on leases for the lifetime of one or more tenants. Wills were becoming more common for even quite modest estates. Retail banking was limited in the provinces and personal loans were commonplace, so recovering unpaid interest on these and even the principal was bread-and-butter work for lawyers. Although JC never considered himself prosperous during these years in Axminster, by the time he was able to leave in the late 1780s he had a cottage and two servants.

Although he must have written huge numbers of letters, both professional and personal, during the period between joining Mr Bunter and leaving Axminster most appear to be lost. From those remaining we can get a picture of what his professional life was like. In 1784 he complained[26] of having "the plague" of conducting "two scurvy lawsuits to the assizes" but there is no doubt that he could be tough-minded[27] when he had to be:

> "...Mr Wale, Mr Read desires me to say that he will have the year's interest (due him from you). If you cannot, or do not, pay this interest as it becomes due, you must expect to be called upon in this way, or by such sort of people as the bearer, and you must at least pay them for their trouble. But as it ought to be altogether unnecessary, I could wish you would give no more occasion for it either to them or your humble servant."

Evidently the technique of sending round a tough customer to 'persuade' a debtor to cough up was applied in Axminster at that time.

> "...Sir, I am desired by your brother here to acquaint you that if £41.19.00 which he alleges to be due to him from the testamentary estate of Edmond Browne deceased and which it is (at least in part) your duty to pay, be not paid within 10 days from the date hereof he will consider the omission as a refusal, and proceed immediately to compel payment by law."

However, a letter[28] of his from 1787 paints a portrait of how he saw himself as having to adopt a false persona as a lawyer and as neither enjoying himself nor making significant money from the law. He was a:

> "...plain-plodding, grave-looking, joltheaded man of business (which every lawyer... that means to shine – that is, to get money – must at least make the world believe he is). But, besides that the business of an attorney is at present in general but an unprofitable one. You know very well that the disagreeable common part of it, which is the foundation of the profession, is not my element. Ah, that 'out of one's element' is the devil. What but a languishing-lingering destruction must be the consequence of either taking a fish out of the water, or of putting a bird into it?"

Surviving correspondence confirms the strains in his relationship with Simon Bunter although after the latter died in 1784, JC was discovered to be his joint executor together with Bunter's nephews, the Clapcotts and also a residuary legatee. Nearly two years were to elapse after the will was proved at London in 1785 before the estate was wound up. During this period he was to write as follows[29]:

> "...I sincerely esteemed the man, and was ever (though in too many instances unsuccessfully) zealous for his real honour and interest...[T]he services I did him [during] a long, laborious and tedious course of years, were important... those I would have done, had I been permitted, were still more so... I served him, in circumstances of all others the most discouraging to a generous mind, in spite of a pernicious weakness in him that was continually leading him to mistake the ostentation of magnanimity for its real action and virtue, by which slanderous persons in whose conversations he delighted, were ever tempting him to sacrifice the merits of his old friends to the pretensions of new ones... [T]hat in fine, my services to this gentleman were essential to him, such as could not have been rendered by any other person and yet were rendered not only without any reward, or assurance of reward, but in defiance of palpable indignities and discouragements, and to the irreparable injury of him who rendered them.

> As to the account of obligations betwixt poor Mr B[unter] and me (which, without any concurrence of ours, the world has been pleased to bring into question) – for the sake of peace, and to avoid giving offence, I have often proposed, and am yet willing, to depreciate the services I rendered that gentleman; to explain away the little wrongs he did me, and in conclusion to consider the suggested account as fairly balanced. But to acknowledge myself obliged to a man (who however respectable, and though I could have loved him as a father, was not capable of esteeming me) merely because he paid for the sacrifices I made to his interests and caprices, by the resignation of a nominal business and by a gift of money, which, before it became mine was no longer his, is a violence upon my convictions that they will not easily submit to."

Thus, even though it seemed that Bunter had eventually handed over the attorney practice to JC this gift was 'nominal' in that JC must by then have been doing all the work anyway and the apparently generous bequests to him of £400 plus books and a collection of old coins (Fig. 4) may not have been all they seemed. Even though JC was also a residuary legatee we can never know exactly how much his total inheritance was worth, if anything. The figure of £2000 bandied about in biographical accounts derived from people who didn't know JC well, or at all, was certainly a guess and almost certainly an exaggeration[30].

Even by 27th June 1787 when JC was distributing Bunter's legacies to others he himself was short of cash, judging by the following letter[31]:

"Mr Hoare, Being in a strait for money, I take the liberty to call upon you again to discharge your note, so long due. If you think me still indebted to you on Mr B[unter]'s account, I'll allow caption fees with all my heart, and still remember it as a kindness and, provided you'll settle with me immediately, I will also forgive all interest of your debt to me. What can I say more? I hope you will not urge to harsh language, or disagreeable measures, one who would thus substantially prove himself to be your friend."

Quite suddenly in 1787 JC's finances improved but even though his role as Bunter's executor must by then have been well known around Axminster the source of this good fortune was still apparently "an inscrutable mystery", although it clearly had something to do with his wealthy friend Mrs Feilder whom he described[32] as his "beloved benefactress". Mrs Feilder was herself the beneficiary of a £600 bequest in Bunter's will. It seems not impossible that she partly forewent this so that JC could at least receive his £400. A fuller account of their relationship will be found in Chapter 3.

As a letter of 26th July, 1787 to John Clapcott, Bunter's nephew reveals, JC's duties as executor were by then almost completed and he was ready to leave relevant documents with Clapcott[33] when he left for London.

"…The mail coach which carries this will also carry a deal box about 2 feet long, 16 inches wide and 18 inches deep, sealed with an elephant and an Apollo in two places and a Hercules strangling the lion in one place … It contains all the writings and papers belonging to our trust remaining in my hands and I hope they will be now safely transferred into yours. Among the most important of them are the mortgage bond and title deeds constituting the security from Messrs Tucker to the estate for £2000 and interest, the probates of the wills of John Bunter, Simon Bunter and Ann Clapcott etc., etc. Permit me to advise that they be not disarranged but carefully preserved 'till no possibility shall exist of their being of any further use. If you wish to have two hampers full of law proceedings, draughts of deeds and miscellaneous obsolete papers I will send them, but would rather advise you to direct me to burn them. They can be of no use but as professional precedents and to put them into the hands of strangers for such a purpose would involve with it the impropriety of disclosing things that were communicated in confidence and meant to be kept secret. [A] chest of 'other people's writings' (as I have always distinguished it) [is] a repository of writings left partly in Mr Bunter's but for the most part in my custody to be kept for other people. I shall save you trouble [by leaving them] with some person of credit here, as my agent, with sufficient instructions as to shewing or delivering them. I do not recollect that I have anything more to say at present only to desire a line of acknowledgement per return of post."

Even after his accession of some wealth JC still pursued quite small sums owing to him which provides further support to the idea that his fortune at this point was not truly substantial. For example, on 20th July, 1787 he wrote[34] to a fellow lawyer, Edward Bellamy, as follows:

> "...My dear friend, being about to leave this country to reside in London, I beg to know if you wish me to keep the writings you left with me or will not (rather) think it proper they should be deposited elsewhere. Whatever be your pleasure herein it shall be cheerfully complied with, my dear Sir, Your obliged humble servant, Cranch. P.S. My best respects attend Mrs Bellamy and the little ones. Mr. Bartlett will remember that he owes me 13s/6d, and if you come this way I shall take it kind if you will be so good to bring it. Please to give my service to him."

Before leaving this account of JC's activities as an attorney in Axminster, it is worth describing a few further surviving records[6] of these activities. In his last few years there he was responsible as steward and trustee for dispersal of the Drake estate whose principal residence was Ashe House near Axminster. This was a complicated business involving much land, often associated with ancient rights and obligations. The Drakes of Ashe were a very old family which finally produced no male heir and on the death of the last Lady Drake much property was sold off. Although the famous Admiral of Spanish Armada fame, Sir Francis Drake, was no relation (and the Drakes of Ashe emphatically refused to let him use their coat of arms) there was a family association with someone just as famous, namely, John Churchill, first Duke of Marlborough, who was born at Ashe House. One of the Drake daughters was married to John Churchill's father, Winston, who as a royalist was impoverished after the English Civil War and lived with his wife's family at Ashe. In a note about John Churchill, JC wrote:

> "...The 'groaning chair' in which Lady Churchill was delivered of her illustrious offspring at Ashe house, was considered as an heirloom, down to the time of Lady Drake's death, and was subsequently bought at auction by the late Sir John William Pole of Shute. In pulling down the Duke's room (as it was called) on the general demolition of Ashe house, about 1782, I am sorry to add that I was obliged as a trustee for the disposal of the estate to consent to that which no man could more feelingly have regretted as a lover of antiquities!"

Of the village of Colyford in East Devonshire, JC wrote:

> "...Having formerly had a trust estate in this borough of Colyford (as a part of the Drake of Ashe estate) and holding, for some time, the

stewardship of that concern, I have myself kept the courts here, alternately with the other part-owners of the borough (I think Lord Petre and Pole of Shute). Though I found this borough almost depopulated, a mayor was still presented and sworn [and] an iron mace, said to be as old as the time of King John, annually transferred to this praetorial dignity; [in other words] from the thatcher to the carpenter, from the carpenter to the blacksmith and then, as the population of the village seldom admitted of its being carried any further, it came round to the thatcher again!"

JC would doubtless be amused to discover that Colyford survives in the present day as a village with a population of around 800 and still guards its ancient privilege of electing a mayor.

At a meeting of the Historic Society of Lancashire and Cheshire in 1864[35] the chairman exhibited a document, labelled 83 car. ii (1682), releasing one Ellesdon of Charmouth from the payment of certain Customs duties received by him, amounting to about four thousand pounds, "in regard that he was instrumentall to our escape after the fatal battell of Worcester." It had attached to it the royal seal, and bore the following endorsement:

> "...Found in the room where the king was concealed in Charmouth manor-house and presented to me by James Warden Esq, Lord of the Manor, 1786. John Cranch"

William Ellesdon was a staunch royalist who bought Charmouth Manor in 1648 and is known to have helped in the escape of Charles II in 1651. Charles visited Charmouth, hoping to board a ship at nearby Lyme. Charmouth is close to Axminster and James Warden bought the manor there in 1783. Perhaps JC accepted such an interesting document from him in lieu of a fee. What later happened to it can only be guessed at although JC likely had to sell it when he fell on hard times.

Another curious piece of history arose from Simon Bunter's will and that concerned his portrait of Sir Walter Raleigh which he had bequeathed to the British Museum. For many years it had been displayed at the Dolphin Inn at Axminster[36]. It was purchased by Bunter for two shillings and sixpence (a low price even then). After the Adams family (see Chapter 2) visited JC's cottage in Axminster, Nabby Adams Smith noted in her journal[15] concerning JC:

> "...He has also a painting of Sir Walter Raleigh, which is thought an original picture; it was lately left by an old gentleman who died, to the British Museum. Mr C[ranch] says he has a great inclination never to deliver it; he thinks it ought to be preserved sacred in this county because

its original was born here in the parish of B[udleigh] and that Sir Walter's character stands very high throughout the county of Devonshire. Papa [John Adams] observed that his character did not appear unexceptionable; he answered that none of his faults were known here; they believed only in his virtues and excellences."

The portrait of Raleigh was supposedly painted by the artist Cornelius Johnson who was born in London to Dutch parents. It is now regarded as lost[37] but whether because JC failed to deliver it is unknown. In general JC was fastidious in his lawyerly duties although quite capable of making a joke about them. More likely he sent it off by mail and, like much else at that time, it got mislaid or stolen. JC later spent many hours doing research in the British Museum and it hardly seems likely that he had intentionally bilked it of an important bequest.

Personality and Appearance of John Cranch

Surviving documents bring JC most sharply into focus at the middle of his life when both known portraits of him were created (see Frontispiece and Fig. 5) and if some of his qualities became apparent before or afterwards, this seems an appropriate place to try and create a word portrait of the man in his prime. Even the most grudging accounts do not deny his talents and the extent to which he developed them. He was a fine natural draughtsman who taught himself to paint in oils. Indeed it is as an artist that he is best remembered today although he was not particularly prolific and several paintings well-known in his lifetime have subsequently disappeared. He developed a very wide and deep base of cultural knowledge through reading and was a writer of prose and poetry of considerable ability. He was reputed to be musical and there is evidence that he could fluently read a score. He was a pioneering antiquary seeking out and where possible preserving ancient remains. There is plenty of evidence in his correspondence that he was generous to a fault to both family and friends when in funds; in fact, later in life, inability to recover his loans caused him many problems. Even before he came into his modest fortune he was giving what he could as a letter[38] to his sister Mrs Willcocks dated 24th April 1787 reveals:

"Dear Mary, I wish it was in my power to do that for you and many other dear friends that I would. I should wish the enclosed paltry ten pounds (which, considering your deserts, I am almost ashamed to ask your acceptance of) were ten thousand, with all my soul, provided too I were not convinced from a long and intense observation and some experience that accessions of wealth are accessions of trouble and that the *summum bonum*, whatever it does, most infallibly does not consist in that."

Note that this letter was written when his expectations, or the lack of them, from the will of Simon Bunter would already have been clear to him which again supports the idea that he really did not anticipate an accession of wealth from that source.

In person, JC was undoubtedly what would now be called an introvert, sometimes given to taciturnity in company which he himself ascribed[39] to having spent more time in reading than in meeting people:

"...for unless I quite mistake my talent, my writing is by no means so absolutely wretched as my oratory and the reason of it may be that I have conversed so much less with men than with books."

He was comfortable with just a few friends who found him a genial, witty companion, but in general he was shy well into middle age. His strong motivation towards self-improvement in a worldly sense may have been hindered by his propensity to form strong opinions, not all of which were popular. He himself would have taken for granted this tendency to be forthright because he was both a Cranch and a Devonian. In fact, his compulsively honest personality seems to have gained him some enemies and it is not clear that he was aware of their enmity even when their spitefulness survives in written form to this day. But, in general, he was quite self-aware and modest to the point of being self-critical. He was not given to obvious display such as flashy clothes. Writing in 1784[40], his American cousin Polly Palmer reproved him for having worn only shoe strings (and not fashionable buckles) for seven years, and only ever having his hair powdered twice (before visiting Abigail Adams in London). He had expressed to her his fear of seeming vain. His preference for lacing his shoes rather than closing them with buckles attracted criticism from his female American relations more than once, but as a great walker the comfort of his feet would have been of greater importance to him than his appearance.

His propensity to be misunderstood owing to the definiteness with which he expressed himself could occur even with those who must have known him well as this letter[41] to his brother-in-law, James Elworthy, dated 12th April, 1787 indicates:

"Dear Brother, You say I am 'warm'. If you mean to charge me with any other warmth than warmth of friendship for you and yours, you do me wrong. I am not tenacious of my opinions. In truth almost my whole life has been but one continued subordination to the opinions of others; but if by 'warmth' you mean (as I fear you do) anger, I can never admit that my last letter indicated (any more than my mind felt) anything at all like it: good God! – to[wards one to] whom I am so highly obliged – scout the idea! I sentence your wife to be fined a roasted goose and you 10 bottles of wine for having suffered yourselves to entertain it… What you took for anger, could be nothing more than a preciseness of expression, to prevent mistakes: but it has ever been and I therefore fear ever will be my fate, to be misunderstood by those whose good graces I am most anxious to preserve. However, take notice that I can't afford to [lo]se such friends as you and Elizabeth Elworthy [JC's sister] and that I defy the world to show one who is more sincerely, or with a stronger or a steadier, affection, hers and yours than J. Cranch."

He acknowledged his 'incurable shyness' in a letter to his uncle Richard[42], and to his friend John Andrews[43] he confided:

"…as much happiness might be enjoyed, and consequently as much unhappiness avoided, in the secluded state in an existence upon the mere necessaries and common benefits of Nature – as in that life-commercial (or, as it may almost be called – life-militant) which, while abounding in higher gusts of enjoyment, is liable to proportionally more exquisite degrees of suffering."

And to Richard Cranch's daughter Eliza he expressed[44] his love of a quiet existence:

"…Your taste, my dear girl, so congenial with my own for domestic and retired pleasures."

As is recounted in more detail in Chapter 2, JC had considerable contact with relations who emigrated to America. JC's uncle Richard was married to Mary, sister of Abigail who was the wife of John Adams who became second President of the United States. Because some of the clearest descriptions of JC's physical presence were written by the Adams family in the period just before JC left Axminster it seems appropriate to place them here. Before he became president, Adams was the first ambassador of the newly independent country to the Court of St James's and while he and his family were in England, at the urging of the extensive Cranch family, a visit was paid to the West of England in July and August of 1787. JC was eager to meet them even though, from the very respectful tone of his letters to them, they evidently seemed rather grand to him. In her diary Abigail Adams[45] recorded that:

"...We... then proceeded for Axminster, the first town in the County of Devonshire... Here we were visited by Mr John Cranch, a nephew of my Brother Cranch, who is an attorney and resides here. The town is a little narrow dirty village but a great thoroughfare, all the Plymouth, Exeter and many other stages passing through it. [We] went with Mr Cranch to see the manufactory of carpets for which this place is famous... Mr Cranch invited us to drink tea with him. He is a single man, of a delicate complexion, small features, about 26 or 27 years old [he was actually 35]. He never looks one in the face and appears as if he had been cramped and cowed in his youth. He has a good understanding, which he has improved by reading, and appears a virtuous amiable man."

Again, Abigail Adams[46] this time writing to her sister Mary on 15th September 1787:

"...From Weymouth our next excursion was to Axminster the first town in the County of Devonshire. Here we found Mr J. Cranch, he dined with us and we drank tea with him; this is a curious genius; he is a middle sized man of a delicate countenance, but quite awkward in his manners. He seldom looks one in the face, and seems as if he had been cramped and cowed in his youth; in company one is pained for him, yet is he a man of reading and an accurate taste in the fine arts, poetry, painting, music, sculpture, architecture; all of them have engaged his attention. His profession does not seem to be the object of his affections, and he has given up the practice with an intention of pursuing some other employment; he appears to me to be a man whose soul wants a wider expansion than his situation and circumstances allow. Dejected spirits he is very liable to; I do not think him a happy man. His sentiments are by no means narrow or contracted, yet he is one by himself."

Abigail writing[47] to her niece Eliza Cranch:

"...Your cousin J. Cranch who travelled a great part of the way with us thinks he has a very accurate knowledge of you. I am not sure that if he was in America, he might put a pair of buckles into his shoes and hold up his head...he is certainly a man of talents but he wants the manner of displaying them to advantage."

Nabby Adams Smith[15] recorded in her journal that:

"... Mr Cranch engaged to dine with us, and came to attend us to take a view of the manufactories of this place, which are of carpet and tape. We then visited the church, which is very old; the paintings and monuments were miserable, except one[f], of which Mr Cranch had the direction[16]; it is to the memory of a lady, the device represents the dove taking the veil from the urn which contains her ashes. Mr C. dined with us, and requested we would take tea at his cottage; he came at six to attend us. He lives in a small, neat cottage, everything around him has an air of taste, united with neatness. He has a variety of small prints, the heads of many eminent persons, and the six prints, Hogarth's representation of *La Marriage a la mode*."

There is no reason to give weight to Mrs Adams' theory about JCs upbringing other than to suggest that it is a rather typical guess that an extravert might make about an introvert. It is reasonable to deduce from his later cheerful correspondence with members of his family that JC's home life as a child had been happy enough. Although lacking confidence in public, JC's inner strength drove his cultural development and made him extraordinary in his own time and worth recalling in ours. We should mention here another characteristic of JC's psychology in that he was clearly intuitive. His employer Simon Bunter said that he "saw too clearly" and JC wrote to his friend Mrs Feilder[48] that he, "always reckoned this 'penetrating faculty' among my misfortunes". In other words, interpreting other people's expressions all too well would have contributed to his wariness about looking them in the face for fear of what he would see there. However, in one respect Abigail Adams was undoubtedly correct in that JC's life as a small-town lawyer both bored him and took him into public duties like court appearances which he loathed.

However, by 1800, in giving advice to his nephew, James Willcocks, JC showed that he must himself have discovered some advantages in at least appearing to be more outgoing. As mentioned above, James Willcocks senior had married JC's sister Mary and after Willcocks died JC seems to have taken a strong paternal interest in his nephews, James and John, helping them to develop their careers. As will be seen later, this kindness was amply repaid since the Willcocks family was actively helpful to JC in his later years. However, when his nephew James was young he got a good wigging[49] from his Uncle Jack:

"…Your profound unaccountable taciturnity and apparent insensibility to everything you saw or heard while I was with you force me, after a very patient observation, to conclude that you were averse, or at least

---

[f] This is the monument dedicated to Meloria Bunter and at the time of writing it still is the most ornate memorial in Axminster church.

indifferent, to any further acquaintance with me or with the men and things of the world that we are got into and must go through with. I certainly thought my time of too much consequence to be trifled away in repeating admonitions over and over, to one who had been represented to me as a young man of good sense, as well as of great good nature. Considering how many things we have to learn, we surely find life short enough without wasting it in vain attempts to inculcate what is not promptly and efficiently attended to. What I told you on the first day of our journey was intended to apprise you in season, as a person entering into the world, (as we phrase it) of the mischievous tendency of morose silence and reserve in our necessary commerce with mankind. These dispositions are always pernicious and sometimes fatal. A cheerful, communicative habit is exactly of the same advantage to him that possesses it which a sail is to a vessel: sooner or later it is sure to catch one of those numerous currents that are continually blowing somebody or other on to prosperity. While an austere gloomy reserve (or the appearance of it which, in the world we are talking of, you will find to amount to exactly the same thing) backs your sails, negatives every wish and battles every attempt to get on. The vessel of your fortune lies a dead weight on the ocean of life and every fool that can but chatter and be cheerful gets ahead of you. If a man will bury his talents (of which silence is to be considered as the grave), he may, and they will, be buried to all eternity, for I'll be shot if the world ever digs for them. A man of this disposition to perpetual sullen silence shuts his door against mankind and then wonders that mankind forsake him!"

JC goes on to encourage James to write often because, "Your welfare cannot be indifferent to me as a child of one of the best of sisters and of women and it will be your own fault if I cannot equally respect you for yourself".

For a final assessment of JC's character here are quotations from two obituarists[50,51] who had evidently known and liked him for a long time. Although they can be assumed to have emphasised favourable aspects of his character their opinion seems to be confirmed by everything else which can be discovered about him:

"...His extensive knowledge of English literature, vigorous conception and reasoning on things, united with the most perfect simplicity and urbanity of manners, rendered his society dear to everyone that had the pleasure of his acquaintance; but his exalted ideas of the duties of friendship, and the practical demonstrations which he gave in their support, will say more than volumes can express, and be a lasting monument of his distinguished benevolence and fidelity."

"...He was a man of the strictest integrity, morals, and humanity, which he eminently displayed in every action of his life – and his words which seemed to flow from the instantaneous feelings of a correct heart, were delivered with the strongest sentiments of reason and profound judgment. The singular meekness or natural modesty which marked his whole conduct through life, he retained with his latest breath, which secured the respect and admiration of all that knew him."

The Perpetual Student

Not all of JC's time in Axminster had been taken up with lawyering and his self-education had continued. For example, he set about learning French and helping him with this was a young friend Thomas Peironnet, the son of Stephen Peironnet who was a dancing master in Axminster. Thomas was baptised in 1771 and was thus a teenager when JC first knew him. His teaching role was described by JC amusingly in a letter to his American cousin Betsy Palmer:

> "…This midsummer eve 1787, sitting with Peironnet in an arbour in my garden.
> Studying French intently
> Therefore declining beautifully
> My robes blowing sweetly
> My cabbages growing rapidly
> Maid Hannah scrubbing the parlour stairs dextrously
> Ditto – singing melodiously
>
> In short in very easy circumstances (while they last). Get out Tom! Get out you French monkey, and don't come again these 3 days – with your flattering *fort biens*, upon vicious pronunciation and conscious dullness. – The petit maitre vanishes – the garden door shuts."

Two more letters from June 1787 mention JC taking advantage of illness to concentrate on French. In one[52] he is,

> "…in bed, sweating out the best end of a cold, but nevertheless reading and translating French 'like a dragon'."

and in the other[53],

> "…a week's illness, from which I am just risen has thrown me upon the French grammar: I can now read a plain story in that language with so tolerable a familiarity that I begin to be in regret for those of my most valued friends who remain unacquainted with it. If you are not, or do not soon get, forward in it I will wish you such an illness."

JC and Peironnet remained friends for a long time because on 15th July 1794 JC was to write[54] from London to his brother William:

"...A friend of mine, a hearty fellow, one Tom Peironnet of Axminster (lately a midshipman on board the Phaeton frigate that took the St Iago) this morning embarked in the ship Barclay, Capt. David Swaine (in the river) for Boston. His present view is to settle at Washington, but that is quite uncertain, Tom being *tam Marte, quam Mercurio*[g]. I have charged him with several letters and messages and some books. He tells me some of the American captains will take passengers (settlers) at a pound a head. Do you really think of going my dear Billy or does it only, as with me, amount to a <u>wish</u>?"

Presumably JC expected William to interpret the Latin tag. In fact this younger brother must also have been something of an autodidact since William and JC exchanged information about shared antiquarian interests throughout their lives. HMS Phaeton was a very successful ship under various captains and *St Iago* was carrying much treasure when captured which resulted in Phaeton's crew getting generous prize money. After emigrating, Thomas Peironnet became a naturalised US citizen, as recorded in Maine in 1796, and went on to have a successful business career, mostly in Pennsylvania.

References

1. Details of JC's siblings are taken from a note written by himself and transcribed into a typescript set of notes about the Cranch family in Kingsbridge Heritage Centre.
2. BPL Ms. Eng. 483 (108)
3. John Cranch, Student career: Taunton Academy (1732-1734) Funding body: Presbyterian Fund Board . Amount: £10 p.a. Source: Presbyterian Fund, Minute Book, vol. 3, Dr Williams's Library, The Presbyterian Board, MS OD69, pp. 167, 171, 182, 197.
4. Richard Cranch wrote an autobiographical note in 1805 which was published in *English Origins of New England Families*, Second Series, vol. 1, Genealogical Pub Co; 2nd edition, May 1985.
5. BPL Ms. Eng. 483 (112)
6. Polwhele, Richard (1797-1806), *The History of Devonshire,* First Edition in three volumes in a single binding. Printed by Trewman and Son, Exeter. John Cranch's own copy with his extensive annotations and pasted insertions. In private hands.
7. Hawkins, Abraham (1819), *Kingsbridge and Salcombe, with the Intermediate Estuary, Historically and Topographically Depicted,* published by R. Southwood, London.

---

[g] Translated variously: "As much for Mars as for Mercury" or "equally disposed to fight or to negotiate" or perhaps most aptly, "fitted as well for war as for business".

8. Hawkins, M.W.S. (1888), *Plymouth Armada Heroes: the Hawkins Family*, published by William Brendan and Son, Plymouth.
9. BPL Ms. Eng. 483 (115)
10. BPL Ms. Eng. 483 (15-60)
11. BPL Ms. Eng. 483 (132)
12. Cited in R. Hansford Worth (1941), *Dartmoor: 1788-1808* from *The Transactions of the Devonshire Association for the Advancement of Science, Literature and Art,* vol. 73, pp. 203-225. Location of original and date of letter not known.
13. Fox, SP (1874), *Kingsbridge and its Surroundings.* Printed by GP Friend, Plymouth.
14. *Journey to Axminster by Waggon* by John Cranch 1771. Kingsbridge History Society Recorders, No. 20. Transcribed by Mrs Kay Coutin.
15. Adams A. (1841) *Journal and Correspondence of Miss Adams, Daughter of John Adams Second President of the United States, Written in France and England.* Wiley and Putnam, New York & London (Journal account of 27th July to 3rd August 1787).
16. Axminster Heritage website: www.axminsterheritage.org/local-history/places Towards the end of the 20th century, Hilary House was demolished and replaced by modern bungalows so, if any trace of JC had remained there, it has certainly now gone forever.
17. *Devon Notes and Queries* (1901), eds.P.F.S. Amery, John S. Amery and J. Brooking Rowe, vol. 1, pp. 193-4, publisher James G. Commin, Exeter
18. BPL Ms. Eng. 483 (108)
19. Davidson, James (1832) *A History of the Town and Parish of Axminster in the County of Devon* (manuscript stored in Devon Heritage Centre, Exeter)
20. BPL Ms. Eng. 483 (110)
21. BPL Ms. Eng. 483 (113)
22. BPL Ms. Eng. 483 (108)
23. BPL Ms. Eng. 483 (64-107)
24. For example, BPL Ms. Eng. 483 (368)
25. Robson, Robert (1959), *The Attorney in Eighteenth-century England,* Cambridge University Press, Cambridge.
26. BPL Ms. Eng. 483 (120)
27. BPL Ms. Eng. 483 (2)
28. BPL Ms. Eng. 483 (15-60)
29. BPL Ms. Eng. 483 (15-60) Two letters in same file
30. For example, Rowe, J.B. (1901) *Devon Notes and Queries*, vol. 1, pp. 193-194, publisher James G. Commin, Exeter]
31. BPL Ms. Eng. 483 (2)
32. BPL Ms. Eng. 483 (15-60)
33. BPL Ms. Eng. 483 (2)
34. BPL Ms. Eng. 483 (2)
35. *Transactions of the Historic Society of Lancashire and Cheshire. New Series* vol. 5, Session 1864-65, published by Adam Holden, Liverpool

36. Detailed in the folder of notes which accompany the manuscript *A History of the Town and Parish of Axminster in the County of Devon* by James Davidson (1832), kept in the Devon Heritage Centre, Exeter.
37. Butterfield, L. H. ed (1961), *The Adams Papers, Diary and Autobiography of John Adams*, vol. 3, Diary, 1782–1804; Autobiography, Part One to October 1776, pp. 206–207 (And notes appended thereto by Massachusetts Historical Society), Harvard University Press, Cambridge
38. BPL Ms. Eng. 483 (2)
39. BPL Ms. Eng. 483 (15-60)
40. BPL Ms. Eng. 483 (416)
41. BPL Ms. Eng 483 (2)
42. BPL Ms. Eng 483 (117)
43. BPL Ms. Eng 483 (2)
44. BPL Ms. Eng. 483 (122)
45. Taylor, C. James *et al.* eds (2007), *Adams Family Correspondence*, vol. 8, March 1787–December 1789, p. 129 (Abigail Adams' Diary of a Tour from London to Plymouth, 20–28 July 1787), Harvard University Press, Cambridge
46. Taylor, C. James *et al.* eds (2007), *Adams Family Correspondence*, vol. 8, March 1787–December 1789, pp. 153–162, Harvard University Press, Cambridge
47. Taylor, C. James *et al.* eds (2007), *Adams Family Correspondence*, vol. 8, March 1787–December 1789, pp. 175–176, Harvard University Press, Cambridge
48. BPL Ms. Eng. 483 (15-60)
49. BPL Ms. Eng. 483 (64-107)
50. *The Bath Herald*, 27th Jan, 1821
51. *The Bath Journal*, 29th Jan, 1821
52. BPL Ms. Eng. 483 (2)
53. BPL Ms. Eng. 483 (2)
54. Transcription of JC's letter found in Kingsbridge Heritage Centre.

Chapter 1

Chapter 2

The American Connection

Although some mention has already been made of JC's interaction with Americans there survives a good deal more information about his relations with three generations of his relatives and their acquaintances. He unequivocally supported the cause of American independence and was fascinated with debates about the form the new nation's government would take.

JC's contact with America began before the War of Independence and arose initially because he corresponded with his uncle Richard Cranch (1726–1811) (Fig. 6) who, as mentioned in Chapter 1, had emigrated to New England. About a decade of silence ensued during the war and when correspondence resumed it widened to include JC's cousins, who had now grown up, and other acquaintances and relations. As already discussed, they included notables such as John Adams, who became second President of the independent America and his wife Abigail whose sister Mary was married to Richard Cranch. The Adams family were based in England for a while during the 1780s and that is the period when they visited the West of England where JC met and assisted them. Awareness of JC's ability among his influential American acquaintances lead to him being made a member of two American learned societies and correspondence about both survives. In order to put all these interactions in context a brief history of relevant individuals and events which formed the background to JC's interactions with America follows. However, he never emigrated or even visited there although it is clear that he would have been made welcome if he had.

Emigration from Devonshire to New England was frequent during the 18th Century and Richard Cranch, sailed to America on the ship Wilmington arriving in Boston on 2nd November 1746 when he was just 21. He was accompanied by his sister Mary and her husband Joseph Palmer (1716–1788) (Fig. 7). Richard and Joseph had been brought up in England to the trade of making cards for the processing of wool preparatory to weaving and they initially set up in that business in School

29

Street, Boston. Evidently that did not pay and they quickly became watchmakers, repairers and retailers in the same shop which remained in their possession until 1755 when Richard moved his watchmaking business to Braintree some thirteen miles south of Boston.

Like JC, Richard was a formidable autodidact and became widely acknowledged as an authority on religious literature. He also evidently acquired extensive legal knowledge since he later had legislative and judicial roles. John Adams described him as having a mathematical, metaphysical, mechanical and systematical head[1]. A long association with Harvard College led to the award to Richard of an honorary degree in 1780. In fact both Richard and JC seem to have allowed business to take second place to their intense intellectual and spiritual interests so it is not surprising that they were mutually sympathetic correspondents. However, Richard's multiple public duties allow us to infer that he was a more outgoing character than JC. Certainly at many periods of life he gave these priority over his watchmaking and other business interests although they never furnished him with more than the barest subsistence financially. In fact in 1781 in order to reliably feed his family he bought a farm, which at times he tilled himself and his wife entertained paying lodgers in the large house they rented.

Owing to his honesty, intelligence, piety and wit, Richard was a popular figure in Braintree, MA, where he lived most of his remaining years[2]. He was chosen as its representative to the Massachusetts General Court (1778-1782), member of the Massachusetts Senate in 1787, Justice of the Suffolk County Court of Common Pleas (1779-1793) and to the Constitutional Convention in 1788 to ratify the federal constitution, which he supported. When in 1792 it was decided to divide Braintree into two towns a new name for the more northerly part was sought and Richard Cranch recommended that it be called Quincy. This was the maiden surname of his mother-in-law who came from a prominent local family and it remains so-called to this day despite the activities of a claque in favour of renaming it Hancock after that other prominent resident, John Hancock. In 1794 a post office was established in Quincy and Richard became Postmaster, an office he held for the rest of his life. This appointment may be connected to the fact that his brother-in-law John Adams was vice-president at the time and Richard's ability to earn a living by other means was deteriorating with age.

After Richard moved to Braintree, and then for a while to the nearby village of Weymouth, he made friends with the family of Reverend William and Elizabeth Smith and courted their eldest, and apparently prettiest, daughter Mary, whom he married on 25th November 1762. Wealth eluded Richard his life long and it must have been other qualities and his respect for women as people which allowed him to captivate a woman 15 years his junior. The three Smith sisters had received the minimum education thought necessary for women destined for domestic life and Richard introduced them to literature and other intellectual fare, a fact for which the second sister Abigail remained noticeably grateful all her life as she journeyed with her husband into the highest reaches of society at home and abroad. Richards's marriage was as firm as any could be and Mary ultimately died the day after him.

In Braintree Richard Cranch became friends with John Adams (1735-1826), the lawyer scion of a prominent local family who was nine years younger than himself[3]. In many ways they were opposite in personality but shared intellectual and philosophical interests. Introduced to the Smith household it took a while for Adams to appreciate Abigail but over time they became romantically involved and were married on 25th October 1764. The very strong bond between the Smith sisters helped keep the Cranch and Adams families intertwined as long as they lived and Richard's continuing interest in his family in England eventually led to JC becoming acquainted either through letters or in person with many of them. On Richard's death, John Adams said of him, "Never shall I see his like again. An invariable friend for sixty years."

Richard's family produced several notable American citizens[a]. His son William (1769–1855), became a prominent judge who himself had a daughter and four sons three of whom became painters including another named John. The existence of this later painter of the same name led some modern auctioneers posthumously to designate JC 'John Cranch of Bath'. It is true that JC was most prolific as a painter in his later years when he lived in that city but this designation is misleading. He himself and his contemporaries always thought of him as John Cranch of Kingsbridge and

---

[a] In passing it can be mentioned that, through William Cranch's daughter, the famous modern poet, TS Eliot, was a descendent of Richard Cranch.

he actually painted for most of his life, albeit much of his early output appears to be lost. Richard's eldest daughter, Elizabeth (1763-1811), usually called Eliza, was the correspondent in several surviving letters to and from JC. From 1781 she was affianced to Thomas Perkins, a school teacher who then went alone to Kentucky to make his fortune. Although courted by others Eliza remained faithful but Perkins never returned, dying in Kentucky from illness in 1786. After a prolonged period of depression she recovered to marry Reverend Jacob Norton in 1789. She had eight children and lived until 1810 despite frequent illness. Her younger sister Lucy (1767-1846) also wrote to JC. In 1795 she married one John Greenleaf.

Inevitably, the War of Independence led to interruptions of family corres- pondence between the nations and because of the conflict, great care needed to be taken over what was put in writing. However, transatlantic cordiality on the personal level persisted throughout. Many inhabitants of the West of England, including JC, had great political sympathy with the Americans and their desire for freedom from British rule. Religious and political dissent were characteristic of Devonians then and, to an extent, still are.

JC and Joseph Palmer, his uncle by marriage, exchanged letters some of which do survive. Although in 1750 Joseph Palmer and Richard Cranch jointly leased land from Colonel Joseph Quincy in the area of Braintree which came to be known as Germantown it was Palmer who most vigorously contributed to the creation of this, the first industrial complex in America. Richard Cranch seems to have sold his interest there to Palmer in 1760. The name of this settlement arose because skilled immigrants came there from Germany to work in a glass factory which ultimately Palmer owned. In 1755 that burned down but by then Palmer was able to offer work to any who wanted it in his other enterprises which included salt, hosiery and chocolate factories, and a spermaceti candle works. He also had two stores on the Long Wharf in Boston together with warehouses which traded in West India goods and various types of hardware. By 1770 these were managed by his son, Joseph Pearse Palmer. Joseph Palmer himself certainly became a wealthy man who lived in some style in Germantown for many years and also had various public roles. It is not exactly clear where his wealth came from since he seems to have brought little money with him from England and, by some accounts, the

Germantown factories were not a great success. Richard Cranch was a quiet supporter of American independence whereas Palmer was a militant one who gave money generously to the cause and became active in the armed conflict between the Americans and the British. He had made a study of fortifications and was responsible for many of the defensive structures around Boston. Despite his enormous sacrifices during the struggle for independence he was, in the end, ill-treated by others in the movement and today enjoys less fame than people who did far less.

He fought in the Battle of Lexington and at Concord, served in the Massachusetts Provincial Congress and on the Cambridge Committee of Safety. He received a commission as a colonel in the Massachusetts militia and in 1776 as brigadier general for Suffolk County, MA. He went on intelligence-gathering missions in Vermont and Rhode Island and led a failed attack on Newport, RI. An attempt was made to scapegoat him for the failure which was actually more attributable to others and although he was exonerated by a public enquiry the impugning of his honour placed appalling strain on an ageing man[4].

His son, Joseph Pearse Palmer, was an actual participant in the Boston Tea Party and as punishment the Palmer properties by the harbour were looted and burned by British soldiers. Later in the war one of Palmer's ships laden with spermaceti candles was captured. The workforce of his factories in Germantown was depleted so much by the demands for fighting men that these businesses failed. Naturally, Palmer fell into debt but far from enjoying understanding and support from other prominent citizens, he eventually had to sell his house and all other property in Germantown. Most conspicuous in causing his ruin was John Hancock, who also lived in the part of Braintree which became Quincy and enjoyed considerable family wealth. He insisted on calling in mortgages he held over Palmer's property. Earlier Hancock, when president of the Continental Congress, refused to supply Palmer with a copy of the charges against him regarding the Rhode Island affair, thus making it impossible for Palmer to prepare a defence against unjust accusations which might have cost him his life.

Palmer tried to recover financially by setting up another salt business but his age and deterioration in his health caused by his extreme wartime exertions and subsequent stresses took their toll and he died in 1788. His son had married Elizabeth (Betsy) Hunt, daughter of a prosperous distiller and the couple had nine children. After various wartime heroics he was rather unsuccessful in a career which included farming and school-teaching. He died in an accidental fall in 1797 aged 47. One letter he wrote to JC survives. The Palmers also had two daughters, the elder baptised Mary after her mother but always called Polly and her sister Elizabeth (Betsy), both of whom exchanged letters with JC. Betsy Palmer was admired for her intelligence and strength of character. She became engaged to Nathaniel Cranch, the son of Richard Cranch's eldest brother, John, and thus her first cousin. The relationship between the two seems to have been stormy. Nathaniel and his brother Joseph had emigrated from England to America and while Nathaniel became successful in business and was liked by Joseph Palmer, Joseph Cranch was a rather un-enterprising gunsmith. Nathaniel died mysteriously having drowned in a river on a cold evening, raising the question as to whether he had taken his own life. When later Betsy Palmer decided to marry Joseph Cranch, her father was vehemently opposed to the engagement but his death not long afterwards allowed the marriage to take place although it produced no children. Richard Cranch brought influence to bear at West Point Military Academy so that Joseph became its armourer but he died quite young and Betsy became a school teacher. Polly became an invalid, never married and died at the age of 44[5,6].

One final correspondent of JC's, whose life story deserves mention, was Eunice Paine (1733-1803). Her brother was Robert Treat Paine (1731-1814) who is best remembered today as a signatory of the Declaration of Independence and who was a friend of Richard Cranch in his early years in Boston. Richard proposed to Eunice in 1753 but her father, Thomas Paine, although not forbidding the match discouraged it given his own reduced circumstances at the time which precluded a dowry. Remarkably, there seems to have been no residual enmity when Eunice respected her father's view and ended the engagement. She and Richard remained friends and Richard's wife Mary seems not to have resented this, so Eunice remained almost a member of the Cranch family and never married. When later in life Eunice was crippled, probably with rheumatism, she was taken in by the Cranches.

Family correspondence

Known survivals of letters between JC and his American relatives must represent a fraction of those written. As a correspondent he was much liked and the manner in which his letters were copied and passed around an appreciative extended family was often mentioned. JC first wrote to his uncle Richard in 1772 to initiate their correspondence, not long after he had started to work in Axminster, and extracts from Richard's reply are given below. Then nothing has been found until the 1780s when conditions became more favourable for exchanges of mail between England and America after the War of Independence ended. Two categories of missives then dominate the surviving letters, firstly, correspondence surrounding the period John Adams spent in Europe with his family when he represented the newly independent America as a diplomat and, secondly, the delightfully chatty letters JC exchanged with the daughters of his uncle Richard Cranch and his aunt Mary Palmer together with Eunice Paine.

So here is Richard Cranch writing to JC[7] from Boston on 29th May 1773:

"...I received your very agreeable favour of last June, and thank you for the respect you express for me. I fear the partiality of friends may have drawn my mental picture in colours much too flattering. I assure you I gladly embrace the overture you have made of a correspondence with me, and should esteem it a happiness to hear from you often. I should have wrote to you sooner, but had no opportunity... until now, and was unwilling to put you to charge of postage for nothing.

I have heard of your inclination to painting, and that nature has given you a good turn that way, and should be glad to know whether or no you have any plan in your mind for pursuing your genius in that employment. We have a limner here, Mr Copley, who by dint of natural genius, with very little instruction, has arrived at surprising perfection in face-painting and drapery, and has in a few years acquired a handsome fortune. I have had thoughts about your going to London, and getting instruction from some master in that branch, and if you should succeed who knows but America might reward your genius, as it has Mr Copley. Perhaps if you was to ...set up business in London, or near it, you might get instructed [without] any great charge; and your having a Sister [living] in London, might also facilitate such a plan. [Having] thrown out these loose hints, you might [let] me know in your next how the thing lays in your [min]d.

I have now a favour to desire of you; and that is, that you would enquire as far as you are able into the origin of the name and family of Cranch, where the first of the name that you can find, came from; especially where our own ancestors came from, and who they were before my Grandfather Andrew Cranch of Kingsbridge. I suspect that our name and family is not originally English, and that the name has not been long in England: and I am led to suspect this, from my not being able to find the name in many books of Heraldry nor have I met with it in any history, or public [documents] either of court, Army, Navy, Subscription Papers, or any other Registers whatever either ancient or modern, many of which I have examined. Neither can I find that any of the name are anywhere to be found except in the county of Devon, or in parts to which they mov'd from thence. And as I am the first of the name that ever had a family in America I have a great curiosity to know if possible, wherefrom [they] sprung. I suppose someone or other of the name either of our family or some other branch or connection may have some records, or at least traditions from whence the family is derived. If you can procure me any satisfaction on this I shall be much gratified and obliged.

I often hear from your Brother [in-Law] Elworthy and have lately rec[eive]d a letter from Cousin Richard Cranch at Exeter, acknowledging the receipt of a watch that I gave him; I hope it behaves well; please to give my love to him and his dear mother and brothers and sister when you see them, and accept the same in the kind manner from your Sincere Friend and Affectionate Uncle, Richard Cran[ch]

[postscript] Please to let your Father and Mother and Uncle William know that I remember them with the tenderest Affection, and give my Kind Regards to your Brothers & Sisters. Our family are in usual health, through the favour of divine Providence. Mrs Cranch joins me in every good Wish for the Temporal and Eternal Happiness of you and all the dear Circle in [Devon].

While I was writing this we were alarmed by a cry of fire, which proved to be in a store-ship which belonged to the Men of War. It burnt furiously for several hours, and the loss I suppose is great. The wind favoured us so as to carry the fire from the town. The ship is burnt down to the water. I [have no] doubt these American expeditions will prove as pernicious to England as offensive to America."

As mentioned in Chapter 1, JC's sister Elizabeth and her husband James Elworthy lived in London at that time. He was a merchant who dealt in oil, candles, soap, glue etc. and was based at 1 Old Broad Street according to trade directories from 1770 to 1790. This is also the first known London postal address for JC although whether he stayed with his sister for long or just used her address is unknown. Certainly the Elworthys seem to have acted at the time as a postbox for family transatlantic mail, a good deal of which must have passed through the capital's port. Abigail Adams met with the Elworthy family several times in 1784 when she stayed in London while John Adams was conducting business at The Hague[8].

Various notes were enclosed with Richard's letter quoted above, among them the first to JC from his first cousin Betsy Palmer. She was to prove one of his most vigorous and sprightly correspondents:

> "My Dear Cousin, Presuming on your candour to put the most favourable construction on my confidence in writing thus uninvited to a young gentleman I proceed to tell you that short as your letter was it gave us all great pleasure and we shall hope for the continuation of your correspondence. Be assured that nothing gives us more real satisfaction than to hear of the welfare and prosperity of our friends your side of the Atlantic, except indeed the extreme pleasure of seeing them in New England, which is a pleasure I dare not indulge the thought of. But if we are never to meet in this world may Heaven grant us all a happy meeting in the Everlasting Mansions of Bliss when time and terrestrial things shall be no more. Duty, Love and best wishes attend my honoured though unknown Uncle and Aunt and all my amiable cousins from their and your Affectionate Cousin, Betsy Palmer"

After the hiatus caused by the war, which is generally accorded the dates 1775 to 1783, family correspondence must have restarted as soon as hostilities ceased. One of the first postwar letters[9] we have from JC was addressed to Joseph Palmer on 12th April 1783. Both international and family relations were becoming more normal by then as the following extracts reveal. Palmer was still living in Germantown, making his doomed attempt to recover financially from the war:

> "Dear Uncle, In some of the few letters we have received from you since the commencement of that tyranny from which the liberties of America have lately been rescued, you were pleased to hint somewhat that (as I remember) amounted to a caution against writing anything to our friends on your side [of] the water touching the current politics of the times. This caution made the deeper impression upon me not only from your very friendly and humane motive for giving it but also from a due consideration of the inefficacy and insignificancy of anything I could utter either against the actors of that tyranny or in behalf of their opponents. It sufficed therefore that under an absolute conviction of the validity of a cause which ought not to have been considered as more the cause of <u>America</u> than of <u>mankind</u> in general, I religiously espoused it in my heart, and awaited in silent patience (though not without strong confidence) the glorious issue it has since produced.
>
> The late peace seems at present to be drawing people to your continent from all parts of Europe. In this country it is certain that America is generally looked to as the grand asylum of persecuted liberty and property. May she long deserve the honorable distinction: very late may the poisons of luxury taint the virtuous simplicity of her national constitution and long may the divine providence continue to her a government worthy of the

noble stand she has made for the rights of humanity! As to the war, I presume you [realise] that it certainly was not the war of the people of Britain, but only ...an effect of a general corruption of the legislative and governing powers – the <u>punishment</u> and not the <u>fault</u> of its people.

The constitution of empire and human government like that of the human frame imbibes with the very aliment [food] by which it is sustained the principles of those vices which sooner or later inevitably destroy it: this is merely in the necessary nature of things, and however mortifying the supposition, and though the decline of America will in all likelihood be from a higher pitch of true grandeur than this country could ever pretend to, yet when I consider her vast internal sources and rudiments of luxury, I cannot help apprehending that America herself may one day be what Britain is – like her sink from the glory of being the protectress of liberty to the infamy of being its greatest oppressor! Pray Sir, pardon me these flights, and I will now endeavour to keep my pen within a humbler sphere."

After this grandly pessimistic prophecy about America JC wrote a long paragraph, recommending to Palmer, his friend Thomas Hopkins, a mercer, who was just then emigrating there, to commend his virtue, energy and business acumen. He went on:

"...I hope that, in consequence of the free navigation restored by the peace, we may now be favoured with American friends which they formerly thought us deserving of; we had but seldom the pleasure of hearing from you in the course of the war. Some letters I once saw which mentioned you having taken the part that became you in cause of your country; and I was informed by a Mr Jackson a refugee whom I saw in London 2 or 3 years ago that you had declined the proposal of your fellow citizens to depute you their representative in the general congress, from a consideration that your services might be more useful in the province.

The last tidings I had of you were happy indeed: Mr Bond (my sister Hannah's husband) wrote me from Plymouth that a Mr Stour had lately brought authentic advices of your being all well – particularly that my old correspondent Uncle Richard Cranch was quite recovered from a severe illness and contrary to expectation.

As to the state of our domestic and family concerns here (which I know you would not forgive me if I omitted to mention), I presume you [have not learned] that your beloved friends my father and mother are both dead: I scarcely need to say to you, my dear Sir, who knew them so well, that they departed <u>rich</u> in that without which every other acquisition serves only to impoverish, or that the memory of those two excellent persons is held in the highest esteem. My brother William succeeded in my father's business. We are all now dispersed in the world but it is great consolation to me that our hearts are nevertheless so knit together in those strong habits of fraternal friendship contracted in our earlier years that we may almost be said to be rather one <u>person</u> than one <u>family</u>: Esto perpetua! And I know this will give you and Aunt Palmer and Uncle Cranch great pleasure and that we shall be sure of your prayers for the future stability of our alliance.

Pray give my affectionate respects to your lady my worthy aunt, and to my other old correspondent cousin Betsy; to your son and Miss Paine and to all the old society. You perceive by this my unwillingness to imagine any of you separated from the rest, or that you are not all continued (or at least restored) to your wonted tranquility at Germantown; but here poor cousin Nat's death comes across my mind like a cloud obscuring the fond prospect and rendering some of the most amiable objects in it indistinct and doubtful. I pray God you may all continue long in good health and safety and in all other blessings here and be rewarded with eternal felicity hereafter. I remain, most affectionately, Sir, your dutiful nephew, J. Cranch"

On 20th June 1783 JC received a letter[10] from his uncle Richard Cranch who had met up with JC's friend, Hopkins, and been brought his first communication from JC in years. He says that the New England climate may be worse than parts of Europe but that in America "…we enjoy **Liberty**!" [his emphasis]. He goes on to extol the information he is receiving about the westward migration of Americans and how they are encountering richly fertile country further inland. He envisages a time when the whole continent will be populated by Europeans and regular interaction established across the Pacific with Asia. His letter was to be carried to England by a close relation of his wife, indicating that the Smiths too were quite recent immigrants to America from Devonshire.

From the same year we have a letter from JC to Eunice Paine and one to his cousin Betsy Palmer. These are already showing signs of the familiar style he adopted with his younger correspondents as their relationships progressed. His letter to Eunice dated 20th September begins with what was evidently a response to her predictions about future governance in the recently liberated America:

"…Politics being the less pleasing subject – (in itself, Eunice, not in your manner of treating it) – let us dispatch politics first: sure the legislators of America could never have dreamt of '<u>perfection</u>' in government, so fond an idea could only have prevailed among the ignorant, inconsiderate and unexperienced. 'Tis true America has at command the collected experience and wisdom of the past ages of the world as materials for a system of government that we may [therefore] reasonably suppose will be <u>original</u>, and superior to the rest: but that very experience at the same time proves that in all human operations, 'perfection' is impossible and visionary and, consequently, that it cannot reasonably be aimed at nor supposed. I can easily conceive the prevalence both of 'tyranny' and 'licentiousness' in the present 'vibrating' state of American policy and power. The thing accounts for itself: Men *absolutely free*, must be subjected <u>gradually</u> and (in every practicable instance) no faster than they can be made sensible of the reasonableness or necessity of the subjection."

JC's reflections show the fruits of his wide reading. He was at this stage a relatively untravelled provincial lawyer and yet his comments seem quite wise. He goes on to draw attention to his current status in what one suspects is rather a mock modest manner. He has spotted that Eunice's letter has been addressed to him by some third party:

"…There lies your letter before me… and I with all the gravity and application of a virtuoso am forming conjectures of who wrote the superscription. The [handwriting] is too good to be yours [and] it can't be uncle Palmer's for he, you say, wasn't at home and yet 'tis in his manner. Perhaps 'twas cousin Joe but, whoever 'twas, I desire to know what provocation you, he, she or they had to insult a poor country retailer of law, with the title of 'Esqr'."

The honorific 'Esqr' would then have been reserved for lawyers called to the bar and it would have been decidedly ironic on JC's part to regard such a 'promotion' as 'an insult'. JC goes on to describe being commissioned by a family called Domett to apply on its behalf to the British government for the compensation guaranteed to loyalists forced out of America. Mr Domett had been comptroller of customs at Falmouth (now Portland, ME) in Casco Bay and had his house there destroyed by the Americans and himself imprisoned in Boston for six weeks, and then banished to England. JC then writes about his friend Hopkins who, on the recommendation of Richard Cranch, has gone to this same Falmouth to sell the goods he had brought from England[11]:

"…H.[opkins] I find is gone to Falmouth, and has opened business just in such a style of intrepidity as might be expected from a man of enterprise, and of his warmth of temper and natural bias to industry. If you see him pray remember me kindly to him and say I wish him all prosperity. Between you and I he has exaggerated my character abominably and you need not have hinted at the dilemma it would put me in if by ever settling among you I should be called upon to make it good; the conscious disproportion makes me blush even at this distance from you… [If] I could do any service by getting translated out of this <u>obsolete</u> country into yours, I should make as light of a voyage from hence to America as of a [trip] from Kingsbridge to Salcombe; Uncle Palmer probably can tell you what a merry sort of voyage that is… I'll talk to Mr Adams when he comes to

England if I can prevail upon myself to solicit the honor of being permitted to pay my tribute of admiration and respect to that illustrious man... I conclude with presuming that it will be a public concern of America that so virtuous and enlightened a citizen as Mr. Palmer shall not sink under the burden of a temporal misfortune, tho' I flatter myself I foresee his redemption by other means. God bless you all, and write whenever you can."

The distance from Kingsbridge to Salcombe in Devonshire is approximately six miles. JC's letter to Betsy Palmer dated 17th December mainly refers to a previous request from her to JC requesting that he procure for her the writings of Hannah More about whom she had obviously heard admiring comments. Later correspondence[12] included several discussions about Miss More, the English author on moral and religious subjects, philanthropist and educator. JC replies[13] that he must send to Bath for the books and hopes to have them nicely bound for her. Presumably her letter accompanied his of the same date to Joseph Palmer[14] which was a rather esoteric discussion of how Congress should be constituted so as to represent the "true-sacred *vox populi*" and that such an institution, "fairly elected by the people ...cannot be trusted with too much power" and that as a result "your empire will most probably be lasting, and it's administration generally happy". Both men seem to have taken the keenest interest in the debate on what structure of government independent America should have. One might comment that at least the result was greatly superior to what arose in the aftermath of the French revolution, which lay so soon in the future.

A good deal of JC's correspondence with his uncles, cousins and Eunice Paine survives from 1784. We can speculate on the reasons for this fertile period. The cousins were mostly still young, living at home and yet to embark on their difficult later adult lives. Transatlantic relations were reviving in all respects after the war which meant an increase in shipping available to carry letters. The Adams family were commencing their most intense involvement with Europe which, as far as it related to JC, led up to their meeting and his accompanying them during their visit to Devonshire in 1787. Almost as soon as that event was over JC moved to London with all its distractions but whether his correspondence with America then declined or whether further letters are yet to be found or have been destroyed is impossible to say. The fact that JC was made a member of the American Antiquarian Society as late as 1818, when William Cranch, son of JC's uncle Richard was also a member, is one indication that he remained in contact. He was also close to his nephew William Cranch Bond and they met more than once towards the end of JC's life. The 1784 letters range in style from excruciatingly polite to skittish and even flirtatious and the summaries and selected quotations given here provide a picture both of JC in unguarded correspondence with those he trusted and also of the infant United States.

Commencing with JC's older relatives, Joseph Palmer was still trying to recover financially and physically from the war and had only four more years to live. On 18th June he wrote at length to JC[15] continuing their discussion about Congress and how it was necessary for it to be given adequate powers to compel uniformity of things like coinage, weights and measures etc. for the Confederation, so as to present a united front to the world, despite the individual states jealously guarding their own way of doing things down to the smallest detail. Palmer clearly saw the possibility that the Confederation would break up and the individual states would go their separate ways. This letter had been carried to England by Mrs Adams and her "very amiable daughter". Palmer concluded, "That these persons are the wife and daughter of an American Ambassador, is enough to command your attention; but when to that is added all those brilliant accomplishments so conspicuous in these ladies and which adorn their religion and virtue, you must be charmed..." On 20th August JC replied[16]:

> "Honoured Sir, Your kind present of political papers came safe at last, and I take the opportunity to thank you both for them and for the honour of your subsequent letter of the 18th June [brought] by Mrs Adams, by which, especially by your sentiments on the relative constitutions of the general Congress and of the separate states, I have been highly gratified. Your reasons for immediately investing Congress with certain powers which are absolutely necessary in the government, and to which none of the states in their separate capacities are competent, appear to me to have been formed on the largest scale of good policy and to be unanswerable.

> Whenever you may have opportunity to resume this theme to communicate any other information concerning either yourself, your neighbourhood, your province or your country, be assured that nothing will afford more pleasure to, Honoured Sir, your (inquisitive correspondent), dutiful nephew and obliged humble servant, JCr. Please to present my most dutiful respects to my Aunt."

The next letter we have from Joseph Palmer to JC was dated 13th October and was carried to JC by his friend John Clapcott who was returning to

England after a visit to America. JC had written[17] to his uncle Richard in June to introduce Clapcott and his project to import Dorsetshire strong beer to America. John was the nephew of Simon Bunter, JC's employer in Axminster, and came from a well-off farming family. His brother was the brewer. Whatever the demerits of the beer project, Clapcott was to be an outstanding social success with JC's American lady correspondents. However, he was to disappoint them by sailing back to England after just a few months.

Palmer's letter[18] is, in fact, the last significant communication from him to JC that we have and merits extensive quotation:

"Dear Sir, I hope you received mine by Mrs Adams [and] that you have had the pleasure of conversing with her and Miss Adams, but as their stay in England was very short, much shorter than I expected, 'tis not probable that you could have much of their good company. I hear that Mr Adams came over to London incognito, tarried only one night, and carried off his Lady next morning for Paris, at which place is to be the negotiation for a Treaty of Commerce between Great Britain and these States. May it be concluded upon terms of reciprocity for unless it be for the mutual and equal benefit of the parties, it can't be expected to be permanent.

I have been confined by the gout and an ulcer on my ankle [for] about 3 months, but am better though still very weak and lame and badly able to write. However, I could not justify myself to myself, unless I sent you a few lines by Mr Clapcott. He was polite enough to pay us a short visit and appears to me a very promising young man. By the account that Mr Hopkins and this young gentleman, give of you and by the general spirit of your letters to us, it seems as though your enthusiasm in favour of America would lead you to pay us a visit, if you can make it convenient. Should that be the case, you will meet with a hearty welcome, not only from your relations, but from many others. And if you should settle among us, I foresee, that your love of liberty and study of governmental matters will, in a few years (if your general conduct be prudent) place you in the House of Representatives and from thence into the Senate. But whether it will be for your interest to come or to settle here, you must judge.

I dare not obtrude my advice but the lawyers here generally find their account in the litigious disposition of the people, which disposition probably arises from an excess of liberty, a kind of ebullition, for there is but a line between liberty and licentiousness. It will be a work of years, to revise and establish the constitutions of the several states and that of Congress, but when well done it will curb the licentious spirit and, as the people grow more orderly and wiser, there will be less business in proportion to their numbers in the executive courts. You will perceive by this and my former letters, that I do not think the Confederation of these States so perfect as it ought to be in order to secure the greatest possible good to the multitude. And you will also observe that the doctrine of *imperium in imperio*, has no place in my political creed. As to the *Vox populi*, when fairly and truly taken I believe it to be the *Vox Dei* but it is in common extremely difficult to collect the real *Vox populi* because the influences of parties mislead the multitudes."

He goes on to recall at length a tale from his youth in England when at an election he encountered a drunken political opponent who, in trying to swing at him with a stick, missed and fell in the mud (so much for *Vox populi*). After recommending a religious tract he concludes:

"…Your Aunt [Mary] Palmer, is in better health than for some years past, but unhappy in the loss of the sight of one eye. We happen to be deep, very deep, sufferers by the late war* and we find it difficult at our time of life to begin the World anew; and this makes me feel much for your good aunt and our children, especially as my health has lately ailed much. However, we trust in him, who is good to all and whose tender mercies are over all his works. Your Aunt sends her love to you; the girls have, or will write for themselves if able but our various troubles have brought them low. My son is getting into business again in Boston and I hope will succeed well and will probably write to you. Adieu, J. Palmer P.S. Miss Eunice P[aine] is in Boston and I hope will write to you.

*This was the fate of many others, who, in that distressing time, gave up themselves, almost entirely, to the public good, little regarding their private interest."

JC had expressed his pleasure at renewed post-war contact with his uncle Richard in an effusive letter[19] dated 14th February 1784:

"…Not a cold, formal, European – No, 'twas a warm – a generous – an American impulse, which urged my revered uncle thus voluntarily to honor me with the first advances towards a renewal of our ancient correspondence; to embrace thus the very earliest opportunity of again striking into those delightful walks of communication which the tedious war had so unkindly shut us out of!

Permit me Sir, to confess also my obligation for the favours you have done me in the person of my friend [Thomas Hopkins]. I trust that friend himself (whom I have now to envy in the character of your fellow citizen) will permanently retain his present lively sense of those favours, so that you may never have cause to regret what you have done for him. At the same time, be assured, I hold myself solely and independently obliged by your kindnesses on that score, be the issue what it may.

I contemplate, with pleasure, your fine picture of the rising grandeur of the new empire, but while that stupendous and delightful prospect so highly gratifies my feelings and imagination, and (by the way) pays so flattering a compliment to my foresight, I am sighing for some vast, comprehensive (perhaps you will add some 'impossible', or 'unnecessary') system of wise and liberal policy to preserve it. The last post brought me a most obliging letter from your brother the ambassador, by which I learn that his excellency got well to the Hague the 17th ult; I am much concerned (and almost ashamed to own to you) that my incurable shyness deprived me of the pleasure of paying my respects to him in England. I have ever esteemed this illustrious man as a public character but now that he calls Mr Palmer his 'friend' and you his 'most valuable brother' I dote upon him.

Do me the favour to present my duty to my aunt and, for the sake of a beloved and excellent friend departed [JC's father, presumably] pray continue to regard, Sir, your affectionate nephew and servant."

Richard responded[20] on 18th June, by expressing pleasure at JC's flattering sentiments towards America. He tells him that Abigail Adams has seen his letters and wishes to meet him. He has asked Mr Elworthy (JC's brother-in-law) to secure accommodation for the Adams family and their staff in London and suggests that JC meet them there.

On 18th August JC wrote[21] to Richard saying that, owing to his commitments and hers, he had failed to converse with Abigail Adams except for the briefest of introductory visits. He mentions his continuing grief over the loss of his father, "one of the best, wisest and most agreeable of men". His next letter[22] dated 19th September was yet another recommendation for an acquaintance named William Pratt who was trying his luck by carrying a cargo of manufactured goods to Boston. JC seems single-handedly to have tried to re-establish Anglo-American trade. On 11th October Richard responded[23] at length to JC's letter which had introduced John Clapcott:

"Dear Sir, I have received your esteemed favour by Mr Clapcott, and have this day had the happiness of entertaining your worthy young friend at our house. He lodged here last night. We are much pleased with his modest agreeable behaviour. I am sorry to find that his adventure of beer is not like to answer very well – there is, comparatively, very little beer used in this country. The gentry generally make use of wine and punch and the common drink is cider (which is very plent[iful] in New England) or rum and water mixed. I wish our friend could have made it agreeable to have spent a few months in America, so that he might have seen the country but he says he has such an aversion to a cold winter passage that he determines to return immediately. 'Tis true he could not here be entertained with those surprising works of art which Europe can now boast and the vanity of which Asia with its ten thousand ruins can demonstrate, but the beautiful and especially the sublime of Nature may be seen here in their original. And though we have not in this western world such gorgeous Palaces as once adorned the East, yet we are happy on reflecting that we are also free from the tyranny that raised them and the slavery that maintained them."

Richard Cranch was being a trifle disingenuous here although Massachusetts only ever had a few slave owners and had recently legally abolished slavery when this letter was written. He went on:

"…I wrote you on the 18th of June by Sister Adams. I hope you have seen her and her children. I rejoice to hear of their safe arrival – I suppose their stay in London was short and that they are now gone to Paris. Should you have an opportunity of writing to his Excellency Mr Adams, I wish you would present my most affectionate regards to him and his family and let him know that I saw his sons Charles and Thomas a few [days] ago, who were very well. Mr Clapcott will inform you about the several branches of our family and your Uncle Palmer's, where he paid a short visit last evening. I hope our young friend will meet you and his other friends in England in health and under the most agreeable circumstances and am, with great Esteem, your affectionate Uncle, Richard Cranch.

P.S. Please to remember me to all our connections in the West [of England]. By Captain Scott, who sails this week for London I have sent a long letter to your worthy brother Mr Bond of Plymouth. It contains some observations on America which possibly may not be disagreeable to you to read. My dear wife and children are well. I hope you will continue to write as often as you have opportunity. If our friend [Thomas] Hopkins is in England give my compliments to him."

JC's reply is taken from an undated draft[24] which included a substantial area of crossing out. Since that is interesting in its own right (one presumes JC decided that it was too disrespectful to send) it is restored here in italics:

"Sir, my friend Clapcott after a troublesome voyage returned safe into this country, I think about ten weeks after the date of those letters which you did me the honour to send by him. His mother (who was ill of a consumption before he left England) had been dead about 3 weeks and his uncle – the gentleman with whom I had been so long connected in business – had also lately died, and in consequence of both events a property of 12 or 15 thousand pounds value had devolved on my friend and his next brother…

The public papers I observe have noticed the arrival of your brother Mr Adams in quality of minister plenipotentiary from the United States of America to the Court of Great Britain some few weeks since. The following paragraph caught my eye just now [in] the Sherborne Mercury. 'It is said, that Mr Adams, the American Ambassador, was so embarrassed at his first audience as not to pronounce the compliment prescribed by etiquette. The great person before whom he stood, very good-naturedly passed by the omission, and told him that though it would not be a pleasing circumstance to receive an embassy from those who were once his subjects, yet as the right was insured to them by treaty, he might depend upon being treated with every mark of regard and protection.

Mr. Adams being at the court of France when your favour of the 11th October arrived, I thought it hazardous for me to trouble his Excellency with a letter, on purpose to do myself the honor of communicating your information respecting his sons, especially considering the probability of that information being superseded by some more direct conveyance from America; though, after all, I fear I may have been wrong in that conception and blameable for not having punctually executed your command.

Being in hopes of seeing my good sister Bond this summer, I have not yet read the letter to which you so obligingly refer me, but I have perused with extreme pleasure one that my brother Elworthy was lately honoured with from the same quarter on the subjects of American commerce and credit and I must confess, Sir, that it tempts me to envy the felicity of your more intimate correspondents, though I must nevertheless acknowledge myself to be, with the utmost affection and respect, Your obliged dutiful nephew"

Evidently the family of JC's sister Elizabeth Elworthy was very much in touch with her American relatives although few traces of that correspondence have been found by the author. JC's next letter[25] to Richard Cranch, dated 27th September concerned another of his sisters, Hannah (Fig. 8), who was married to William Bond as mentioned previously:

"Sir, It is not without some confusion of mind and some disagreeable apprehension of offending you that after having in my letters [sent] by Mr Pratt, in effect renounced my late practice of troubling you with testimonies in behalf of emigrants from this country, I should yet have occasion to infringe that resolution. My motive now is indeed more forcible, and such a one as I am more inclined to expect your pardon for being the advantage of one to whom, besides his valuable character in general, we are all obliged for his particular attachment to an amiable and virtuous sister. Some knowledge of Mr Bond's merits has I observe already found its way to America, having drawn some very flattering testimonies of approbation from some of my correspondents in that quarter and on that account it will be the less necessary for me to attempt to describe a character to which I am conscious I cannot express the justice it deserves.

By a very odd succession of incidents Mr Bond found out [about] and has to his entire satisfaction been induced to join Mr. Hopkins's corps of adventurers from this part; and they are all I find to sail from Lyme this morning. Mr Bond's view (therefore) being at present directed to the

Casco [Bay, Maine] settlements he will most probably stand in need only of such informations and advices as you may be pleased to honour him with on that head. I will only add that I cannot but expect that his principles as a man and his abilities as a mechanic and a tradesman added to the abundant good nature and humanity of his disposition will not fail to gain him all due esteem and patronage from his connections in the new world. I am with much affection and respect, Sir, your dutiful nephew and faithful humble servant, J. Cr. Being straitened in time I shall not be able to write to any of my other friends by this opportunity."

The Bond family counts as another American immigrant success story among JC's relatives[26]. William Bond, although apprenticed originally as a goldsmith became a clockmaker in America. His son, William Cranch Bond (Fig. 9), was born in America and also became a highly regarded clockmaker who produced the first chronometer made in America. He also showed strong interest in astronomy from an early age and established his own observatory from which he made several discoveries whose importance is still acknowledged today. In 1815 he was commissioned by Harvard University to gather information on European observatories with a view to establishing astronomy there as an academic discipline and was appointed the first director of the Harvard University Observatory in 1839. However, the Bonds as a family rather regretted their emigration and kept to English ways. On 18th July 1819 in Kingsbridge, Devon, William Cranch Bond married his first cousin, Selina Cranch. In the marriage record he is described as a citizen of Boston and certainly the Bonds' clockmaker's shop existed in that city until modern times. Selina bore him four sons and two daughters and after Selina's death in 1831, Bond married her older sister, Mary Roope Cranch. His son George joined the astronomical enterprise and further important joint discoveries with his father followed. However, William Cranch Bond yearned to live in England[27], liking neither the business environment nor the climate of Massachusetts. But, he was never able to accumulate or borrow the capital required to set up a business in England though he was a frequent visitor and met JC on more than one occasion, as mentioned above.

1784 also yielded a good deal of correspondence with JC's Palmer cousins. As mentioned previously, we should here recall again that Elizabeth was much used as a girls' given name at that time but it was common within families to use one of the common contractions. Thus Elizabeth Palmer was, as described above, usually 'Betsy' and Elizabeth

Cranch was usually 'Eliza' and those names have been adopted for them consistently below. On 13th February of that year JC wrote[28] to Betsy bewailing his inability to obtain for her a fine copy of Hannah More's works: "Under this disappointment I am mortifyingly obliged to forward Miss More in a very uncouth draggled condition which considering her merit, I can scarcely expect you will pardon me for". Much of the rest of his letter is devoted to literary criticism of Miss More's work, for example:

"...The first thing I dipped into in poor Hannah's books was *Sensibility*, a poem, and I must own I began to read it totally with the air and disposition of one who expected to find nothing more in it than the common cant upon that subject: judge then how agreeably I must have been surprised when it caught my attention and fairly held it fast by uncommon thoughts and the finest philosophical and moral distinctions adorned with every grace of poetry...*The Search After Happiness*, though abounding in fine morals and good versification is very dull and the whole dramatic plan of it to the last degree unnatural... The 'Essays' are above all praise, though of so different a cast of merit, they have actually pleased me as much as Lord Bacon's."

Even Joseph Pearse Palmer's wife Elizabeth wrote[29] to JC during May of 1784 in a letter which included enquiries about Hannah More who was obviously the subject of admiration and fascination among the young ladies of New England:

"...And now, Sir, permit me to ask you some questions [about] your own countrywoman. Hannah More, as you are pleased to call her, has gained many, very many, admirers on this side [of] the water and I as one of them wish exceedingly to know her history. Who she is? Where [does] she live and what have been her misfortunes? I think she must have been unfortunate or she would not have been so good. Her mind must have been softened by calamity or she would not have painted compassion and humanity in such striking colours. Above all she appears to be a very good woman. I want to know how old she is...by your letters I should suppose you were acquainted with her, if not personally you undoubtedly are with her history and your good nature will prompt you to gratify the curiosity of one who has suffered her gratitude to overcome her pride in thus exposing herself in comparison with those who are so much her superiors in this mode of communication."

May 23rd saw Betsy Palmer writing[30] again at length to JC after being particularly asked to do so by Abigail Adams who was shortly sailing for England and expected to visit the western parts and "wishes for letters to other friends, to Cousin Jack... in particular, for she wants to see him". Hannah More was on her mind too:

49

"...About a month ago we had the pleasure of being introduced to Miss More and though in her deshabille I was never more pleased with any lady, even in full dress. Yet I cannot boast the honour of having had a great share of her company; a few domestic engagements have prevented my conversing so much with her as I wish and intend. She has however given me her sentiments on several important subjects, and I never was more pleased than with her delicate distinction between the Silence of Listless Ignorance and the Silence of Sparkling Intelligence. It was an idea that I had felt the force of a thousand times but had never found language to express it...You seem to be acquainted with Miss More – I wish to know everything you can tell me of her character – how she looks – how old she is, what station of life she is in and why she isn't married – but I suppose she is too sensible – don't mistake me – I mean that your Sex in general are so terribly afraid of being out-shone – that they dare scarcely venture to marry a woman who can write grammatically much less... a wife who writes for the press."

In the same letter she also recalls an idyllic afternoon spent in beautiful country near the coast with friends including Nathaniel Cranch who, as mentioned above, died mysteriously:

"...Youth innocence and hope were our companions. We neither anticipated the future nor regretted the past and our enjoyment was pure. We plucked the flowers in our way, delighted our eyes with their beauty and were regaled with their fragrance without recollecting that they would soon fade and be forgotten... Will you my Dear Cousin Jack accept the enclosed little ornament for your watch. Accept it as a tribute to departed worth; wear it my Cousin for His sake, wear it for mine."

Later she describes overhearing her brother reading one of JC's letters addressed to her father, which prompts her to write:

"...Now there is a glow of enthusiasm in some of your letters... Do you know that a degree of this said enthusiasm is a favourite ingredient (with me) in a character, not being one of the mighty prudent sort of folks myself I don't love those that are so. Your clever sort of people that never take a wrong step, who walk straight forward and look neither to the right nor left, [I wish] peace to their quiet souls; may their path be level before them; but let it not be connected with mine."

She concludes with family news and descriptions of several relatives. There is also speculation and enquiry about JC's love life; she assumes that despite his retiring existence he must have formed an attachment of some sort:

"...If you are absolutely in love, I shall like you the better for it; it makes folks mighty agreeable."

Cousin marriage was quite common in the family and it is not difficult to imagine that the quite flirtatious tone of several of these ladies' letters had some slight ulterior motive. They probably yearned to assess JC in person but were to be disappointed.

In another letter[31] dated 13 June to JC carried to England by Abigail Adams, Joseph Pearse Palmer, the hero of the Boston Tea Party, wrote to his cousin JC in exquisite handwriting:

"Dear Cousin, I am an admirer of your letters and wish to become one of your correspondents; yet my present condition of life is one of those which naturally unfits one for social writing. How to supply the wants of my family is the necessary and constant object of my attention. It is hard for a man in the midst of a battle to fix his mind in search of truth and sentiment. I very much expected to have gone in company with Mrs Adams to Europe and had an opportunity to know and be known among our English friends, but cannot be: perhaps another season may be fraught with more favourable circumstances.

I am now about to take a store in Boston and transact business, on commissions. If any of your friends will make consignments to me, they may depend upon the strictest attention to their interest. Had our Plenipotentiaries, been invested with powers to settle a treaty of commerce with Great Britain at the time they were concluding the treaty of peace it would (in my humble opinion) have been a happy circumstance to the commercial interest of this country, especially New England. I cannot but apprehend many difficulties will now arise to obstruct the settling of such a treaty for the embarrassing, if not destroying our fishery. I suppose [it] to be a great object of British Policy, not only as it is a source of wealth but as it will be the grand nursery of seamen and a consequent foundation for our future strength by sea.

I thank you for *Percy*. I have not yet had opportunity to read it; however, being wrote by H. More and a present from you, are strong inducements, to presume it very good. My Betsy [Elizabeth Hunt Palmer] has wrote you so I have only to add, that I thank her for the pretty things she says of her husband; good nature or good policy, you know, may induce ladies to speak well of those they are legally bound to. Which of the above was her motive I won't pretend to say. However, plain honesty obliges me to affirm she is possessed of both and many, very many, loveable and amicable qualities beside. But as I suppose she will read this letter, I shall suppress mentioning them; she is not without some vanity, I assure you. Would to God, I could make her as happy as she deserves!

I suppose all the circle at Germantown have, or will, write you; yet I cannot avoid saying, it seems hard [that] so good a man as my father [Joseph Palmer] should have such severe trials at so advanced an age but, 'The ways of Providence etc.'. Heaven grant that it may be in my power, by a faithful discharge of filial duty, to lighten the burdens of an unjustly oppressed father and to alleviate the over-anxious solicitudes, of a tender feeling mother! [Mary Cranch Palmer] – And, …by the tender duties of brotherly love, help to [restore my] two beloved sisters to health and cheerfulness! Who[ever] can do all this… shall with strictest truth, be Your (happy) friend and Cousin Jos. P. P[almer]"

His wife did append a few comments to this letter, such as:

"… [I] would inform you that when we first embarked together in the voyage of matrimony, his Papa told him by all means to keep peace at home and his knowledge of the human heart, of its fondness for praise, especially from those we love has induced him to write thus; but let me tell you it has not saved him from a box on the ear."

She is also one of several relatives to warn JC to be careful of the attractions of John and Abigail Adams' daughter, "… she is indeed a sweet girl, but you have eyes – and take care to veil them."

On 20th June JC wrote to Betsy Palmer[32] opening by telling her how he is hatching a plan with Captain Callahan to transport his friend John Clapcott to America. He goes on skittishly:

"…[Betsy] you are a sweet correspondent! Only promise to spell a little better and to write legibly and I swear to be constant to you. But only think of Mrs Adams's being obliged to me for the most recent advices of the welfare of her good man! Need I own to you that this lucky hit makes me proud?

I will own the truth to thee, [Betsy], my curiosity in regard to America and American persons and things is unbounded and I should read an account of a mere merry meeting of three or four gossips at Braintree or German-town, with more avidity than an account of a jubilee or even a coronation, at Westminster. But to be serious Elizabeth, did you ever see a rattle snake, or a wild Indian? Have you any vineyards, or orangeries or orchards of apples about you. How far back in the wild parts of your country have you ventured? Are your horses and cows *ab origines*, or were they brought from Europe? Have you slaves? Are you yet persuaded that the war was the war of a detestable faction and not [the responsibility of] this abused unhappy nation, which has suffered by it more by half than you have? Lastly have you got any money? If I send over a ship load of the best strong beer in the world will any of you buy it and pay for it? It is confidently said that you have in general got more money than we have.

Did you see any battle or skirmish in the course of the war, and how many did you kill or wound? What adventures, either droll or dreadful, did any of you meet with? We are made to suppose that half of you went without clothes during the war. Speak the truth now Betsy, had you any shoes, or more than one stocking for a long time? Do you dress *á la Anglais*, or after the fashion of your new allies [the French], or do they suffer you to have a taste of your own? Finally, (for I think I have said 'lastly' before) did you ever read such a parcel of stuff as your loving cousin has wrote here? I conclude in a pet – because you say nothing about your father or mother. Adieu!

P.S. I sent a miserable long letter to Miss Eunice a good while ago. It began about politics and treated an abundance of other subjects both high and low, I don't remember when, or which way it was sent, but can't help wishing she may have received it though it were ever so great a farrago of nonsense, for (without affectation) I had rather be guilty of that, than of ill manners.

My duty to Uncle Palmer and I have at last received his valuable present: I have no demand on him now but for a long letter which I am strongly addicted to think he owes me and shall be most happy to receive. Uncle Cranch is in the same predicament."

Polly Palmer took it upon herself on 29th September to answer[33] the series of enquiries he had made to her sister about life in New England. The nearest rattlesnakes were five miles away from Germantown and whilst their bites were venomous, wearing boots was usually a sufficient protection. Native Americans had receded 2 to 300 miles inland, settlers having bought their land nearer the coast. She had seen some chiefs and expressed fear of their "ferocious countenances". Fruit of many sorts was in good supply and her father had planted a large orchard. Massachusetts was legally a slave-free state and blacks were not numerous there. The War of Independence had largely occurred elsewhere and only during the first year had guns and drums been audible in Germantown. Boston was, "a large town and a very handsome one containing near 30,000 inhabitants" who dressed fashionably with clothes imported easily from London. Some had money and others not, as in England, but beggars were few and labour was expensive to hire. However, crime was treated far more leniently than in England of the time:

"...Robberies and housebreaking are too frequent but those who are guilty are chiefly from Europe. We seldom hang any for our laws are very tender of life. Imprisonment, sitting on the gallows for one hour and 39 stripes besides paying costs is what the worst of them suffer. For the first offence of breaking open a dwelling house [there are] severer penalties but juries are very merciful."

Both Palmer sisters wrote again to JC in October. Polly[34] had met Mr Clapcott and thought him "a very pretty young fellow; he was so pretty that I wanted him to be an American. He speaks in high terms of you; I fancy that you are indeed an uncommon genius". However, Clapcott had also described JC's carelessness about his appearance and Polly devotes a quarter of a folio sheet in detailed admonition for what she deems a fault in JC. This letter shows that the seeds were already sown of the melancholy disposition which eventually caused her to withdraw from life. She wrote:

> "...Cousin Jack, I fear you think too well of us Americans. We should be very glad indeed to see you but your imagination has pictured us too flatteringly; we are no saints I'll assure you, quite the reverse, nor have we great plenty of money neither are we politically prudent. Finery is the thing our ladies covet and their obliging fathers and husbands bankrupt themselves to gratify their vanity. Indeed you would be sick of us in a month. It is only the fear of your disappointment in us and the expense you must be at to come and go that prevents my arguing you to come, for we wish to see you."

She describes how ill her father has been with an infected wound complicated by a severe attack of gout which might have been worse but for his temperance in diet, "seldom eating flesh and very rarely tasting anything stronger than cyder". She suggests that:

> "...few men could inform you better of what you are so desirous of the knowledge of American concerns than he who had a great hand in bringing us out of bondage, as may appear by his papers and many plans of fortification. In the first year of the war we were mere novices, knew nothing at all about it. Every man it is true was obliged to keep a gun and proper ammunition but not 5 in 10 had them. And they were also by the law obliged to train, that is, exercise their arms four times a year, but they had not done it. The magistrates and the people were alike remiss till danger roused the latter and then they had not wherewithal. The God of Hosts was with us or we never could have done as we did! Very few amongst us understood fortification; Papa in his younger days had made it his study [and] he now brought it into actual service. By that means [he] did greater good to his American Country than by the active service... in the many battles he was in."

She then dwells on personal and public misfortunes until, "I find I grow low spirited so I'll leave off for this time and go take bitters".

Betsy's letter[35] to JC starts with a similar assessment of Mr Clapcott's 'prettiness'. As to the shipload of strong beer, "I'm rather apt to think we can much easier drink than pay for it, but this your friend knows best about – who I fancy was rather disappointed". She goes on to give a detailed description of their cousin Eliza Cranch: "...gentleness and all the truly feminine virtues give a mild lustre to her fine eyes. In a word, her manners are universally pleasing, her mind well cultivated and her face rather agreeable than handsome". After this she gives her own answers to some of the questions JC had asked to which Polly had also responded:

"… I never saw a wild Indian but during our army's stay at Cambridge in '75. I was gratified with the sight of some of the chiefs who took up the hatchet in our behalf and fine looking fellows they were; yet there was a ferociousness in their visages that made me tremble. I have not been far into the heart of the country, perhaps 70 miles or thereabouts is the utmost extent of my peregrinations. The Indian women or as we vulgarly term them, Old Squaws, come among us with brooms and baskets to sell which they make very neat. I once saw a wigwam and was much delighted with the neatness of [it]. There is a pamphlet I have lately seen which if you have not [yet seen it] would gratify you much. It is a *Tour Through the Interior Part of North America* by Captain Carver.

Have we got any money? Yes, some of us have and some have not. Those that have spend it for frippery and those who have none sign for the balloon hats, caps and fringed waistcoats. The wise ones talk much against the merchants for sending such quantities of coin out of the country. It must be a great damage to an infant state. [It is] a pity we can't consent to do without so much of your European finery till our pine-trees, codfish, potash etc. could be exchanged for them.

I saw no battles nor did I do any kind of mischief, except tearing my gown to pieces clambering the rocks to see the cannonade when Charlestown was burned. But Polly has told you all about this matter: scenes of various kinds we were witnesses of and frequently partakers in [but] this would lead into too large a field. I will only observe that the first year of the war called forth each latent spark of virtue. Then a (I had almost said) divine enthusiasm took possession of every bosom. All ages and denominations felt its influence; every heart was open to the sufferer and every hand held forth relief. Alas! The Angel of Benevolence; whither has she fled?! Your Cousin, Betsy Palmer"

A fragment of a letter[36] from JC to Betsy of unknown date responds to the queries about Hannah More:

"…To be serious – I know Hannah More. She has few external charms but there is an easy elegance in her manners and her eye is expressive of the keenest sensibility. Her mind is stored with the richest materials:

A wisdom solid and a judgement clear
A smile indulgent and a soul sincere;
But she won't do for a wife to an attorney,
Unless he has a mind to draw his briefs in hexameter verse.

Your next inquiry… 'who are my friends?' Shall I speak truth of fact, at the expense of rectitude of principle? Then of all my brothers and sisters, dear as they all are, William is the nearest to my heart and yet this young man's external temper is by no means so amiably engaging as some of the sisters. Why is this? It can't be described but only (as Sterne apologises for not describing it) – 'it is sweet to feel by what fine-spun threads our affections are drawn together'.

Next to my relations, stands the companion and cooperator of all the little plans and projects of my earliest youth, my constant friend and correspondent for twenty years past Mr. [John] Andrews (of Modbury)…This learned and ingenious, good and modest man is (very improperly) of the same profession with myself, and equally in love with it. …With three other literati (besides Mr. Andrews) and two or three excellent (non-literary) characters compose the whole circle of my intimate friends in England.

Love to cousin Joseph Cranch; and if he won't venture on a letter let him try at a postscript; as those who can't aspire to an inside passage in a stage coach, politically put up with that safer (tho' less convenient) honour of riding in the basket. J. Cr."

1784 also yielded considerable correspondence with the children of Richard Cranch. On 7th June Eliza wrote[37] at length to JC. Hers seems to have been a quiet soul much attached to domestic life:

"…Did I frequent the gay and brilliant circles, I might perhaps find more entertaining subjects to amuse you with; but as I never had a taste for them I seem to avoid them. You will not doubt this when I tell you I have spent two months in [Boston] these nine years. I live but 11 miles from it and have many relations, all good and hospitable, residing there, but this is my choice – the repose of rural life suits best my disposition. My Papa's business confines him almost all the time in Boston. This is not just as we could wish but we must submit to some undesirable things. A small farm supplies us with butter and cheese which we make in the house and we have been enabled to live comfortably though not in affluence. My Mama is an excellent economist and looks well to the cares of her house. Never were children blessed with more indulgent parents; every reasonable wish of our hearts is gratified so far as circumstances will allow."

She writes at length to describe her own appearance and that of her siblings and then describes her relationships with members of the Adams family:

"…my Aunt Adams expects to sail from Boston in a very few days – by whom I forward this letter…Mayhap you have felt that pang of separation which in a short time our family and myself particularly must suffer at the departure of my Aunt and her only daughter. Ere you read this they will be on the British shore. My Mama and her Sister Adams were near of the same age, raised in the retirement of rural shades and vales. They were almost the only company for each other and formed a friendship, uncommonly strong for sisters. They were both married young to two persons as strongly connected by the bonds of friendship as themselves – my Father and Mr Adams. We live at only half a mile's distance from each other and have lived in love. My cousin Nabby Adams and myself have been friends from earliest infancy; we went to the same schools and united in the same amusements. Her Mama seems almost the parent to me. In all my frequent indispositions she has attended my bed and administerd with tender anxiety the wholesome restoratives. Think my cousin what I shall feel at parting with them! ...Novelty and variety will spread forth all their charms to amuse them whilst we have nothing to do but reflect upon the past, compare it with the present and regret the absence of our friends."

She concludes by expressing "an ardent desire to visit England" and suggests that if JC was to visit America she might travel in his company on his return. "I wish you would petition your neighbours the French to send us over a balloon, then we would all come and make you a visit".

Writing briefly to her on 17th August[38] JC tells her how her American acquaintances have expressed high opinions of her and this combined with her own letter, his respect for her father and their shared taste for a quiet life arouses in him affection for her. He then criticizes himself for expressing such sentiments, "so totally unsuited to the circumstances of a life, which having unhappily begun without aim continues and will most probably end without success!" JC had in fact made great strides in developing his intellect and artistic talent and had procured a modestly profitable profession, albeit one which bored him. His sense of inferiority was to subside as he matured and while his great ability was always recognized by his American acquaintances his lack of just one obsessive focus for his creativity may have set a limit to his fame.

Eliza Cranch had obviously not yet received JC's August letter and did not reply directly until December, such were the vagaries of the post, and in the interval she wrote to him again[39] on 11th October, evidently in an excited state of mind. She too is regretting the early departure of the agreeable Mr Clapcott, then goes on at length to excuse herself for lack of 'female delicacy' in writing to him, supposing he has not written her. She has received his present of a Hannah More book and read his letters to her father and Betsy Palmer and now she hopes to get the same treatment by writing to him. She then gives a flattering description of Betsy Palmer, including the "amiableness and delicacy of her disposition". Next her stream of consciousness expresses her wish for she and JC to exchange visits; she has even dreamed of being in Devon: "seen some great folks and some dear friends and have awoke sadly disappointed". She had evidently sent this letter, together with some notes written earlier, in the care of Mr Clapcott:

> "...I have mentioned several little scraps I have written to you today and I ought to say something more of the enclosures contained in them. I fear that you will think I am somewhat bewildered in my reason by the singular appearance of the valuable presents I have troubled Mr Clapcott with the care of. I was sitting by him turning over my pocket book when this little Indian Hunting Song appeared. I told him I would send it to you to set it to music and then beg the favour of you to return it to me to practise upon. He said you would certainly do it and I gave it him. I proposed spending some of this winter in Boston in order to learn to play upon the harpsichord and when your song comes I hope I shall have made proficiency enough to play it."

This is another of the rare mentions of JC's undoubted musical ability already mentioned in Chapter 1. Via Mr Clapcott she and her sister Lucy had also sent an acorn and a piece of savin (*Juniperus Sabina*) and the accompanying letter[40] written earlier the same day goes as follows:

> "...Will my Cousin Jack accept these small tributes of the affection of his three cousins? My sister and myself would have sent our profiles if we could have had them taken but at present we could not. Will you in return [sic] send us your likeness? We hear you have taken one yourself. We shall [regard it as] a proof of your Love for your American friends. I hear you are a painter; let me have some of your landscapes to adorn my chamber – I will place them just opposite my bed and they shall be objects of my affection. Mr Clapcott is here sitting at breakfast while I am writing; I shall if possible write again before he sails but you must not expect me to write much while he is here; I talk to him all the time – do pray make [apology] to him for my impertinence. I am very awkward at an apology and I assure you one is necessary. [Why] did you let such an agreeable young man come here for to stay so little time – but perhaps a little longer might be dangerous to the heart of your Cousin Eliza Cranch.

> [P.S.] I have just been with my sister, Betsy Palmer and Mr Clapcott to visit a favourite tree upon which are carved the names of many of my friends. Mr C. has put his thereon and the next I hope will be yours. Enclosed is an acorn, the fruit of this said tree. The Savin is a little bush which grows near it; accept them both as the product of the whimsical disposition of your E. Cranch"

Lucy contributed a wrapper for the acorn writing on it[41], "Accept this acorn from the Tree Sacred to Friendship from your friend and cousin Lucy Cranch".

To conclude 1784's busy correspondence between JC and his Cranch cousins, Eliza wrote again[42] on 2nd December as follows:

"...I feel a much more pleasing sensation at sitting down to acknowledge the receipt of a letter from you, my dear Cousin, than I did at writing my last letter to you when the ideas of impropriety and too great presumption were presenting themselves constantly to my mind. But your very kind and affectionate letter of the 17th August has banished them entirely and I shall now write with that confidence which your goodness, candour and indulgence have inspired. The very first sentence of your letter has given me uneasiness as I foresee from it that a store of disappointment is laid up for you and mortification for me if ever we are personally, or by letter, much acquainted. Indeed I cannot thank my friends for that description of the character of E.C. [Eliza Cranch] which their partiality for her (for I will not attribute it to a worse cause) has led them to give you, but I will not say more upon the subject lest you should think she is opening the way for a compliment and will only warn you against that too common error, credulity. Your expressions of tender affection for my Father could not fail of creating an agreeable impression upon the heart of a child who is fully sensible of his exalted worth and who knows no pleasure equal to that of hearing the praises of the friends she loves.

December 11th. This sheet has been thrown by for some time and I had given up the idea of sending it as I did not think it probable I should have an opportunity this season but I hear that [Captain] Callahan sails directly and shall send this on board tomorrow. My Papa and Mama received letters from you about a fortnight since, by Mr [William] Bond, who has arrived at Falmouth. We have not yet seen him but hope to very soon; most cordially shall we welcome him to our habitation. I am much pleased at the idea of his settling with us but could have wished it might have been nearer ...but...I have already laid the plan for paying Mrs Bond [JC's sister Hannah] a visit when she arrives and bringing of her away with me to pass some weeks. Perhaps you may come with her and so gallant me back again; pray how do you like the scheme?

I suppose ere this you have had the pleasure of congratulating your friend Mr Clapcott upon his safe return. Should you see him, be so good as to present my congratulations upon the same happy occasion... In your last letter to my Mama you requested the profiles of my Papa and your eldest cousin and as many more as Mama can find leisure to obtain. You have also promised as an encouragement to the artist that she shall be made a toast of as soon as the shades arrive if she hits the likenesses. So great a temptation cannot be resisted. I must tell you that it is E[liza] C[ranch] but before she is rewarded she must deserve it. It is said she takes good likenesses in general and be assured she will use her best endeavours to gain the prize. Lucy has undertaken to draw my shade and it is said to be a good resemblance; she must come in for a share of the reward but she is quite high I assure you and declares that you shall not be honoured with her profile till you very humbly request it.

I have been to Germantown for a month past and you have been often the subject of our conversations. Your picture, as it hung over the chimney, has been curtsey'd to [and] talked to many times. Sometimes we say you look intolerably saucy, sometimes severe and a great variety of observations are made upon you - Uncle P[alme]r says it's no resemblance of you – when you come we will judge.

I most sincerely sympathise in your disappointment at not seeing Miss Adams but perhaps it is best you should not and I would advise you to console yourself. Please to make my respects and Love to all our Friends and believe me your Friend and Cousin, Eliza Cranch"

Joseph Palmer almost certainly never met JC since he left for America before JC was born and there is no evidence that he ever returned; so his comment was presumably a leg-pull.

As well as JC's cousins, Eunice Paine took advantage of Mrs Adams's passage to England in June of 1784 to send JC a long letter[43] dated 14th. Appended to this is another letter which she had written on May 24th and it is not clear whether the two ended up being delivered together but here the earlier is dealt with first. Eunice, like Eliza Cranch, was inclined to write as her stream of consciousness dictated but with possibly an even less structured approach. She began with the agonies she had suffered at the possible impropriety of having taken the initiative in writing to him first and how relieved she felt when he had replied so urbanely:

"...I was at your Uncle Cranch's and mentioned our having sent along a large packet and that I had wrote to Jack Cranch. 'You have?', 'Yes Sir.' 'What to the lawyer?' Now, there was neither approbation nor disapprobation in the query but all the impropriety which can be imagined stared me in the face. I [would] have recalled it if it had been in my power but it was impossible."

She then said how Abigail Adams had been "exceedingly pleased" with JC's letter and had "laughed heartily". She had been sorry JC had not gone in person to see her husband and she intended to meet him when in England. Not for the first time JC was counselled to be cautious in his dealings with Nabby Adams who was "a fine girl", though shy. The image of "Werter" was raised which presumably was a reference to *The Sorrows of Young Werther* which Goethe had written in 1774 and which had taken the world by storm. Eunice need not have worried; JC's confident tone in letter-writing was belied by his shyness in person and though he met Nabby later there was no awkwardness. Eunice went on to "lament, as other old folks do, the effects of our independence…young folks who always look forward see a thousand alluring scenes to press toward, it's natural and proper, but to those who look back to the simple days before tyranny disturbed us, there's much to be regretted." She must have been writing at Joseph Palmer's house because he had "mended her pen" and as a consequence she now "hopes to do better". She alluded to the extreme difficulties Joseph has suffered after the war:

> "…His steadfastness and diligent application can hardly be equalled. Almost any other man would have been entirely ruined… He now stands firmer and his prospects are clearer. Your Aunt [Mary Cranch Palmer] enjoys herself better in consequence but her strength is small, yet she's much the spryest of us all and was it not for the weakness of her optic nerves would write you and her other friends better letters than any of us can."

Unfortunately her optimism about Joseph Palmer's affairs was unjustified, which by June she was ready to recognize. She was however optimistically predicting to JC an almost immediate visit to the West of England by the Adams family but in fact that did not take place until 1787 because, for the time being, John Adams's duties took precedence. The first paragraphs of her letter were dedicated almost entirely to compliments about Abigail Adams. In Abigail's retinue apparently was one John Briesler and by recounting his history she revealed more about the fate of the Palmer enterprises in Germantown:

> "…He was brought up in your Uncle Palmer's family from a child but has been free six or seven years. [He] is in very poor health and hopes the voyage and rest from labour may restore him…His parents were Germans who came over in the year '53 as settlers to…Germantown and he was a glassmaker when the first proprietors [made use of] children. Your Uncle bought the land and employed the artificers as long as he could [until] want of materials and public disturbances broke up the business. [Your Uncle] then went [into] the spermaceti business [and] employed as many of the hands as liked at that. [The Brieslers] held out as long as any work was to be done [until] the war called off everyone. Oh this cruel, cruel war – what ravages it has made; the blessings of peace and free trade will to very many make up the losses they have sustain'd but to a man far

advanced in life as your Uncle [although] not to say impossible [it is] very unlikely."

Eunice went on to excuse how she had at first addressed JC as 'Esquire' telling him that it was a reasonable assumption considering that lawyers tended to be called to the bar at an earlier age in America, "Vegetation is much more rapid here than in your mild climate; a man that is regularly bred will arrive at his zenith by six and twenty".

> "...I forgot what I said to you of your friends' encomiums but you need not be afraid to appear among your American friends; they all know how to distinguish betwixt real merit and advancement. That you are a retail country lawyer was your friend [Hopkins's] mortification but happiness is not confined to any circumstance nor is merit increased by title; we can all respect plain John Cranch. An interview with our truly illustrious Friend [John Adams] will compose all your flutteration."

Finally she sent greetings to all JC's brothers and sisters expressing particular affection for Mrs Willcocks whose "cheerful disposition pleased me much", and William Bond: "I am quite in love with this Brother of yours. Hannah must be very happy we think".

Her letters called forth a lengthy reply from JC dated 21st August[44] in which, among other topics, he pulled no punches about her awful handwriting:

> "...Not a little of the pleasure I derive from your first letters consists in their being volunteers: so never blame yourself for taking liberties with me: I love them, Eunice, as much as I detest the false appearances of reserve with which the females of this country hide the real coquetism and vanity in which they have the misfortune to be brought up. It was but consistent with my good uncle's wisdom and love of liberty not to blame you for writing to me unasked; for as he only proposed the question, leaving your answer unencumbered with those most grave commentaries – which are commonly bestowed upon the most trifling indecorums. You had certainly, in that instance, a right to take his honour's 'silence for consent'.
>
> I am obliged vastly by the numerous and necessary cautions respecting Miss Adams; female beauty and accomplishments I must own lose none of their force upon me and had I seen the fair maid we are talking of, I am by no means sure that the armour which even you (my Thetis) have furnished me with would have been proof against so powerful a combination of charms.
>
> But do you know I have paid a visit to the Ambassadress? I have, and am mad to think of it; how so? Why I stayed but half an hour; and some

impertinent man of rank interrupted the preface to one of the finest *tete a tetes* that ever was going to begin in the world. The next day her excellency had an engagement at Windsor, and I was obliged to post home.

It's lucky that I am peculiarly well versed in the science of reading difficult and bad penmanship, though I must confess there are passages in yours so singularly disintelligible that I have had much ado to refrain from avenging myself by answering you in the barbarous abbreviated law Latin and Gothic characters of my predecessors, 'learned in the law'.

If Mr Hopkins only talked of my coming to America he was within the bounds of truth. It is true I am heartily tired of this corrupted, worn-out obsolete country, and have long wish'd to be translated out of it and to change the scene. I dabble, you must know, in all the fine arts but my proper hobby horse among them is painting, which has been so long in my service (or rather keeping, for it has wanted actual <u>service)</u> that believing it would hardly carry me conveniently to the end of my journey I have of late been looking about for another."

He went on fancifully to imagine himself joining John Adams's retinue as undersecretary and visiting France and Holland with him but acknowledged the "egregious vanity" of this and asked Eunice, "in the eye of a friend is it the more disagreeable alternative to be vain or to be reserved?". It is revealing of JC's psychology that he thought these qualities to be opposites since he was obviously aware that his introversion – his reserve – caused him to be rather unappreciated in society but at the same time he considered extraverted assertiveness to be 'vanity'.

Letters to and from JC's mainly female American correspondents from the next few years survive and, whilst it isn't certain, it is likely that there was then a slackening off as the individuals pursued their own lives. However some transatlantic contact continued well into JC's old age, demonstrated not least by the conferring on him of membership of the American Antiquarian Society as late as 1818, which he affirmed by sending to the society his thesis on the Roman relics of Bath in the same year, as discussed in more detail in later chapters. He had also made a presentation to the Bath Literary and Philosophical Society on 17th February 1817 concerning a paper he had received from Dorchester, MA which described the mummified corpse of a woman found in a cave in Kentucky. Dorchester was then the home of William Cranch Bond who was therefore quite possibly his correspondent[45].

Chapter 2

Returning to the correspondence with Richard Cranch's daughters JC addressed lighthearted short notes[46,47] to them on 15th June 1785. To Lucy he acknowledged receipt of the 'acorn of friendship' and commissioned from her an account of a week's transactions of an American country household. Eliza's note was written in a phonetic rendition of Devonshire speech (which recalled to the author the still similar talk of old country people of Devonshire heard by him in the 1950s). JC promised to send Eliza some "beautiful elegies and canzonettes by Jackson of Exeter" by the next ship.

The last letter[48] from Eliza Cranch to JC to be found in the Boston Public Library collection was dated 19th November 1786. JC had sent her a bundle of musical scores (although none of his own composition as far as we can tell) of which she acknowledged receipt. Since for this biography, at least, this is our farewell to Eliza her letter is quoted extensively:

> "...I am afraid that I have incurred the charge of ingratitude by my long silence and am apprehensive that assuming the pen now will not acquit me: but you must forgive and accept, though at this late period my sincere thanks for one letter yet unanswered and for the quantity of music you have been so good as to send me; when am I to repay all these kindnesses my good Cousin? I feel my present inability and cannot foresee the manner in future. Perhaps the time may come; till then the consciousness of exalted benevolence and the assurance that you have enlarged my pleasures and happiness must be your satisfaction.
>
> I have not told you how great pleasure the company of your amiable sisters afforded us [Ebbett Cranch and Hannah Cranch Bond had visited]. I could only regret the necessity of their leaving us so soon. I feel sorry they are settled so far distant from us; I should not be more apprehensive at taking a voyage to England than to Portland. I do hope however that I shall some time or other make them a visit. Cousin Ebbett promised to come here and spend some months next spring. We depend upon it. When will you come? I have an unbounded desire to see you; I am prepared to love you very well so you need not [doubt] a most welcome reception. I will insure one equally sincere to your Lady, for I depend upon her accompanying you.
>
> I am afraid that we grow so wicked here and show ourselves to be such ungrateful, unsteady, discontented sort of people that you will not wish to come amongst us. But we are not all such. We are however much affected by the conduct of others and at present our public affairs wear a most unpromising aspect – quarrelling amongst ourselves and most wickedly abusing our Liberty. Our wise folks say it will come to rights in time. Totally unversed in the arcana of state politics, I can only say my wishes are ardent and sincere for the good of our country. Our own domestic

affairs, which I know you are most interested in, are very little altered within these [recent] years; only that we are dependent upon public treasuries and find them generally empty. [So] we live as we can for the present and depend upon promises for the future. Thank Heaven we have not yet suffered; our wishes are circumscribed as well as the means to gratify them so that we enjoy content."

It is ironic that scrip notes, issued by Massachusetts at that time and signed by Richard Cranch, frequently appear today at auction and yet he found it difficult to get paid himself for his public duties. Eliza went on:

"...My Papa spends most of his time in Boston upon public business. My Brother continues at his studies in Cambridge. Next July he leaves them to seek his fortune. I sometimes feel a degree of anxiety for him but it is soon checked. Heaven will direct him; he is yet very good and there never was a more dutiful child or a more tenderly affectionate brother. I fear I love him too much but the affection is so pleasing to my heart that I cherish it and cannot wish it less. My Mama and Sister are well and at present we are all at home. For myself I have little to say; I live on without any essential variation in person, mind, or circumstances endeavouring to fulfil the duties dependent upon the relations of a daughter, sister, friend and acquaintance to the extent of my power. Dependent upon these connections are my pains and pleasures; consequently they must be variable [and] it's true I find them so. My happiest hours are derived from these sources and, alas, my bitterest moments.

My Uncle Palmer's family are now removing from [Germantown] to Charlestown; *And must we leave thee Paradise?* I hope it may prove advantageous for them. They are as usual in health and I wish the change of scenes may raise their spirits.

The loss of the [Adams] family we shall fe[el] [strongly]; they always came to see us two or three times [a] week and now we are deprived of almost all society out of our own family. Aunt Adams must [surely] return or we shall be quite alone. I do not like that England should so long detain what America alone knows how to value.

When you write, tell me I am forgiven for past neglect and reassure me of your continued affection; I hate excuses but this stupid letter stands much in need of one. The weather is excessively cold and though by a good fire I can scarcely hold my pen. Adieu! Continue to love your really affectionate cousin, Eliza Cranch"

There was also further correspondence with the Palmer family during 1785. Betsy in her letter[49] of 13th November was inclined to scold JC for not visiting America. Having their mutual cousin, Joseph Cranch to hand, she pressed him into appending an account of himself. Betsy was eventually to marry Joseph, as mentioned above.

"…It is now six o'clock on Sunday evening. I have ordered a fire here on purpose to employ this evening in writing… The good folks below (by which I would be understood to mean Papa, Mama, Polly and a young lady by the name of Leppington) are supping upon cold roast pork, oysters etc. I have took my bowl of Indian hasty pudding and milk with a few oysters and am seated at my little table to thank you my cousin for your letter of 16th June which I received at my uncle's at noon this day.

It is a long time since we have received a line from any of our friends your side [of] the Atlantic; we have often talked of it and wondered what was the matter. For my own part I acknowledge that I was apprehensive you had taken some offence at some freedom which might inadvertently [have] flow[ed] from some of your friends' pens… Often have I addressed your picture which hangs over the parlour chimney by the side of our friend Charles's with, 'my Cousin Jack, why don't you write to us? What's the matter with you? Have you forgot your American friends?' [With] every vessel that we saw go up to town, we would anticipate the pleasure of a packet, but none has arrived till this of June and I rejoice that we are not blotted from your memory."

She now gets down to some serious discussion of JC's psychology based on her reading of his letters. One might think that she is putting two and two together and making five; were JC's flippant tone when he wrote to her and his reluctance to talk about himself signs of an underlying unhappiness or were they just reticence occasioned by his shyness? Maybe it was partly a fear of being put under an emotional microscope which kept JC from visiting his American relations.

"…I love my friends; I feel interested in their happiness and dearly do I love to be permitted to participate in all their pleasures but above all to share in their pains – but I fear to be impertinent. Was my pen to dictate from my heart it would say, 'why do you thus do violence to your own feeling by assuming a gaiety foreign to your heart? What grief do you thus endeavour to conceal?' Indeed my cousin, all your letter bespeaks a heart but ill at ease, at least I read th[is] so; if I am mistaken I shall be happy in my error. But you would not tell me. You mention some particulars respecting Mr Clapcott's accession of fortune; it sounded domestic and I was pleased to hear it. But not a word of yourself. Do you not think us worthy or why are you thus reserved? Thus should I go on was I to follow the dictates of my heart. But this is serious and you are determined to laugh. Ah! My friend it will not do – I have tried it…in the war…an <u>effort</u> to be happy always…increases…our uneasiness.

[H]ow is it possible to tell what your character is unless you'll come and spend one winter with us; I wish you would. My imagination is apt to take the rein. I pleased myself [for a] while that the reason we had no letters from you was because you had determined to make us a visit. No sooner was the idea started than – whip – the horses were in the sleigh and away we drove to Braintree, to Boston, to Cambridge, to Newton. In a trice you were introduced to the whole circle of friends, and a charming time we had galloping over the snowbanks. Then again how delightfully glided the winter evenings with such a sprightly animated companion. It was indeed a sweet delusion. Why cannot you come and really [do] it?

I beg you to present my affections to all your brothers, sisters, and their families; I hope they [will] not entirely forget their American friends…I was just going to tell you something of Cousin Jo Cranch but as he is here to tell his own story [I] will not say one word more about him, but leave a space for him to fill up – and if he refuses I shall scold, nay, I shall quarrel with him. So adieu, says your Cousin [Betsy].

[Appended by Joseph Cranch] Well I have had the scolding, and for fear of quarrelling I now take up my pen, to say something, although I confess I do not know what to say, but as write I must, perhaps it may be as well to say something tow[ards] where I have spent the summer which has been at Springfield, a very pleasant town in the western part of this State about 96 miles from Boston lying on the Connecticut River and is the best place for res[toring] public stores, to be found in all New England… During [the war] there were I suppose the amount of three-hundred artisans employed, such as wheelwrights, carpenters, blacksmiths and armourers. [T]here are shops now standing fit to carry on all these kinds of business. There are also two store houses, of 100 feet long each which contain about eight thousand stands of small arms, a few large mortars, [a] considerable number of howitzers and about seventy or eighty field pieces with their carriages. But after all this what I want to say about myself was this, that I was appointed by General Knox, our Minister at War (in the month of June last) as superintendent, for the purpose of cleaning the arms. Accordingly I went and remained there until the 23rd of November. My pay was 9 pounds lawful money per month by which I could support myself very well as an old bachelor. [T]he rest of the arms are to be cleaned on contract, but I am afraid the terms are too low for me to take up with. Adieu. P.S. Remember me to Molly, Betty, Hannah etc., etc."

Polly Palmer writing on 27th November[50] also joined in the admonitions to JC, this time for his indifference to his appearance and other eccentricities. How accurate the reports of JC were which led to these comments one has no means of knowing. In any case, she started with a little lecture on the ordinariness of the paper she is writing on because, evidently, when writing to the Adams family when they were staying in France it was deemed desirable only to use the very finest vellum with gilt edges.

"Sir, It is very impolite to begin a letter on such a sheet as this which is the only one I have at hand. When I was to write to a certain lady then in

France I happened to say I had no post-paper and besides, I supposed it must be gilt; a gentleman present, no stranger to that lady, said it was also lately necessary to have gilt paper for a French ship would [not] carry one wrote on plain, for that their very ropes were gilt. Now mayhap this may go by one of your British ones who won't happen to be so nice as our illustrious allies were said to be.

But to your letter, you are a very strange young man. My Sister has given you a good serious lecture, so I won't meddle with that part any further than by my concurrence with her sentiments. But I do say that a man ought not to think himself perfectly at liberty to affect such a singularity in his habit as to make folks stare as he walks the streets. It is an unpardonable vanity for you who are by all accounts a handsome fellow, thus to draw the eyes of the multitude upon yourself to the mortification of other handsome fellows who are unnoticed merely because they are modest enough to appear in the garb of the country they live in. I say too that standing upon one leg, whistling, or star-gazing is censurable in company because it shews a want of deference to the company. If one is inclined to any of those freaks you mention let them retire or ask leave of the company to practise them and all is well. You promise to reform however and disclaim vanity, so I ask your pardon for having again mentioned the word.

You are a satirical creature but I forgive you for my share of it; I am not an enemy to delicate satire, such as only rubs one up a little without bruising. Good even[ing] to you; the folks are just come from meeting and I hope to hear some news of our Charles [Adams] but will he be the same after five years absence in foreign countries? I am afraid to see him lest he should look down upon us.

Well Charles is not come yet; New York is a charming place to be sure for he has been there some weeks and has letters for us in his possession; I hope we shall have them in time. Master Adams stayed at that place six weeks after his arrival and kept everybody waiting and longing for his coming till they were out of all patience. When he did come the letters were so old and so long in coming that they had not the same relish that they would have had some weeks before…If they had been received as soon as they arrived in America the answers might have reached the kind authors and their replies have been part of the way back to us, if the voyages had been propitious. New York I think is but 300 Miles by land from Boston…yet you see how long people are in coming, whereas the 3000 Miles across the Atlantic is frequently performed in four or five weeks.

Betsy has just received a letter from Miss Adams and who mentioning you in a particular manner, not to your disadvantage, supposes that some presents of salmon and partridges must have been sent or procured to be sent by you; her letter is dated the 29th of September [and] Betsy I suppose will write all about it.

I make as strange work in replying to your letters as you do in replying to mine, for neither can be called answering, which by the way I don't like to do in such kind of epistles. I think the word itself quite improper[ly] used as it often is: letters of business should be <u>answered</u> punctually paragraph by paragraph but those of amusement one may take more liberty with and make excursions, as you and I have done... I have already said enough if not too much upon the first paragraph of your letter; the second mentioning your connections you purposely avoid answering and call one of your sisters Moll. If my brother called <u>me</u> so, we should be [at odds]. Poor fellow I wonder where he is?... He [her brother Joseph Pearse Palmer] is gone to the eastward from Boston, somewhere not far from Falmouth (one or two hundred miles we don't call <u>far</u>) upon business but as we have not heard from him lately we feel uneasy. One of our maids in the kitchen, for we have two, asked me just now when we heard from Mr Palmer. I told her not for a great while and that we began to be uneasy about him. 'Oh' said she, 'the voyages to the eastward are more dangerous than they used to be; there have been more vessels cast away lately than ever and, before I could speak, told a dreadful story of one that happened this fall and dwelling on the particular distressful circumstances. I had like to have given up all thoughts of finishing this letter but recollecting myself, I told her I was sorry for what had happened and retired into the parlour. This is one of Job's Comforters. May my brother be preserved.

When you speak of the inland parts of our country you seem to forget the savages, the very thoughts of whom make my blood cold, yet if there were no such cruel men there are many wild beasts who would dispute the quiet possession of those lands. Naturally the lands that are newly discovered are by all accounts extremely fertile; those which are unknown I have not the liberty of saying anything about.

Let me by the favour of you to present my love to all of the Cranches and Palmers, particularly Uncle Andrew, if living, and his family. Let him know that he is as much esteemed and beloved by his Brother [Richard Cranch] and Sister [Mary Cranch Palmer] as ever, but a multitude of distressing scenes have kept them from writing. For months together we had always somebody very sick and to tend. We had but just got rested after such a series of sickness, when a boy was brought home, as everybody thought, mortally wounded with a scythe. The men even fancied that they saw his inward parts; it was a dreadful wound indeed. For a fortnight the doctor would hardly give hopes of him. This happened the 5th of August. It was a flesh wound on his back and over his left shoulder. In ten weeks after he was able to go to a trade a[s] ship's carpenter; perhaps one day you may see him, he is a fine boy and longs to see foreign lands; his Name is Thomas Field. Good Night, the letters must be made up directly, Your Cousin, Polly Palmer"

The next letter found[51], which JC wrote to Betsy Palmer was dated 1st July 1787. The address written on the envelope was Charlestown so evidently the forced move of the Palmers away from Germantown had now taken place and JC was aware of it. He had evidently just finished the French lesson from Thomas Peironnet described in Chapter 1 and goes on:

"...The first thing I find to admire is the moderation of your scolding. Certainly I deserved greater severity; but I begin to believe that the new world does not in general produce scolds to equal the old one and that I may yet be tempted to come over and choose my rib from among the placid daughters of Columbus. Any encouragement cousin?

I've brought down from my closet this parcel of American letters. In my conscience, some of them have not been acknowledged! So my dear cousin, in that rambling free-and-easy way which we have agreed to tolerate in each other, let us now alternately read what is written, and write 'what comes uppermost', without design, without method, without ceremony. Allons!

I think your account of young Mr Adams too pleasing to be kept to myself and therefore I resolve to communicate that part of your letter to his mother tomorrow morning. But what you and she will say to this freedom, I am almost afraid to conjecture. I severely feel for you the pain of quitting Germantown and so does Eliza Cranch. A heavy sigh indeed did the good maid send me over, with that pathetic apostrophe from Milton. Everybody allows sorrow to be weakness but who is superior to it. The counsel of the stoics is like the project of Aesop's mouse, to hang a bell upon the cat's neck; effectual enough if it could be <u>done</u>, but impossible to <u>do</u>!

How dare you fancy that any Cranch or anybody else that ever <u>knew</u>, can have <u>forgot</u> you? Cousin Polly! If you catch her thinking such nonsense again, pinch her ears. I'll indemnify you!

I sensibly felt the goodness of your anxiety for my situation and circumstances and as I perceive it's vain to attempt evading your penetration I may as well confess that you did indeed touch the strings on sorrow full hard in comparing me with the hero of that dreadful German fiction which, in my opinion, ought never to be read but by those who are capable of forgetting it. However, don't believe that the resemblance of my fate to that exquisite picture is by any means striking. <u>My</u> prospects, I can thankfully assure you, <u>brighten</u>.

For past infelicities, peace and oblivion go with them. My life, indeed, upon the retrospect seems to have consisted in an immense variety; pains and pleasures of almost every sort and degree. But why should I be wishing to exhibit it to you? Good God, that Vanity should perk up its little ridiculous head even from the depths of misery! Mine indeed shall be suppressed in this instance but as I know that this information of a friend's growing happier is to some folk the very music of consolation, I shall further gratify your humanity and kindness by devising that my sisters may learn my situation from <u>you</u>. We shall all fancy it has derived a stronger tincture of happiness from the friendly medium.

Don't you smile sometimes at the <u>confidence</u> of far-separated corres-pondents? How does one know, while writing in all the confident hilarity and cheerfulness of being, but it may be to the dead – the dangerously ill – the unhappy! But this, you'll say, is ungenerous – to anticipate calamity: Pray correct me!

How I enjoyed our excursion to Boston, Braintree, Newtown etc.; aye, and with some happy incidents, I must tell you, that were neither set down nor thought of in <u>your</u> scheme of it. O imagination – O Hope – (amiable delusions!); will ye indeed, tarry ...with us thus, sweetly beguile even to its end the tedious, unavailing pilgrimage of life!

Now tell me, my dear girls, should I write to each of you a <u>separate epistle</u>? Don't there seem to be a quaintness, a queerness, a stiffness, a formality – a confounded 'something or other' in it? Suppose, as it's so fine an afternoon, that instead of writing we sit round our tea and coffee upon this grass plot here (about 5 yards off) and <u>talk</u> over everything. Edwin, you rascal, bring another table and some chairs, instantly! Hannah, the tea kettle over in a moment!"

There follows a rather zany imagined conversation between the various relatives and friends in course of which JC imagines that the development of conversation itself is analogous to a piece of music which begins discordantly and builds towards sublimity. This he illustrates rather confusingly with a diagram depicting this progress as like building a wall (Fig. 10).

Then he goes on:

"...So, now 'twill do; now I can hear you, hear you all and all at once. Upon my life, the very music of the spheres! But one may as well attempt to comprehend and write down at once the eight or ten different parts that constitute the harmony of an ode to fancy, or an ode to drollery. Well ladies, you have run on in a full flow of <u>harmony</u> I think I called it (to my undoubted edification) near half an hour. Now (if you please) for the ceremony of opening 'my mouth'. "

Whereupon he restores a more normal epistolary tone with responses to previous letters from America and news of his own:

"...I was much gratified by the account Miss Leppington furnished us with of the dedication of Charles River bridge. Pray let us have some more of these stories. You know (for I heard you say it one day to Charles Storer) 'how fond this fool is of incident and anecdote and domestic gossip', and yet none of you tell me anything. Pray who, and what, are your neighbours and what are all your employments... How do my respected friends

Chapter 2

(animate and inanimate) the horse, dogs, cows, cats and birds, farms, woods, orchards and gardens belonging to all your families? The 'Oak of Friendship' in particular: may it flourish till you injure it!

Mary Palmer, did you and I finish our squabble upon 'affectation'? If you've anything more to say, say it – you shall have the last word upon everything. Pardon me for calling you 'Mary'. But why didn't they christen you so; you deserved a name of respectability; and I remember I have heard of a <u>Mary</u> Palmer worth half the Pollys either in the old England or the New.

Many thanks for the songs and, mentioning songs, reminds me to tell you that <u>negligent</u> as I have been (and as hath been hereinbefore mentioned, confessed, expressed, manifested, declared and set forth) I verily believe that I have been so unfortunate as to have sent letters to you that have miscarried. For the future, let us specify what we receive by the <u>Dates</u>; else we shall never know what we are about. And we should give larger allowance too, for distance, accidents, inabilities and improbabilities.

Somebody should tell my Uncle Cranch, in reference to an enquiry which he did me the honour to make some years ago, that a Dr Oliver Krantz (I suppose) was the author of a history of Greenland, of some note, and minister plenipotentiary for Sweden at the Treaty of Nijmegen. That exclusive of the Cranches of Totnes and our other remote relations of the same name in the south of Devonshire, I have heard of some at Ludlow in Shropshire, and others at Marazion in Cornwall. My notes of other information, collected and intended for our venerable friend on this subject, are mislaid, but I will endeavour to recover them if possible. I see the name of Peter Cranch in the present list of our East India Company's officers abroad, but suspect he may be one of the Totnes family, another branch of which is at the head of a considerable silk business in Spitalfields.

Tell Joe Cranch he is a very good fellow for writing to me and shall be obliged for your vote and interest to make him write again. We all remember the old gentleman with pleasure and kindness.

Was I to be whipped, I can't recollect where or how I spent my 10th April; not so happily, I believe, as you spent yours, though I must own my mind has enjoyed some gleams of sunshine since that. Will Cousin William Cranch ever write to me? Their Excellencies (Adams) have condescended to honor and oblige me very much by some letters and presents of books. I wish they would afford themselves time to make a short excursion into this country. My compliments to everybody. Adieu!

This has been wrote by snatches at 3 or 4 different times and places. It is finished (or stopped I should rather say) here at Southampton – a delightful town and neighbourhood ninety miles from my home. Tomorrow to the Isle of Wight; afterwards to sweet Lyndhurst and the New Forest. You begin to conjecture that this looks like a <u>love</u>-excursion.

You shall not be undeceived; but if it be so, the parties will not forget their transatlantic friends, and particularly to drink to their good healths this day at dinner in the very zenith of their own felicity."

The last letter[52] to JC from Betsy Palmer which is preserved in the Boston Public Library archives is dated 17th June 1788 and strikes a cheerful tone belied by some of the facts conveyed. Unbeknownst to her, her father Joseph Palmer would die on Christmas Day the same year, which did at least remove the obstacle to her marrying Joseph Cranch. But by then, as already mentioned, the family had had to move from their beloved home in Germantown. JC himself was now resident most of the time in London.

"...One, two, three, four – thirteen cannon discharged – and now again they rend the air. The feast is over and the toasts begin, at each of which there is thirteen guns fired. But what is the meaning of all this? I'll tell you my Cousin; this day is the anniversary of that on which eleven years ago Charlestown was burnt to ashes by the Britons. And this day the two towns of Boston and Charlestown join in celebrating with joy and festivity the new town which has arisen with added beauty from the ashes of the former and, in particular, the dedication of the new Bridge over the Charles River [that] was this day opened [with] a grand Procession. But I'll tell you more about it when Papa and Betsy Leppington return, who set off this morning to be present at this scene of real joy and wonder.

They are returned very much gratified with their excursion. We will send you the account as it is in the Monday paper which will give you a better description than can be obtained from recollections a week old and a mind agitated by comparing the past scenes of [17]75 with the present joyous ones of sentiments of a people who that day eleven years [ago] were reduced to poverty by fire and sword, and dispersed to seek an asylum where it might be found, now rebuilding by their own industry... with great addition and style of elegance much superior to the former one. If you could walk this afternoon over Bunker Hill you would be enchanted with the prospect of the adjacent country. The day is fine and it is the season of hay-making and cheerfulness in every face adds pleasure to the view. The beautiful variety of hills, woods, lawns and rivers, corn fields and gardens would afford fine subjects for a poetical genius.

August: Bill Cranch tells me there is a vessel to sail for London in a few days, by which I think to write to your sister Elworthy and enclose this; don't you think I change my hand writing strangely? I had a letter not long ago from Ebbett. She admires the situation of Falmouth. Pray heaven they may feel happy and find friends disposed to supply the place of those they have left. These parting of friends I don't like; I won't think of it. This life is a dream; when we wake to real life shall we not be all together? I think with much pleasure of taking a trip to Casco to see my cousins. Perhaps I may [but] if I never do I have the pleasure in prospect and that is something.

I wish you was here this moment, sitting in this delightful closet that commands an extensive prospect of the harbor and Islands. But why should I lead you to such a distance; only cast your eye down from the window and see what a beautiful parcel of cucumber and melon vines there are. What [a] pretty little enclosure; how green and flourishing they look, and that mulberry tree upon one side. But we have eaten all the fruit; I'm sorry – if you had come a few days sooner. However to comfort you for that loss, look across the northeast part of this young orchard to that stately field of corn. Of what a deep and glossy green are the leaves; how tall, easy and graceful hang the tassels from the top, which promise an early feast of roasting ears. It is lovely good cousin; do take an ear; don't you like it?

I thank you my dear Cousin for your letter [brought] by your sisters. Believe me, we were happy to see them [Hannah Bond and Ebbett Cranch]; I loved them before but feel an increase of affection now I have seen the tear of sensibility, heard the voice of affection. Your sisters both flatter us with the idea of a visit from you; how is this matter cousin? I have heard a hint – of a certain lady – a little older it is true but what of that; good, amiable, rich. No more of this; may happiness attend you whether with or without a female friend.

With such a genius for painting, I can't excuse you for not taking the faces of your whole family and sending them over to your friends here – but don't put their hats on.

Papa, Mama [and] Polly all join in best wishes to you and [the] whole group of Cranches. Polly is very low in health, Papa & Mama better…We remain at Germ[antown] but in a most [pitia]ble state of uncertainty

To make amends for my own dullness [I] shall enclose you some genuine American poetry. The Banks of Kentucky we were pleased with, more perhaps from the idea that it was possibly the production of a friend of ours [Thomas Perkins] who is gone to that remote part of the world than from the real merit of the poem.

I have been long expecting the fulfillment of your promise to write soon; do not continue to disappoint the expectations of your friend."

The visit which the Palmers received from JC's sisters, Hannah Bond and Ebbett Cranch had evidently been a long one. Ebbett had emigrated to America with the Bonds and lived with them for the rest of her fairly short life (she died at the age of 49). Older by just one year than JC she does not seem to have been particularly close to him as evidenced by a plaintive paragraph in her letter[53] to her sister Mary dated 1st April 1788:

"...Is Brother John married yet, where does he live, what is he doing? – I am at a loss to know the reason that he has never wrote me one single line since I have been in America. He writes to my cousins I find; he certainly cannot have forgot that he has a sister called Tib [nickname for Ebbett] and she is gone to America. I think it's very unkind indeed."

One more letter[54] to Eunice Paine from JC dated 15th June 1785 has been found. Whether their correspondence continued after this with the same skittish tone or indeed, at all, is hard to know.

"...You are valued by your neighbours, no doubt, for I am honoured with rebukes from all quarters, for having abused you, for having dared for to venture for to find fault with your handwriting, for having attempted to frighten you with great black letters and scraps of Latin and (among other curious misdemeanours) for not calling you 'Madam'!

Now, 'Madam' (since that must be your name) now for giving you satisfaction. As to Mr T. ~~Tyler~~ considering the irreparable mischief I have committed against that gentleman (referring to the melancholy accident of metamorphosing his fair one) I shall esteem it very good luck if he lets me off without fighting; and with respect to the same gentleman's obliging criticism, I do observe, and here humbly confess, that there may have been [a]... scholar called 'Prician'[b] (of Welsh extraction I presume by his name) though I never heard of a better than Priscian, and that certainly [an] early, learned flagellator of bad Latin, if he be an alien, may lip our gracious King's English, with impunity. As to genders, pronouns, prosody, terminations, and such like crabbed business, your orator confesses that he knoweth no more of them and what is yet more in his favour hath never pretended to know any more of them than the king of [Nepal]. I should not banter in this style but that Mr T.'s grave reflections upon my blunders happen to be totally inapplicable. When I am weak or ill-bred enough to speak or to write to a lady in a language I don't understand, he shall whip me as severely as he pleases; but this was an instance not of speaking or of writing but of laughing. Now according to Bracton a man may laughfully laugh in any language he pleaseth, or (to come home to our own case) in o language at all; and I am so unhappily given to this same villainous vice of laughing that it is as much as I can do to keep my muscles steady even while I acknowledge that Mr T.'s letters speak him a polite scholar and a gentleman; that I beg he will accept my thanks and respectful compliments and permit me to claim the honour of his acquaintance.

I had determined, Madam, to marry, and not go to America, Madam, before I was honoured with your advice on these heads, so that you need not vex yourself, Madam, for having given that advice, when hereafter you

---

[b] Priscian was an early Grammarian who wrote a textbook of Latin which was standard during the Middle Ages. It appears that JC knew more about him than Tyler.

come to find the want of me on the other side the Atlantic, and so, Madam Beatrice, having now done my best to be even with you in complaisance and brevity and snip-snappery, Mr Benedict has nothing more to say than that he too 'is in a great hurry' having 'many engagements on hand' &c.

'You saucy impudent; I've a good mind never to write. 'Marry' – indeed! – I wonder who the deuce will be plagued with such a hare brained, frightful Leddy deddy di tum [to music] Good night ~~Eliza,~~ Eunice, 'Madam' I mean!"

Clearly JC was not taking remarks about his lack of decorum in his letters at all seriously even when he had evidently received an admonishing letter from Mr Royall Tyler. This was indeed ironic since Tyler was a scallywag[3], albeit an educated, charming and initially well-off one. He wanted Nabby Adams's hand in marriage and towards this end charmed Abigail Adams thoroughly. But Nabby who was initially cool towards so bold a suitor was further warned off by Mary Smith Cranch in whose house Tyler was a paying guest and who was aware of his dissolute ways. However, an understanding was reached between them before Nabby went abroad but in Europe she met Colonel William Smith whom she did find attractive and whom she did marry. Sadly, he was no more uxorious than, one suspects, Tyler would have been. Given that we do not have Tyler's letter to JC some of the latter's comments are obscure. Indeed after selected omissions have been made in quoting the above letter, some of it is still hard to follow but worth including as a good example of a particularly frivolous style he often adopted with women correspondents with whom he was on familiar terms.

JC's Relations with the Adams Family

In Chapter 1 some encounters between the Adams family and JC were described, since they are the only source of descriptions of what it was like to meet him in his Axminster days. What follows is a more general account of his interaction with the family.

JC initially held John Adams in awe but he found him quite approachable when they did meet. Adams seemed always to have had time for interesting people, especially those near relatives by marriage such as JC. A rather humble letter[55] from JC initiated correspondence on 17th January, 1784. Adams had been one of the American diplomats sent to negotiate the 1779 Treaty of Paris, which brought an end to the War of Independence. Afterwards, he remained in Europe to try and gain recognition of the newly independent country and secure desperately needed financial support. He was most successful in both respects while he was ambassador to the Dutch Republic from 1780 to 1785. He then became the first American ambassador to Britain. At the beginning of 1784 when he was just setting off for Holland again after a visit to England, a letter from JC just failed to catch him before he left, causing JC great anxiety when he thought that his approach might have been rejected. It is almost painful to read so humble an epistle as that written on 17th January 1784 although one can still detect JC's underlying sense of self-worth:

"Sir; I have never found so much difficulty in prevailing upon myself to do any indifferent [questionable] action, as in this of convincing myself that it is not too great a presumption to address a few lines to you, with the little present of game which will wait your acceptance about the same instant. In truth I could willingly have sent the gift, without at all disclosing the giver, could I, at the same time, have been less sensible of that awkward distress which the ingenerous mind ever feels, on finding itself obliged to an unknown benefactor; and it is upon this consideration, Sir, added to the faith which the whole world warrants me to place in that candour and liberality of sentiment which illustrate the solid parts of your great character, that I am induced to avail myself of the same opportunity to profess the duty and respect I owe to you, both as my relation (Mr Cranch of Braintree is my uncle) and as the most eminent patriot and statesman of the age.

But Sir, I may not thus trespass on your delicacy or your time. Suffer me only to entreat that you will have the goodness not to reject my humble present nor, if possible, this my still humbler overture towards obtaining the honour of being known to you; and permit me to add, that if I can render you any service during your stay in Europe, I shall esteem it no less a pleasure to execute, than an honour, to receive any commands you may think proper to oblige me with. I am, most respectfully, and with best wishes for your good health and welfare, Sir, your obedient, humble servant, John Cranch.

P.S. As I cannot repress the vanity of imagining that you may possibly think me not unworthy of some slight inquiry, it is expedient I should request you to direct any letter you may be pleased to favor me with, "To Mr Cranch, an attorney, at Axminster, in Devonshire" and any question concerning my character or situation, to my agent, Mr Harrison senior, to be heard of at his son's chambers in Barnard's Inn.

I have a strong inclination (but, without your permission, cannot presume so far) to send you a copy of an interesting letter that I have received by this day's post from a friend of mine just settled in Casco bay. By "interesting" I would be understood to mean peculiarly so to yourself, as a principal guardian and patron of the interests of the illustrious Republic."

JC had sent a basket containing two hares at the same time as his letter, intended for the Adams family table. In their absence they had to be eaten by others. The interesting letter[56] to which JC referred was from his friend Thomas Hopkins, mentioned above, and written when he was in Falmouth, ME. John Adams in his reply asked JC to send a copy of the letter in which Hopkins described a thriving port, populated by an industrious people with access to abundant raw materials including lumber, fish, and furs. Hopkins concluded that America offered unmatched opportunities for commerce and lamented, "Foolish Britain, wretched country – what hast thou lost?"

John Adams, notwithstanding JC's fears, in fact replied promptly from the Hague on 31st January 1784:

"Sir, Your favour of the seventeenth of this month was delivered to me, last night. I left London on the third of this month so that your kind present of game, afforded a Regall [feast], to Mr Stockdale in Piccadilly, but I am not less obliged to you for it, than if I had been so fortunate as to receive it myself. I beg you sir to accept my sincere thanks for it.

As the Nephew of my most valuable Brother Cranch I should have been happy to have met you in England if the time would have permitted, I should have wished to have made an excursion to that part of England where the relations of my friend Mr Palmer and those of my brother reside and if you Sir, or any of your friends should travel in Holland, I should be very glad to see them at the Hague.

I should esteem it, as a favour, if you would send me a copy of the letter you allude to from Casco Bay. You may address your letter to me, at the Hague, by the post. I am, with great Regard for yourself and your Connections, Sir, your most obedient and obliged humble servant, J. Adams"

JC had already attracted the attention of an amused Abigail Adams who, in writing to her son John Quincy[58] on 25th April 1784 said:

"…This same Mr John Cranch appears an original. He writes his cousin Betsy Palmer, that out of the great respect he entertained for the public character of your Papa he sent him a basket of hares, but not having heard from him he is in great tribulation lest it should be construed presumption. He adds a postscript to his letter in which he calls upon her to congratulate him upon having received a letter full of civility and urbanity. He observes in a droll way, that he would only dip his pen once more, to tell her that having mended his pen, he finds that he can when he has mind to, …write a handsomer hand than his illustrious correspondent with all his accomplishments, therefore he desires her to recommend him as a secretary."

Abigail visited London quite briefly in 1784 and spent time with JC's sister Elizabeth Elworthy, but she was soon taken off to France where John Adams was to be involved in negotiating the peace treaty with Britain. Writing to his sister[59] on 24th July JC excuses his failure to visit Abigail because of work commitments:

"...I suffer in reflecting that two scurvy lawsuits, which I am to have the plague of conducting to the assizes, will inevitably deprive me of the pleasure of obeying those agreeable commands which my good aunt and yourself have laid upon me. In these mortifying circumstances, and in the utmost confusion, I can only entreat you, my dear sister, to represent me at the feet of our illustrious relation [Abigail Adams], and to beg her forgiveness; to assure her of the stability of my duty and kind regards; and that, should any happy alteration of the present embarrassments on one side, or of travelling arrangements on the other, yet render it practicable for me to see her, I will most certainly avail myself of it."

The disappointment felt by West Country English relatives at the lack of a visit by the Adams family in 1784 was conveyed to America by William Bond and passed on to Abigail by her sister Mary Cranch in a letter[60] of 16th January 1785:

"...Mr. Bond is a little sprilly, kind, good-natured, sensible man. They hoped to have seen you in the West. You would be diverted to hear him give an account of the preparations that were made to receive you. Their houses were all set in order, and new clothes purchased to wait upon your Ladyship in. John Cranch had his hair dressed and powdered – a thing which was never done but twice before in his life. A new hat was procured and a pair of buckles were put into his shoes which had not been fastened with anything but shoe strings for seven years before. John Palmer had a new coat etc. and was greatly concerned lest the lane leading to his house should not be wide enough to admit your carriage to come up to the door. But poor creatures how you disappointed them by landing at Dover. If you should go to England again you must if you can, make them a visit."

Albeit a somewhat tongue-in-cheek and second-hand view it can be assumed that being polite to his honoured American acquaintances temporarily overcame JC's general indifference to his appearance. After the Adams family returned to England, JC resumed his practise of sending them presents of game. Abigail Adams wrote[61] from London to thank him on 21st October 1786:

"Dear Sir, A fine salmon by the Exeter stage a week ago informed me that the gentleman from whom I had before received a similar favour; was still mindful of his friends by his deeds, though he seldom favoured them with his personal presence. Accept, Sir, my thanks not only for the salmon but for the partridges and woodcocks which I presume came from the same quarter last Spring, though you have not suffered [yo]ur right hand, to disclose what your left hand has performed. It pains me to receive these repeated [in]stances of your politeness and attention, having nothing to offer you by way of acknowledgment, unless a literary American production may prove agreeable to you.

As I know you to possess a liberality of sentiment beyond many of your countrymen, I have taken the liberty to offer to your acceptance what a dread of truth and a just representation of facts prevents the printer to whom they were sent for sale, to offer to the public. The conduct of Britain towards America in the late revolution, though recorded by the pen of truth and the spirit of candour is considered as a libel upon the actors who are too wealthy and powerful to suffer a just representation of those very deeds which they blushed not to perpetrate.

Adulation, and the wealth of the East Indies may silence a venal age but a Cornwallis and a Rawdon will still be recorded in the historic page of America with all the dark shades of their characters. Mr Ramsey the writer of the *Revolution of Carolina*, is a gentleman of fortune and respectable character and was lately president of Congress.

By my last letters from America dated in August I had the pleasure of hearing that our [friends] were well. I had promised myself the pleasure of visiting Devonshire during the Summer, but an unexpected [call] obliged Mr Adams to go to Holland, whither I accompanied him, and returned too late to think of another excursion this season. Whenever you come to London be assured, Sir, that I should be very happy to see you; Mr Adams presents his compliments to you. I am Sir, with Sentiments of Esteem, your Friend and Humble Servant, A. Adams"

Abigail had sent JC a copy of *The History of the Revolution of South Carolina* by David Ramsay who had difficulty getting the book published in London in case its controversial content would be ill-received. Lord Cornwallis who had commanded British forces during the War of Independence was made Governor-General of India in 1786. Francis Lord Rawdon was another British general officer during that war and much hated in America for his cruel conduct. Incidentally, the various salmon JC sent must have been princes of the species. Nabby Adams had written[62] about the earlier consignments as follows to her brother John Quincy Adams on 24th September, 1785:

"…We have a most admirable friend in Exeter. The week before last we received a basket containing two fine large salmon directed to Papa and the porter who brought it told us that it came in the stage from Exeter which was all we could find about it, there being no letter nor anything but a simple direction to Papa. And the last week a porter brought a box from the same place under the same direction which upon opening we found to contain a dozen partridges, but no letter. We have been upon the round of conjecture and have concluded they must come from Mr Jack Cranch. He does not intend to be known, to be sure. These kind of attentions are very flattering, but the obligation one feels under for them is not very light, especially when one knows of no good way to return them.

The day we had the salmon Colonel Franks dined with us. He drunk the health of the donor in a bumper, and entitled him Fish Monger to the United States of America. It was the finest I ever tasted, and the partridges were very fine. They are called *game* here you know, and the laws are very strict against those persons that buy it. Indeed a person who purchases game is subject to a penalty. It often happens that people of whom it is purchased will give information of the purchasers and the penalty is severe, so that those people who have not parks are obliged to receive it through the courtesy of their friends if they have it at all. Papa says he intends to rally Mr Jefferson upon the civilities he receives here, but says I must not let Congress know it for 'they will assuredly lessen my salary, and to be sure they have no reason to do that'."

One can assume that JC had remained on friendly terms with the gamekeepers on Lord Petre's estate; versatile he may have been but there is no reason to think that poaching was part of his skillset. JC replied[63] to Abigail on 7th November 1786, again expatiating on the war:

"Madam, Being much ignorant of the republican distinctions of pre-eminency in title, as well as of American etiquette in general, I must anticipate your pardon for any errors in that kind, while I acknowledge the honour of your Excellency's obliging letter and present of books. Both have afforded me great satisfaction only the latter moving now and then to some untempered gusts of resentment against those *Execrables*, Balfour [and] Cunningham. But the sentiments and actions of such beings as Rutledge, Greene, La Fayette, Gadsden, and others soon allayed those little indignations and the mind, lit up by such splendid examples of courage, generosity and divine patriotism, no longer perceived itself shaded by the feeble rancours of an expiring petty tyranny.

It is impossible to conceive his Majesty in any larger idea than that of a respectable private gentleman [who] in disagreeable circumstances without much inclination of his own, was urged to it by a Scotch-infested junto consisting of the Navy, the Army, the contractors and a larger banditti than usual of plunder-inspired, profligate adventurers… But I should not thus, Madam, impertinently trespass on your attention and I beg your pardon. We had entertained hopes in the summer, that this country would be honoured with at least a transitory presence of His Excellency and yourself (agreeably to the plan you mention to have been frustrated by your journey to Holland). The season is slipped away, but our disappointed cottages will again be trimmed for your reception at a more genial and auspicious season.

You charge me with total silence when I sent some of the birds last winter, I meant to trouble our illustrious friend with a line of advice about them and such a note was certainly carried to the post though I must now conclude by your imputation that it miscarried. I am gratefully sensible of the honour His Excellency does me by his obliging remembrance. It is not unlikely that I shall be in London sometime this winter; if so Madam, be assured, I shall accept the civilities you condescend to offer me with great pleasure and with the respect and gratitude which becomes Your Excellency's Most Obliged Faithfull Humble servant, J. Cranch"

He concludes with a postscript congratulating Abigail on the union of Miss Adams and Colonel Smith, adding a jocular allusion to "the ecclesiastical gluepot". Abigail Adams replied[64] on 7th March 1787 and, again, an interesting passage struck out in the original draft is restored here in italics:

"Dear Sir, your obliging Letter of November 7th came safe to hand, as well as a couple of hares since received, for which accept my acknowledgments. I was happy to find that the books I sent were acceptable to you though they painted some of your countrymen in very black colours and one cannot refrain from being affected by the disgraces brought upon their country from the evil conduct of its members, though they abhor the measures and detest the authors.

I wish I could say that a change of administration since the peace had effected a change of sentiment with respect to America but this nation, Sir, is still pursuing measures which daily more and more alienate America from her and force her into a closer connection with France; *they will not enter into a treaty with America nor have they deigned to send a minister in return for the one sent to this court. The consequence will be a recall of the American minister and I can truly say the sooner that event takes place the more agreeable it will be to me, though there are individuals in this nation for whom I shall ever entertain the highest respect and esteem.* How much this will benefit England, time will discover:

I take the liberty of sending you a late publication styled the *Defence of the American Constitutions*, which has been attacked, as you will see, by great men. How ably they are defended the public will judge but something appeared necessary at this time to settle the minds of the Americans, who appear to feel inconveniences without tracing them to their true source. It will perhaps afford you some amusement, not only as a Friend to America, but to the Liberties of Mankind.

By my last letters from America our friends were well, though somewhat troubled by a number of insurgents who had molested the peace and good order of society by unlawfully assembling and stopping the courts of justice. By the latest accounts ... General Lincoln had marched against the insurgents, dispersed and quelled them so that I hope they will no longer impede the course of Justice, or disturb the good order of society. Ebullitions of this kind will break out in all free governments, like humours in a healthy body; but I presume they cannot proceed to any dangerous height.

Mr and Mrs Smith present their compliments and thanks for your kind congratulations. Mr Adams joins me in the sentiments of Esteem and Regard with which I am, Dear Sir, your Humble Servant, A. Adams"

The planned visit to the West Country was at last afoot by the time JC wrote again[65] to Abigail Adams on 13th June 1787 and he seemed nervous at the prospect:

"Madam, I should have addressed your Excellency sooner but that my mind which is the weakest (or, as I had rather settle your Excellency's idea of it, the most delicate) thing in the world, has been for some time suspended between the contrary fears of trespassing upon your more important attentions, on the one hand, or against the obligations of gratitude and decorum on the other. The last has finally prevailed and I will now submit to be thought as 'impertinent' as your Excellency pleases, provided I may be acquitted of the 'ingratitude'.

But, in presenting me with the Defence of the political constitutions of America what did you, my dear Madam, but make me your debtor for one of the greatest pleasures of my life? Should I [then] withhold acknowledgements which it is even duty to make or should I dare apprehend from a noble American Matron, such coquetry of benevolence, as first to excite the sensibilities of a grateful heart, and then either to refuse or condemn its humble returns?

This delightful season being so far advanced, I begin to fear that I may not enjoy the promised pleasure of attending your excursions into this part of England. May I presume to intimate that the accommodations of my cottage, though humble, and (what is worse) not yet hallowed by the arrangements of a prudent 'Goody Baucis', are not despicable and that its deficiencies can be supplied by very excellent inns. The expectation of entertaining (though but for an hour) the father of American Liberty, will stimulate my endeavours to make that entertainment agreeable. The remembrance of such an honour will amply reward them. I would, by way of inducement, add but that his excellency already knows it (perhaps better than myself) that, to say nothing of the amusing varieties of Devonshire in general, we have in this town in which I live some capital peculiar manufactories; and that those of wool and thin cloths about Exeter are also of great consideration. But one hint more will I dare give – you shall be as public, or as private as you please.

I shall be highly obliged to you, Madam, or to Mrs Smith, for any information relative to our friends at home – I mean America. Be persuaded, nothing can be trivial to me that comes from those friends and that country. Pray accept my respectful compliments of thanks and good wishes, for yourself and for Doctor Adams and Mr and Mrs Smith and permit me, Madam, to have the honour of confessing, and on every occasion demonstrating, myself to be your Excellency's obliged, faithful, humble servant J. Cranch"

In referring to Baucis JC was acknowledging his lack of a wife although, as mentioned in Chapter 1, he was by then employing two servants. In classical mythology Baucis and Philemon were an elderly couple who offered hospitality to the gods Jupiter and Mercury when others refused to do so and as a reward had their cottage transformed into a temple. JC was here probably directly quoting Jonathan Swift's poem, *Baucis and Philemon* which specifically mentions 'Goody Baucis'. By mid-July JC was energetically making arrangements. In response to a letter he had received from Abigail Adams of the 16th July 1787 he had replied the next day[66] to her enquiry about staying in Axminster:

"…In obedience to your command about the inns, permit me to acquaint you, that I think you will be accommodated much to your satisfaction at the George[c], here; and I shall expect to be honoured in due time with your preparatory commands to the host and hostess (Ellard) as to beds, horses, time &c, if necessary, that you may suffer no inconvenience which it might have been put into my power to prevent."

JC immediately contacted West Country relatives and acquaintances asking them to make preparations and on 20th July the expedition

---

[c] The George Hotel in Axminster functioned in its present building from 1760 until 2008 and then lay unused until it was sold in 2017 with the new owners planning to re-open it as a hotel. When the Adams family visited it, it was at the peak of its glory as one of the finest coaching inns in the country. Although Axminster was rather undistinguished in itself at the time, it was a convenient place to rest and change horses on the main coaching route between London and the important Devonshire cities of Exeter and Plymouth. Its assembly room was reputedly designed by Robert Adam and appears to have been an addition to the original 1760 building so whether it was there when the Adams family visited is hard to say. The years when Adam practiced architecture would make that a possibility. As mentioned in Chapter 1, Axminster supported a dancing master in the 1780s which implies that refined social activities went on there.

commenced, the party consisting of John and Abigail Adams, Nabby Adams Smith and her 3 month-old son and his nurserymaid, Abigail's maid, Esther, a footman, Edward, the Adams's coachman and a postillion. John Adams recorded their arrival in his journal[67]:

"...Our next Stage was Bridport a small sea port but a very bad harbour. No trade [except] coal which is carried there by water for the supply of the inhabitants. We dined there, and then proceeded for Axminster, the first town in the County of Devonshire. Here we put up at the best Inn I ever saw, the George kept by a Mr [Ellard]. The apartments were not only neat and convenient, but everything had an air of elegance and taste. Here we were visited by Mr John Cranch a nephew of my Brother Cranch who is an Attorney and resides here. The town is a little narrow dirty village, but a great thoroughfare, all the Plymouth, Exeter and many other stages passing through it. Went with Mr Cranch to see the manufactory of carpets for which this place is famous. The building in which this business is carried on is by no means equal to an American barn. The whole Business is performed by women and children. The carpets are equally durable with the Turkey, but surpass them in colours and figure. They are made of coarse wool and the best are 24 shillings a square yard – others at fourteen. They have but two prices. From thence we went to a tape manufactory which are the only two manufactories in the town. Mr Cranch invited us to drink tea with him. He is a single man, of a delicate complexion, small features, about 26 or 27 years old. He never looks one in the face and appears as if he had been cramped and cowed in his youth. He has a good understanding, which he has improved by reading, and appears a virtuous amiable man. He accompanied us to Exeter and Plymouth."

As mentioned in Chapter 1, JC was actually 35 when this was written.

Nabby Adams Smith also wrote in her journal:

"...We left Axminster at nine in the morning. Mr Cranch took a seat in the post-chaise with papa; mama rode in the coach. The road continues very mountainous to Honiton, a stage of ten miles from Axminster, just before you enter the former, there is a valley which is much admired for its fertility and beauty. The latter part of the road answers Mr Boylston's description – that the roads were cut or worn down many feet, and the hedges so thick and so high, that one had no prospect of the country around, which is the case. Mr Cranch bore these inconveniences with but little patience; he pulled down walls and tore gates up from hinges, bolts and bars, like a Samson."

Another glimpse of JC came when Abigail wrote[69] to JC's cousin in America, Eliza Cranch, on 1st October 1787:

"...Whilst we were at Plymouth we proposed a visit to Horsham about 8 miles distant but a part of the road only was turnpike. We inquired if we could go in a carriage, and we were told that we might, but the persons who gave us this advice did not attend to the difference between a coach and a post chaise. We set out in our own carriage and four but not being a turnpike we took a wrong course and squeezed through the narrowest way that a carriage ever passed before the hedges on both sides meeting, I expected every moment when the coach man and postilion would have shared the fate of Absolom[d]. About two miles before we came to the house we were completely stopped. A good man seeing our difficulty advised [us] to pass through two wheat fields, but there we were obliged to dismount and leave the carriage for the servants to get on as well as they could. The lane which led to the house was so wet and springy that we could not walk it without being over our shoes and this as I had silk on was not quite so convenient…Through the fields the hedges which we had to climb over were so high that it was totally impracticable to attempt. Mr J. Cranch who had never been at the place before, scratched his head and scolded his cousin for permitting the road to be so obstructed but, finding a gate, Sampson like, he lifted it from the hinges and made it serve for a ladder to pass over the hedges, but still we could not avoid near a mile of wet and mud."

Naturally enough, after this West Country adventure, interaction between JC and the Adams family subsided and this explains why little further correspondence with JC has come to light. The last discovered letter that he wrote to Abigail[70] when he was himself living in London was dated 11th April 1788 and John Adams's embassy to London ended the same year and the family returned to the America:

"…Understanding by my sister Elworthy, that your Excellency complains of having read yourself out of books, I am tempted to send you down the latest publication that I can find promises amusement enough to justify me, and accordingly I have to entreat your excellency's acceptance of Costigan's *View of Society and Manners in Portugal*[e]. I was just now in hopes to have gratified your excellency another way – with some letters addressed to you by a ship arrived at the Isle of Wight from Portsmouth in America which we were informed lay at the General Post Office; but finding upon enquiry that these letters have been forwarded to Grosvenor Square I confide that they will be sent to you by some other hand.

---

[d] Absolom, the son of David, was killed when his head was caught in the boughs of an oak tree as he rode under it (2 Samuel, 18:9 &10).

[e] This volume, Arthur William Costigan's (1787) *Sketches of Society and Manners in Portugal*, published in London, is still in John Adams's personal library which is now housed in Boston Public Library.

My brother [in-law, Elworthy] here would run away with all the honour of serving your Excellencies but that I contrive, now and then, to push myself into some employment subordinate to him, in order to engross as much of that honour as I reasonably can, and with the utmost avidity catch every occasion of shewing that I am, most truly, your Excellency's grateful, humble servant, J. Cranch"

Also, one more letter has been found from JC to John Adams[71] written on 8th July 1794:

"Honoured Sir, I hope your Excellency will pardon my presumption in sending to you these books, with the specimens; and condescend to accept the same in acknowledgment of my gratitude for the notices you have honoured me with: I send two other copies to Uncle Cranch, one for himself, and the other for the Academy; and 3 or 4 more for other friends in New England – having some apprehension that the work neither is, nor will be published, and on that account dreading a mortification of my own vanity – (being I observe honourably mentioned in it) – no less than a disappointment of the more laudable views of the ingenious author.

I hope my respectful Compliments may be acceptable to Mrs Adams and yourself; being, most faithfully, Sir, Your Excellency's obliged, obedient, humble servant, John Cranch.

P.S. The person who does me the favor to take these things to America, is Mr Peironnet, lately an officer in our navy, who is going to settle in your country and is an intelligent and deserving young man, and much attached to me."

This was the Thomas Peironnet who we encountered in Chapter 1 as JC's French teacher in Axminster. The title of the books he took to John Adams appears to be unknown.

JC's Membership of American Learned Societies

JC was made a member of two American learned societies, both of which still exist today. The American Academy of Arts and Sciences was founded in 1780 by sixty-two individuals including John Adams and Robert Treat Paine. John Adams was its president from 1791 to 1814. The American Antiquarian Society was founded in 1812 by printer and patriotic newspaper publisher Isaiah Thomas. JC's nomination to the Academy will likely have been a result of his association with John Adams to whom he wrote[72] from London as follows on 24th Feb 1790:

"Honoured Sir, I grow so ignorant of anything out of my profession, that I really know not where, nor what the 'American academy' is, to which the enclosed treatise is addressed. In this situation, I had judged [it] fair to suppose that as the title of the institution (whatever be its form or its nature) implies it to be <u>national</u> and equally relative to all the countries of the American empire. It is more likely to be established in the Metropolis, than in any other place: and if there be ought of philosophy or patriotism in its objects, cannot but have a place in the esteem, as well as in the knowledge of Mr Adams. Should I therefore be so far right I shall make the less difficulty of committing, to a candour and condescension that I have already so happily experienced, the good will of my ingenious friend and the liberty I take of commending his work to your excellency's notice, or to that disposal of it which he solicits, and which I trust I will be found to deserve. The author, Mr Crocker, the master of a respectable seminary of the common learning (the Free School at Frome in Somersetshire), has rendered no little services to the important cause of education, is well known to Mr Wales, Doctor Hutton, and other eminent mathematicians of this country and wherever he is known, much esteemed. Perhaps the economy of "apple trees and cider" is already better understood in your country than my friend may have imagined. However, as his tribute is merely voluntary, and he does not pretend to have been "requested" to teach America horticulture (as poor Mr Twigot fancied he had been requested to teach her the principles of government) I feel tolerably confident that we shall give no offence upon the whole.

May I venture, while my pen is on the paper, to beg my grateful and respectful compliments to Mrs Adams, and to remind her of the promise she was pleased to make, at her departure from the Isle of Wight, that she would write to me after her arrival in America. My vanity, she may be assured, will not suffer me to forget it, and the indelible impression of her Excellency's liberalities while here would make it equally painful to imagine any diminution of a friendship I have much cause to value. I know not well the forms of respect with which I should treat your Excellency at this time, and on these occasions but perhaps it need not be mentioned, and methinks I have the pleasure to hear your excellency say, with your wonted benignity, 'John, I would have you be a <u>good painter</u> and by no means a <u>good courtier</u>'. Brother Elworthy was favoured with a letter from Doctor Tufts[f] lately which mentioned that our friends at Braintree were well. I will only add to this my respectful compliments to Colonel and Mrs Smith, if at hand, and trespass no further on your Excellency's valuable time and patience, than while I acknowledge myself to be Sir, your most obliged, faithful, humble servant, J. Cranch

If your excellency see Mr Trumbull[g], I refer it to your discretion to tell him (what Mr Horace Walpole lately told me) of the *Sally at Gibraltar*

---

[f] Cotton Tufts (1734-1815) was a physician who practiced in Weymouth, MA and was Richard Cranch's family doctor and friend. He was a cousin of John Adams.

[g] John Trumbull (1756-1843) was an artist born in Connecticut and although he fought as an officer in the War of Independence spent much time in London both before and

that he found it difficult to be persuaded 'that so fine a picture had yet been painted in England', though I mention it rather to give you pleasure, than from any other consideration, as it is more probable that Mr Trumbull already knows it, than that his modesty has suffered him to communicate it to his friends."

Evidently JC had been persuaded by his friend Abraham Crocker to submit this work on cider[73] to the Academy via John Adams. The correspondence confirming JC's election as a fellow evidently took a while to find its way to him and he did not write in acknowledgement to the corresponding secretary Eliphalet Pearson until 10th July 1792[74]:

"Sir, I feel extremely distressed that the honour which the American Society of Arts and Sciences conferred on me by electing me one of their fellows, so long ago as August 1791 should remain unacknowledged until now, that it is almost August 1792. But as I have only lodgings in London, and as the packet which contained my certificate with the favour of your letter happened to be addressed generally, nothing but one of those lucky chances which did not happen or some advices from a third person which fortunately did (just now) come to my hands, could have secured to me this valuable token of the affection of my friends, of the liberality of the society and of the polite attention of their Corresponding Secretary.

I have then at last, Sir, the very great pleasure of addressing myself to you to desire that you will signify to the Society, that I thankfully acknowledge their favour and without affecting to think myself unworthy a situation that requires so much less of talent than of benevolence – without despairing on account of ill health, or want of fortune – without being abashed by superior abilities, since even those superior abilities may be meliorated and subdued to my level by superior virtues (and men can no more be equally wise than they can perhaps be equally good), I will cheerfully proceed to meditate some act that, conducing (in however small a degree) to the noble intentions of our institution may furnish my honoured friends with some apology for their having connected an obscure and remote stranger with the wisest and best men in your happy country. I remain with all respect, Sir, your obedient, obliged and humble servant, J. Cranch"

If JC did fulfil his idea of performing some 'act' relating to his membership there appears to be no trace of it. The opposite is true of his election on 15th April 1818 to the American Antiquarian Society since on 23rd October 1818 he sent it a substantial thesis on the Roman remains in Bath. The scope of this document is more wide-ranging than the account he

---

after the war. His painting *The Sortie Made by the Garrison of Gibraltar* was painted in 1789 and commemorated an event during the siege at Gibraltar in 1781. Both Trumbull and JC were elected to the American Academy of Arts and Sciences in 1791.

wrote for the Bath authorities which was placed in the first museum there commemorating its Roman past. The document sent to the Academy was prefaced with a splendid heraldic device shown herein as Fig. 11. A fuller account of this is given in Chapter 6.

Other Late Contact with America

Clearly contact amongst the wider Cranch clan in Britain and America continued during the remainder of JC's life, and beyond, but surviving transatlantic letters to and from JC personally have not been found. He was sometimes mentioned in the correspondence of others, for example, his friend William Langworthy (see Chapter 4) emigrated to America where he became acquainted with John Adams's son-in-law, William Stephens Smith. On 21st January 1796, Smith wrote to Adams requesting that he arrange a meeting for Langworthy with the President and mentioning that he was, "the intimate friend and companion of Mr Cranch in England". To his daughter on February 6, 1796 Adams wrote[75], "Mr. Langworthy appears to me, as he does to you, a man of information and good sense... I have learned from him that Mr John Cranch is a charming painter, but without much encouragement; which I always expected would be his destination."

JC's sister, Mary Willcocks, writing to her son on 23rd March 1800[76] had the following to say:

> "...I had a letter from your good Uncle John [Cranch] yesterday in which he says he shall write you by the next post and he thinks shall advise you to quit Bath and make best of your way to London that he may have the pleasure of seeing you established there before he sets off for Devonshire which he still holds his intention of doing early in the Summer. Your uncle mentions that there are letters from America which he has sent to Brother Joe. I hope we shall have them soon; one is from our dear old Uncle [Richard] Cranch. I am sure I never expected to have seen a letter of his handwriting any more; he is now 74 years of age. I suppose you will see the letters when you go to town as I imagine these are only copies."

At that time the Willcocks family were based in Devonshire although they were later to move to London where, after the death of her husband, JC's sister Mary then went to stay with her daughter, also called Mary, who had married one John Moginie. JC himself was still then living mainly in London. Letters do survive of JC in correspondence with others both when he was in London and later in Bath which make his continuing relations with America clear. Indeed, for a while he seems to have been the 'postbox' for transatlantic communications, receiving and distributing packets of letters. However in 1807 Mary Willcocks in writing to her son[77] lamented, "What can be the reason of our not hearing from our dear American friends in so long a time. I think it must be two or three years ago we had any letters from thence."

In 1811 when JC was at his lowest ebb financially he was greatly distressed by the discovery that he still owed money to a friend, the furniture maker John Seymour, who had emigrated to America. A more detailed account of JC's financial woes is given in Chapter 6. This particular one was still not resolved by 1815 when JC's nephew, William Cranch Bond, visited JC in Bath[78]. That visit might well be the occasion when two documents which undoubtedly had been owned by JC found their way to America. The first is dealt with in Chapter 4 and was a receipt for the purchase of a putative head of Oliver Cromwell. The second was a splendid detailed drawing of Falmouth, now Portland, ME, which had been created by John Seymour Jr, the son of JC's creditor mentioned above and reproduced in a book about the Seymours by Stoneman[79]. On it, the details of its provenance were inscribed in JC's unmistakable handwriting and signed by him. However it appears that the original document has subsequently been lost.

Finally, a melancholy coda to half a century of rewarding international family friendship survives in a letter[80] from William Cranch Bond to his cousin John Willcocks dated 9th June 1821:

> "Dear Cousin, We have just been informed by Mr. George Andrews of the sudden and unexpected death of our dear Uncle John Cranch. He received a letter from his brother John Andrews of Traine more than a month since, giving him the intelligence. We are much surprised and cannot account for it that there have been no letters for us as within two weeks several vessels have arrived direct from Liverpool."

References

1. Adams, John. *Diary* vol. 16 (10 January 1771 - 28 [i.e. 27] November 1772). Held by Massachusetts Historical Society. Internet ref: Adams Family Papers Electronic Archive: www.masshist.org/digitaladams/archive/doc?id=D16.
2. Adams, Charles Francis (1891), *History of Braintree, Massachusetts (1639-1708) North Precinct of Braintree(1708-1792) and the Town of Quincy(1792-1889)*,The Riverside Press, Cambridge

3. Nagel, Paul C. (1987), *The Adams Women. Abigail and Louisa Adams, their sisters and daughters* ,Harvard University Press, Cambridge MA and London
4. Shipton, Nathaniel N. (1966), *General Joseph Palmer: Scapegoat for The Rhode Island Fiasco of October, 1777.* The New England Quarterly, vol. 39, pp. 498-512.
5. Greenspan, Ezra (2000), *George Palmer Putnam: Representative American Publisher*, Pennsylvania State University Press
6. Marshall, Megan (2005), *The Peabody Sisters. Three women who ignited American Romanticism*, Houghton Mifflin Company, Boston & New York
7. BPL Ms. Eng. 483 (392)
8. Ryerson, Richard Alan *et al.* eds (1992) *Adams Family Correspondence*, vols. 5 and 6: October 1782 - December 1785, Harvard University Press, Cambridge.
9. BPL Ms. Eng. 483 (112)
10. BPL Ms. Eng. 483 (393)
11. BPL Ms. Eng. 483 (113)
12. For example, BPL Ms. Eng. 483 (116)
13. BPL Ms. Eng. 483 (115)
14. BPL Ms. Eng. 483 (114)
15. BPL Ms. Eng. 483 (405)
16. BPL Ms. Eng. 483 (124)
17. BPL Ms. Eng. 483 (119)
18. BPL Ms. Eng. 483 (406)
19. BPL Ms. Eng. 483 (117)
20. BPL Ms. Eng. 483 (394)
21. BPL Ms. Eng. 483 (123)
22. BPL Ms. Eng. 483 (126)
23. BPL Ms. Eng. 483 (395)
24. BPL Ms. Eng. 483 (130)
25. BPL Ms. Eng. 483 (128)
26. Bond family papers, 1724-1931. Harvard University Historical Scientific Instruments Collection.
27. BPL Ms. Eng. 483 (326), (327), (329), (330), (332)
28. BPL Ms. Eng. 483 (116)
29. BPL Ms. Eng. 483 (419)
30. BPL Ms. Eng. 483 (408)
31. BPL Ms. Eng. 483 (418)
32. BPL Ms. Eng. 483 (118)
33. BPL Ms. Eng. 483 (414)
34. BPL Ms. Eng. 483 (415)
35. BPL Ms. Eng. 483 (410)
36. BPL Ms. Eng. 483 (121)
37. BPL Ms. Eng. 483 (398)
38. BPL Ms. Eng. 483 (122)
39. BPL Ms. Eng. 483 (400)
40. BPL Ms. Eng. 483 (399)
41. BPL Ms. Eng. 483 (404)

42. BPL Ms. Eng. 483 (402)

43. BPL Ms. Eng. 483 (427)

44. BPL Ms. Eng. 483 (125)

45. *The Bristol Mirror,* 12th April 1817

46. BPL Ms. Eng. 483 (131)

47. BPL Ms. Eng. 483 (132)

48. BPL Ms. Eng. 483 (403)

49. BPL Ms. Eng. 483 (411)

50. BPL Ms. Eng. 483 (417)

51. American Antiquarian Society Letterbook, Catalog entry #271394

52. BPL Ms. Eng. 483 (412)

53. BPL Ms. Eng. 483 (389)

54. BPL Ms. Eng. 483 (129)

55. Lint, Gregg L. *et al.* eds (2010), *The Adams Papers*, Papers of John Adams, vol. 15, June 1783–January 1784, pp. 459–460, Harvard University Press, Cambridge

56. See note appended to JC's letter to John Adams dated 11th February 1784 on p 31 of The Papers of John Adams vol. 16, Feb 1784-Mar 1785, Lint G.L. *et al*, eds, (2012), Harvard University Press, Cambridge

57. Lint, Gregg L. *et al.* eds (2010) *The Adams Papers*, Papers of John Adams, vol. 15, June 1783–January 1784, pp. 473–474, Harvard University Press, Cambridge

58. Ryerson, Richard Alan ed (1993), *The Adams Papers*, Adams Family Correspondence, vol. 5, October 1782–November 1784, pp. 325–326, Harvard University Press, Cambridge

59. BPL Ms. Eng. 483 (120)

60. Ryerson, Richard Alan ed (1993), *The Adams Papers*, Adams Family Correspondence, vol. 6, December 1784–December 1785, pp. 59–61, Harvard University Press, Cambridge

61. Taylor, C. James *et al.* eds (2005) *The Adams Papers*, Adams Family Correspondence, vol. 7, January 1786–February 1787, pp. 378–379 (letter and notes appended thereto by Massachusetts Historical Society), Harvard University Press, Cambridge

62. Ryerson, Richard Alan ed (1993) *The Adams Papers*, Adams Family Correspondence, vol. 6, December 1784–December 1785, pp. 378–390, Harvard University Press, Cambridge

63. Taylor, C. James *et al.* eds (2005) *The Adams Papers*, Adams Family Correspondence, vol. 7, January 1786–February 1787, pp. 389–390, Harvard University Press, Cambridge

64. BPL Ms. Eng. 483 (420)

65. Taylor, C. James *et al.* (2007), *The Adams Papers*, Adams Family Correspondence, vol. 8, March 1787–December 1789, pp. 87–88, (letter and notes appended thereto by Massachusetts Historical Society) Harvard University Press, Cambridge

66. Facsimile of Letter supplied to the author by Massachusetts Historical Society Adams Papers collection

67. Butterfield, L. H. ed (1961), *The Adams Papers,* Diary and Autobiography of John Adams, vol. 3, Diary, 1782–1804; Autobiography, Part One to October 1776, pp. 206–207 Harvard University Press, Cambridge

68. *Journal and Correspondence of Miss Adams Daughter of John Adams Second President of the United States* Edited by her Daughter (1841), Wiley and Putnam, New York & London (account of 27th July to 3rd August 1787)

69. Taylor, C. James *et al.* eds (2007), *The Adams Papers*, Adams Family Correspondence, vol. 8, March 1787–December 1789, pp. 175–176 (and notes appended thereto by Massachusetts Historical Society), Harvard University Press, Cambridge

70. Taylor, C. James *et al.* eds (2007), *The Adams Papers*, Adams Family Correspondence, vol. 8, March 1787–December 1789, p 256 (and note appended thereto by the Massachusetts Historical Society), Harvard University Press, Cambridge

71. Unpublished manuscript held by Massachusetts Historical Society

72. From the Letterbook of the American Academy of Arts and Sciences

73. Crocker, Abraham (1799), *The art of making and managing cyder; deduced from rational principles and actual experience.* Printed by R. Crutwell, Bath

74. Letter to E. Pearson Esq, Cambridge. To the care of the Hon Richard Cranch, Boston. Letterbook of the American Academy of Arts and Sciences

75. Hogan, Margaret A. *et al.* (2013) *The Adams Papers*, Adams Family Correspondence, vol. 11, July 1795–February 1797, pp. 160–162 (and notes appended thereto by Massachusetts Historical Society), Harvard University Press, Cambridge

76. BPL Ms. Eng. 483 (155-201)

77. BPL Ms. Eng. 483 (155-201)

78. BPL Ms. Eng. 483 (64-107)

79. Stoneman, Vernon C. (1959), *John and Thomas Seymour, Cabinet Makers in Boston, 1794-1816*, Special Publications, Boston MA, p19

80. BPL Ms. Eng. 483 (321)

Chapter 3

Relationships with Women

JC never married although clearly he wanted to well into middle age. Not a great deal of information about this area of his life survives, but that he was often in love cannot be doubted as judged by his sympathetic letter[1] of August 1805 to his much younger friend Philip Crocker about a disappointment in love:

> "...Now to your affair. Is the old love renewed or is it barred for ever? Tell me all about it, for I must suppose love to be uppermost in your heart though painting may be so in mine. I know exactly how 'tis. You'd give your ears that I could see your divinity, and hear you prattle forth her perfections as I'd give mine to have you here admiring my *Old Quarrymen*, my *Preparation for Haymaking*, my – what not, and hearkening to this nonsense I should have to spout concerning <u>my</u> goddess! Don't fancy, however, from this flippancy that I think it a joke or a light matter to lose the girl of one's heart or to get rid of the scrapes usually consequent to such serious disappointment. Far from it; I have gone through too many of them myself for that and, indeed, nobody can <u>really</u> commiserate you that has not."

By the time this was written it is fair to assume that JC had given up any matrimonial ambition and his relationship with Miss Argles described below, which must have occurred around the turn of the century, must be assumed to be the last such disappointment he had to endure.

It is difficult to get inside the head of a young 18th century man today, especially given the current state of sexual politics. JC was no social revolutionary and seems simply to have accepted the mores of his day. His women relatives were all 'respectable' and most got married. His immediate Cranch family, although not noticeably prosperous, clearly valued learning a great deal and was proud of JC whose abilities and ambition took him to a degree of recognition at national level. In his immediate Kingsbridge family there was no money for schooling for either boys or girls but most learned to write more or less well. In America the first generation of immigrant Devonians seem mostly to have earned a living at some trade acquired in England and become sufficiently prosperous to secure an education for their sons, several of whom went on to become figures of national importance, but there too, in the generation that arrived and in the generation immediately following, education for girls was patchy. Having said all that, there is never any hint in JC's correspondence of intellectual condescension to women. He might be a little flirtatious with his female cousins but otherwise theirs was a cheerful correspondence of equals. As already described in Chapter 2 JC's contemporary, the bluestocking Hannah More, whom he had obviously met and who was of interest to his American women cousins, he simply admired as a writer at the generally accepted high valuation of the day although his romantic attraction to her was obviously nil.

If JC ever expatiated on his thoughts about relations between the sexes, no record of it can be found. However, his oldest friend, John Andrews, who seems to have had a successful marriage himself, wrote to him[2] on 18th December 1797, obviously after JC had complained of the frustrations of his unmarried state

> "...What you say of the taxes on a bachelor I suppose refers to a different kind of taxes from those laid by your friend Will[iam] Pitt. Being Sunday night, I may be allowed to moralise a little upon that subject. I have sometimes thought that considering oneself merely as a man of the world, it is (in general) cheaper gratifying the passions as a bachelor than otherwise. Children are allowed to be provided for in a much less expensive way and the occasional gratuities to the fair objects, and other charges which may occur, are not likely to be so heavy as to constant maintaining of a wife (as it often happens) in pride and extravagance.

> Add to this, that connections which are found ineligible or tiresome may be quitted and pleasure followed (as the saying is) 'just when the maggot likes'. However, I believe it will be found in experience that there is what we call a good and bad luck attendant on this plan of life, as well as on matrimony, and that when the latter turns out well the real satisfactions enjoyed are greatly in its favour. The advantages above stated on the side of celibacy are not always sure of being had and there are hazards, anxieties and cares peculiar to a pursuit of pleasure in that state, as well as to a married life. If the plan be keeping a mistress in that way, [it] is likely to be more expensive and less constant than a wife; the only advantage is the liberty of parting and even that may not be always easy."

Andrews then starts discussing the health risks attendant on what he euphemistically calls 'vague amours', but a page seems to be missing from his letter at this point. As an aside one might comment that these risks were very real and that James Boswell, Dr Johnson's biographer, frequently suffered from 'clap,' i.e. gonorrhoea, as a result of casual dalliances[3]. Exactly what JC made of his friend's comments cannot be known, but he was a very principled man who evidently deplored vice. Clearly 'celibate' in the sense Andrews used it simply meant 'unmarried', but whether JC had sexual relationships outside marriage we cannot know for certain.

And so to the relationships with women about which we know at least a little. JC's time in Axminster from his early 20s to his mid-thirties was the period when correspondence with his unmarried American women cousins seems to have been at its peak. They unsurprisingly took considerable interest in his marital fortunes and he may have felt it safe to confide in them to a degree. Thus we learn of a 'Charlotte'. On 23rd May, 1784 JC's cousin Betsy Palmer wrote[4] to JC from Massachusetts and evidently in a previous letter he had suggested that they exchange pictures of each other for she says:

> "…My Picture! And pray what will your Charlotte say to it? 'Tis true the ocean rolls between us and I can promise your head would be in no danger from the lifeless representation of a very plain face. A lock of hair you shall have Coz… You mention your retired way of life; do in your next, tell me how you live, whether you have an agreeable neighbourhood, who your friends are and what sort of a girl your Charlotte is, for I presume a person of your complexion could never have… fill[ed] these years without having formed some attachment. Let me know all about it. If you are absolutely in love, I shall like you the better for it – it makes folks might[y] agreeable, at least I think it would have this effect on you. But take care Cozn Jack that there is no 'Albert' in the way."

He evidently made determined proposals of marriage to two women when young because he discussed them with a third whom he was courting. This latter lady was Elizabeth Feilder (known as Eliza) and their friendship was evidently one of the most important in his life. But whether the woman who JC "sincerely loved" was Charlotte remains unknown although in his letter[5] to Eliza Feilder on 28th January 1786 he said:

> "…I must now add a circumstance suggested by your last as not improper for me to be more explicit upon, viz, that I am under no matrimonial engagements whatever. In consequence of the misfortune I had, not to be accepted by one whom I most sincerely loved and to whom I had presumed to offer my addresses, I did, lately, transfer those addresses (not the passion I must own) to one with whom I was far from being even intimately acquainted. This person being pre-engaged very properly and positively declined my suit; and I must now lay in my stock of dogs and cats and old easy chairs and pipes of tobacco; in short, set myself and house in order to live and die a forlorn old bachelor."

JC got to know Eliza Feilder when he was in Axminster because she was an acquaintance of Simon Bunter although, according to a letter from her to JC, her relationship with Bunter[6] had been "short and interrupted". She had stayed at nearby Lyme (now Lyme Regis) where Bunter had built a small house (which still survives although greatly extended by subsequent owners and is now owned by The Landmark Trust). She was quite wealthy and that may have been the basis for the title 'Mrs' which she used. No record of her having been married has been found and it seems likely that her fortune was inherited from her father who appears to have been a wealthy official. From more than one source we know that she was, for some time, housekeeper to Lord Romney (Charles Marsham 1744-1811) at this home, The Mote, near Maidstone in Kent. She seems to have been a close friend of the Marsham family, especially Harriet, sister of Charles, so the role of housekeeper may have been something of a sinecure. Her birth date has not been found but clearly she was older than JC. News of their relationship again seems to have reached America and come back to JC in the form of another letter[7] from Betsy Palmer who, as mentioned in Chapter 2 had, "…heard a hint of a Certain Lady, a little older it is true but what of that – good, amiable, rich – no more of this."

Several letters written by JC to Eliza Feilder survive though none of hers to him has been found. Later in their relationship both were in London obviating the need for much correspondence. Clearly JC persisted with his pursuit of her for some years and even after he gave up hope of marrying her their friendship must have continued because she made him executor and residuary legatee of her will, dated 25th February 1799, which is still to be found in the British National Archives. She made her mark on the will rather than signing it so she was evidently too ill by then to write and was very likely on her death bed. JC proved the will at a London court as soon afterwards as 29th March of the same year.

What must be an early but undated draft of a letter[8] to her by JC must be from before 1775 because the undesirability of his leaving his employment with Simon Bunter is one objection to marriage which had been put to him by Eliza. It reveals early discouragement for JC and is worth quoting from at length; however, he clearly persisted and she obviously never decisively drove him away.

"...Really Madam if you should not be able to fancy me as a sweetheart I foresee very much misery to myself and it would be only prudent to restrain myself from the dangerous experiment of seeing or hearing from you; though I suppose the wisdom and prudence of a man in pursuit of an unsuccessful amour would be at least equal to that of a moth which to enjoy the <u>light</u> scorches itself to death by the <u>fire</u>.

I am much apprehensive that your object[ion]s of the inequality of our ages, of the delicacy of your own constitution, of the consequences of my leaving Mr B[unter] etc., as supposed grounds of future disagreeablenesses between us are to be considered not so much in the light of real defences against my suit as in that of masked batteries to conceal more substantial objections, and such as perhaps I ought to apprehend as invincible.

My object is to possess no less than what I deem to be the *summmum bonum* itself, the privilege of sharing with a virtuous woman not (as the noble author calls 'em) those 'trinkets' of fortune, wealth, title and place but the richer treasures of a retired and virtuous contentment."

Certainly at the beginning of his relationship with Mrs Feilder JC had no idea that his finances would radically improve. But as made clear in Chapter 1, his developing relationship with her may have been responsible for this anyway. He would obviously be aware of the disparity of social position between himself and her, albeit not feeling that it should matter much. But her awareness of their age disparity and her dubious health seem to be quite adequate reasons for her not to marry although in practice she lived another quarter of a century and might have lived longer if JC had persuaded her to move to a healthier part of the country. It does seem possible that she may have feared losing contact with her friends in Kent to whom, judging by the generous bequests to them in her will, she must have been close.

The correspondence which survives from this relationship consists almost entirely of drafts and copies of JC's letters to Eliza which he himself kept. They date from 1781 to 1787 and their frequency and the fact that he kept these letters indicates the strength of their relationship. If JC's primary motive for removing to London in 1787 was to be at the centre of British cultural life it seems probable that he also relished pursuing his relationship with Eliza Feilder whose life during this period seems to have been centred on London and nearby Kent. However, one or two affectionate letters from JC to other women during this period also survive suggesting that he may sensibly have 'hedged his bets' somewhat.

It is difficult to select material to quote from these letters to Eliza because of their many brief references to matters of shared interest which are obscure to us two centuries later. However, his attraction to her must have arisen almost as soon as they met and if she rebuffed his ideas of marriage she obviously valued their acquaintance. On the 25th April 1781 he wrote[9]:

> "...After assuring you (then) that I love you better than any other person... in the world (not excepting even that important person Myself) I shall conclude with a presumption that I think no woman besides yourself is capable of pardoning, that if you do not accept of me for a lover – you must inevitably lose me as an acquaintance ...I have seen it asserted by a great divine, that the punishments in a certain place consist of nothing worse than a perception of the joys of an infinitely better place, with the consciousness of being excluded from them."

Thus, already, separation from her draws a mild comparison with hell which he is not sure he can withstand. However they evidently stayed in touch because there are two more letters from JC in 1781 the tone of which implies that hers are just friendly whilst he continued to hope for more. With the first in September he sent her three drawings including one he had done of himself[10].

In the second[11], in October of that year, she had told him she wanted to leave London and he applauded this. He talked of a house, presumably near to Axminster, which evidently they both knew and he was going to investigate as possible accommodation for her. At the thought of her being nearby his, "...heart rose up at the recollection of a thousand extravagant ideas which had been indulged there; rose to entertain wishes that had been long banished and to embrace another happiness, of visions and impossibility." We have to assume that nothing came of this plan because the next surviving letter from JC to Eliza Feilder is a businesslike response to a query she has made in 1784 concerning the whereabouts of a model artificial leg[12].

However, when Simon Bunter died in 1785, if the number of surviving letters is any indication, the correspondence accelerated and exchanges were then frequent until JC moved to London where he was closer to Eliza. In fact, the beginning of this period was marked by something resembling a tiff because she had apparently accused JC of slighting

Bunter which resulted in JC's criticisms of his former employer which were quoted in Chapter 1.

By 13th October 1785, JC was at last smarting less about his ambiguous relationship with Bunter. Earlier that year he had written to Eliza offering coins and medals he had inherited from Bunter to Lord Romney, her employer. Now JC was ready to submit to her kinder judgement [13]:

"...I know not whether your sentiments respecting our good friend departed do more honour to your head or to your heart. It is plain that you had discovered at least as much of his character in the course of your short and interrupted acquaintance with him as I had by twelve years direct observation and study. But you have the start of me in another respect; you have taught me to set a higher value – perhaps to entertain a stronger affection – for his memory than my severer disposition would of itself have admitted. How beautiful is this mild and gentle candour diffused over the virtues of my honoured friend. Indeed I find [you] can teach me everything and I have only to be as good a copyist as I can."

In November of 1785 JC visited London staying in Broad Street with his sister Elizabeth Elworthy. Eliza Feilder was also staying in the capital at Portland Street and JC announced his arrival by sending her a basket of game birds. By the 26th of the month, presumably after he had returned to Axminster, he made clear[14] his feelings about being parted from her:

"...it was with such a reluctance on my part as I had never felt on any other occasion; nor can I yet be consoled but in the hope of soon meeting you again ...and yet more blessed be that guardian spirit who shall blend, with my ardent wishes for it, the gentler inclinations of her I love! But I tremble while I indulge in this (perhaps unhallowed) strain. Will my sweet friend forgive me? Write soon – if possible your whole heart! I embrace you with the tenderest affection. Farewell!"

Evidently his desire to marry Eliza was now out in the open and the letter[6] from JC of January 1776, quoted above, would indicate that she was at least giving this consideration because she had evidently sought assurance that he was not committed to another. The same letter went on:

"...May this find both yourself, and our good Mrs Marsham, better! Poor dear Peter [his dog presumably] has had a thousand extraordinary caresses since you ordered him to be 'much'd' – (how has your humanity taught me to love this word!) and a commodious bed is speedily to be made for him by one Will Drower, my carpenter, a very humane honest fellow and a great friend of Peter's. I have the pleasure to assure you that this faithful adherent, though blind, is otherwise quite well. You'd be delighted to see the little cottage we are got into. Is it impossible that you may yet see me in it? …I will …suffer nothing to check the delightful idea. Farewell my dear Madam; I kiss your hands most affectionately!"

Harriet Marsham, as Eliza Feilder's close friend, JC clearly got to know quite well. Although JC and Eliza remained close until the end of her life it seems likely that around now she, at least, finally shelved any idea of marrying him. For the most part during the remainder of 1776 and in 1777 his numerous letters to Eliza remained very affectionate and from time to time his hopes for more than friendship continued to surface. As well as writing about matters of ill-health and proposals to meet they occasionally mildly argued. On 12th October 1776 he had a fright when she seemed to have written to decline an expected meeting in Southampton[15]:

> "…Good heaven, what can occasion so heavy a dejection of so noble a spirit. I am astonished and overwhelmed with [fear] – insomuch that I cannot but with difficulty write these few lines. Oh, my Eliza, if you still regard me (and sure I will never doubt that, any more than I will cease to love you beyond all other women in the world) make me, if it be possible, instrumental in restoring your tranquility. Christ what can have happened? Or is it possible that you do not esteem me as you once did: God enable me to resist it! Oh Eliza, why would you torture me – can't we yet love – be united – be happy?
>
> P.S. I will endeavour to write again if you do not forbid, after you shall have dispelled my present horrible apprehensions."

By the 19th October she had reassured him somewhat[16] though he told her that "…the quiet of her servant is now grown so absolutely dependent upon hers", that she should do nothing for him, "after the instant it shall become in any degree either painful to her feelings or inconvenient to her situation". He was writing this near midnight and concluded by toasting her: "…here is one temperate glass [wishing] peaceful slumbers and health to my sleeping love. Adieu Eliza; I would imprint a thousand good nights on your dear thin lips."

Shortly afterwards they obviously did manage to meet because on 9th November he wrote[17]:

> "…Your letter would have been answered instantly but that, just before its arrival, I was called off, on a sudden, to assist in celebrating the nuptials of my friend John Clapcott who, after a long term of sighing and wishing is, at length, made as happy as I think him capable of being made, in the possession of his amiable cousin, the nymph of [illegible]. They are settled prettily enough, near Blandford...In the mean time, does Eliza take care of her health and spirits? For I fear she goes not to rest so early, nor rises so

early, nor exercises in the fresh air, so often as these high advantages are practicable. After our dear engagements at the *Oak-branches*, need I add professions that my little life and fortunes are wholly at your disposal or (with the good father in the parable) repeat, 'Thou art ever with me and all that I have is thine!' Reluctantly – fondly – Adieu!"

By December 28th 1776[18] he was anxious to meet again:

"...Now as to our meeting – must it depend on information from you or may I indulge the ardent inclination I have to see you soon, at all events? Pray have the goodness to govern me in this particular and permit me to wish many Christmasses and New Years, first to your dear self, Eliza, and next to your noble friends at the Mote... I triumph in the very anticipation! Adieu!"

For the first few months of 1787 there was a more practical tone to his letters although he continued to address her with fondness. On 2nd February he was in hourly expectation of being summoned to her presence[19] and, "...having already been explicit on the principal subject of our late conversations, I have now only to add that I continue steadfastly resigned to whatever advices or commands my most beloved friend shall be pleased to favour me with." On 23rd March he says[20] "...I shall keep myself clearly disengaged from appointments of business, until you shall be pleased to signify where and when I may be permitted to kiss your hands; and the sooner I learn these particulars, the sooner I shall enjoy a great increase of pleasure. Adieu!" On 5th of April he had returned from his trip to Blandford, Dorsetshire to find that a letter from her had been delivered. His reply[21] informed her that among other matters of mutual interest he had been finalising accounts for Bunter's estate, then he went on:

"...Will you have the goodness to instruct me more especially respecting the pyrites that you wish to have from Charmouth? I shall be highly gratified by this commission, and entreat to know immediately, but more precisely what the article wanted is, and if I may be permitted to fill out the parcel with some curious fossils from my own collection. If you think my Lord Romney or any other of your noble friends might be gratified by anything of this sort."

Why Eliza wanted pyrites can only be guessed at. Was she obtaining it for someone else or was she interested in the supposed health benefits of its crystals? Was it the beauty of 'fool's gold' which attracted her or was she a student of the infant subject of geology? Anyway, shortly afterwards a box containing 18 or 20 pounds of pyrites was dispatched to her in London by the mail coach and his note[22] confirming this also wished her good health and sent his compliments to his friends at "The Mote" and especially to Mrs Marsham. He closes with, "My dearest Friend, Adieu."

Interestingly, among the stream of letters to Eliza Feilder is a long one JC wrote to one Isabella dated 16th April 1787. She was obviously a longstanding acquaintance for whom he had considerable affection, albeit he expresses confidence in "...the rectitude of our friendly attachment". His letter[23] was a reply to one she had written to him and he chided her gently for not sealing it properly because it had been opened in the post. The previous afternoon he had been for a walk "tracing our old haunts" and imagining her as his companion:

> "...In enlarging my walk I discovered some other pretty enough recesses, which I could not but begrudge myself the solitary enjoyment of. The image (however) of my fair friend was not absent, but partook largely of the pleasures of our ramble. It leaned on me, sat by me, read to me, talked with me and, to convince me of her returning strength (would you believe it) jumped over two ...molehills at once!"

Later, as he referred to her small stature, he was distinctly ribald:

> "...Depend upon it you are little; and that perhaps not the worst of it – perhaps the 'little' can't be made bigger without spoiling the 'maid'. Insufferable! Hold your tongue!"

In May 1787 Eliza Feilder paid a visit to Southampton, which seems to have been a regular occurrence, and on the 19th JC sent her a jolly little note[24] written in Chaucerian English and intended to follow it with a visit:

> "...I trust this noteys shall be followyd by your most lovynge and faythefull knyghte."

On 1st June he wrote her a letter[25] which is significant in terms of his later move to London. He had been staying in Blandford and she is in London:

> "...I set out well at eight o'clock yesterday morning. The beauties of Salisbury, of the country and of the weather, served among other things to remind me of your (Irish) observation, that solitude is one of the happiest things in the world, with a friend or two to partake of it... Should we hit on nothing of business that will settle me near you in town, what will hinder our retiring thither ...or from enjoying the mild climate and arcadian simplicities of the south ... or some other scheme of pleasant life which I shall wish you [to] form... Again farewell, best of friends – purest of lovers!"

By now he must have known how much or little he had inherited from Bunter so it cannot have been an amount which would allow him to move to the metropolis to be near her without some lawyering business to justify the move. He was to change his mind about moving quite soon after and apparently without clear business reasons. Subsequent correspondence with Eliza suggests some mutual change of fortune but its exact nature remains mysterious. His letter[26] of 12th June confirms the impression that he still felt poor and obliged to remain an attorney. He opened with a fanciful list of proposals for joint expeditions, perhaps even to the continent, while he acknowledged that they were 'elegant and voluptuous' notions for someone in his unprofitable profession.

From JC's letters on the 18th and 19th of June[27,28] it is clear that they had agreed on a joint stay in Southampton later in the month and he commended her for preferring it to, "...the elegant converse and dissipations of Bath." In the meantime his servant Hannah was sending Eliza some loaves and biscuits and his other servant, Peter, sent congratulations on her restored health. Peter seems at that time to have been the name of both JC's dog and his servant in Axminster.

> "...My heart, already far advanced on its way to meet its beloved object, already feels the soft tumults of expected pleasure. Adieu!"

Immediately after their return to their respective homes came the distraction of the visit to the West Country by the American ambassador John Adams and his family. JC kept Eliza informed and on 18th July he wrote to her as follows[29]:

> "...Upon my return hither, I found a long and kind letter from Mrs. Adams, and yesterday's post brought me the foregoing [he had copied his correspondence with Abigail Adams into his letter]. Does it not look probable that I shall attend them into the west as a sort of Cicerone? All this pleases you (I know) highly...I thought it prudent to dispatch my answer, together with this, not by the mail, but by the mail coach by way of parcel, directed to be delivered instantly to Mr Elworthy, that it may reach them before they set out to morrow morning. Adieu, Adieu!"

His cover note[30] to James Elworthy included the following:

> "...As their excellencies (Adams) leave town tomorrow, and I know not at what hour, and would wish them to have my letter before they set out, I must trouble you to step with it in a coach to Grosvenor square on your receiving this parcel which I have therefore directed to be delivered to you immediately. The letters for Mrs Feilder and Mr Harrison you may clap

into the post as you go along…I wrote you lately from Southhampton, and I continue firm in the expectation of seeing you within a few weeks…Our dear brother Will writes me that…his wife has been lately brought to bed, and I am to be married soon: so that you see the family of Cranch is not likely to be exterminated this year."

Obviously his time spent with Eliza had done nothing to discourage his optimism about his relationship with her. Indeed the remaining letters that exist sustain the belief that their mutual fondness remained intact and so the precise reason for their not marrying is unknown.

Another letter[31] from JC to Isabella written on 23rd of the same month survives and it is clear that she knew Eliza and about JC's relationship with her. It is worth quoting from extensively since it contained much information about JC's life at the time:

"…A great revolution is taking place at Axminster. I lately spent a happy month at Southampton and in delightful excursions from that place with a person who is very dear to both you and me. I may confidently include you, for that person has all your own virtues and attractive qualities, expanded by a larger education and more experience. Don't fancy that I defraud you of any merit by this expression, for it leaves you the practicability of being, in time, everything that this amiable friend is: but I was going to mention a revolution – a more interesting one perhaps to my dear friend than that going on in Holland. I am quitting Axminster for ever and am to settle for the present in London. You shall be acquainted with all the movements of this business in due time. Meanwhile accept my thanks for your charming long letter and depend on having the picture when I shall be sufficiently settled to do it. I hourly expect my illustrious friend Mr A.[dams] with his lady and suite to honour me with a call in their way westward, and possibly shall be permitted to accompany them to Plymouth. Won't this be charmingly lucky if I should see you. You can easily conceive that my mind does not remain unagitated by such circumstances as I must necessarily be in at this busy juncture, and therefore will excuse you that I remain sincerely your friend & humble servant. I cannot help adding some expression of the pleasure I feel at the calmness and complacence of mind apparent in your letter. Pray God increase this blessing to you with every other. Depend on my writing again when I am quiet, for I have much to say to your sweet letter. How fine is that expression – 'the little day of life' – I kiss it with enthusiasm!"

The very next day JC was writing to Eliza again[32]. Exactly what happened to change his view about his own fortune we cannot know but obviously some improvement gave him confidence quickly to wind up his business in Axminster and go to live in London. From the following letter it is clear that details of this remained a secret in Axminster whereas his role as

Simon Bunter's executor and residuary legatee cannot possibly have been secret, since many people must have known about it. His previous comments to her about Bunter's legacy seemed pessimistic so whether something suddenly occurred to make it more valuable to him or whether there was some other but unknown accession of funds we cannot know for certain but it seems likely that it had something to do with Eliza being his 'benefactress'.

> "... 'Tis all happily past, my sweet friend! The little foolish attachments to place and persons are weaned. My affairs, in consequence of very earnest exertions, almost all arranged and I shall soon leave this country (I believe I must flatter myself) with general regret, and every testimony of respect...My good fortune is yet a secret, so that I am at once enjoying the grave homage due to an inscrutable mystery, and an applause which cannot be denied to a long and steady course of honest and generous conduct.
>
> I am in hourly expectation of their Excellencies (Adams) and suite; and whether I hear from you or no, shall remain confident that you will not disapprove of my attending them westward, if I find no discouragement on their part; and soon after, I purpose to bid adieu to this neighbourhood, and throw myself into the dear embrace of my beloved benefactress."

JC's own surviving correspondence yields but one further glimpse of this most important relationship with Eliza Feilder and it is a letter[33] written by him some seven years later addressed to her friend Harriet Marsham and dated 2nd June 1794. He hoped his letter of Friday to Mrs Marsham reached her, informing her that Mrs Feilder's health was better. Nothing occurred the previous night to make him believe otherwise. She would, as advised, go into the country for better air as soon as she found it practical.

> "...My regard to our friend will no longer let me refrain from observing to you – that I think her situation and circumstances in P[ortland] Street not at all proper for her – among people of dispositions so very repugnant to her own, that what with their unfeeling tempers and vulgar manners – what with the noises inevitable in a small house, full of various people, and little factions and contentions necessarily and continually arising among these people, and a thousand like indescribables, I have often wondered that a woman with a mind like hers, should feel any reluctance to rid herself at once of what was continually making her unhappy and remove where she could be treated with that <u>voluntary</u> respect and tenderness she is so eminently entitled to, and enjoy tranquility without the awkward necessity of <u>compelling</u> it. It became my duty and the friendship I owed her to mention all this, and have mentioned it often and long ago."

It seems that Eliza had given up her housekeeping role in Kent and was now domiciled in London. She now had only five more years to live and it seems safe to suggest that they will have been dogged by ill-health. JC went on to ask Mrs Marsham to keep his comments to herself and wrote a postscript saying, "In the course of writing this letter, I was called suddenly to Hampstead where I write the latter part of it within three or four doors from the house where I remember our dear Mrs F[eilder] has told me she was born."

No baptismal record for Eliza has been found but her will reveals some interesting facts about her and JC. As mentioned above, she appointed him residuary legatee and executor. She gives his address as Frith Street, Soho which, at that time, was the street where his friend J.T. Smith was living, of whom a full account is given in subsequent chapters. She took the unusual step of naming an alternative executor so there must have been some concern in her mind that JC might predecease her or be unable to act. This individual was Michael Bowman who one deduces was a close mutual acquaintance and possibly Mrs Feilder's business manager (see Chapter 6). Bowman's failure in business was later to cause much grief to JC. Eliza made extensive cash bequests, many to the Marsham, Argles and Griffin families. She also left £50 pounds to her god-daughter Sophia Elizabeth Bowman and £100 to Michael Bowman who was the godchild's father. The total of her cash bequests was £1350 and the list of these had clearly been drawn up some time before the will itself because it was separately witnessed by a Mrs James and a Mrs Bowman, presumably Michael Bowman's wife.

No fewer than eleven members of the Argles family of Maidstone in Kent had cash bequests including a goddaughter and a godson. This family would have been of little interest to the author were it not for another surprising documentary survival which necessitates an introduction to the Reverend Mark Noble, Rector of Barming in Kent. Noble was the author of a book about the Cromwell family, the third edition of which was published in 1787 after the first two editions had been much criticised by other Cromwell experts. Unsurprisingly, Noble was much interested in the exhibition of Cromwell's head organised by JC which is described in Chapter 4. His extensively annotated copy of the pamphlet which JC wrote about the head[34] came at some point into the hands of the Wilkinson family who in modern times owned it and much ancillary documentation all of which finally came into the possession of Sidney Sussex College, Cambridge where it remains in its archives. Noble never met JC although arrangements to do so had been attempted. However, his notes included a small handwritten biography of JC, which must have been written after JC died because much of it is recognisably derived from newspaper obituaries of the time. However, it also included intriguing personal knowledge evidently resulting from his personal acquaintance with the Argles family who lived nearby. If his account was gossipy and somewhat garbled it is the only extant description of what may have been JC's final attempt to marry and its facts are confirmed to some extent from other sources.

Noble stated that JC proposed marriage to Ann Argles, daughter of Thomas Argles and that the latter sent someone to spy on JC and then claimed that JC was too old, lived in an unfurnished house and had no means to support a wife. He therefore discouraged Ann from accepting the proposal. According to Noble, Thomas Argles had a 'liberal' (i.e. profligate) way of life which left no means to endower his daughter and we might suspect that his rejection of JC's suit may well have been selfishly motivated. Noble described Ann as personally being in favour of the match. She was then 39, "...never had been handsome but was...the best of daughters and a good and benevolent person." Noble says that she never subsequently married.

Noble knew a little about Eliza Feilder and was in possession of an engraving connected in some way to her "well-known" father (although, as mentioned above, the author has been unable to uncover any details about Mr Feilder). Noble knew that Eliza had been housekeeper to Lord Romney but obviously knew nothing of her long relationship with JC. He describes "the astonishment of most" when she left him "her whole fortune" and implied that Feilder had in her life-time encouraged Ann to marry JC with promises of a legacy. But we know that being a residuary legatee was no guarantee that JC inherited anything and, while Ann received a £50 bequest in Eliza's will, this does not amount to much encouragement to marry. However, we have to accept Noble's word that he himself had been consulted about JC's suit by Thomas and Ann Argles and therefore must have had his basic facts right. He himself had just recommended delaying the marriage but obviously Thomas Argles had quickly decided otherwise.

JC's failure to marry may have been attributable in part to his relative poverty and shyness when young and later to his elevated notions of what that relationship should be. After two centuries it just seems a pity that such a clever and nice man never achieved the settled domestic life he clearly wanted.

References

1. BPL Ms. Eng. 483 (147)
2. BPL Ms. Eng. 483 (423)
3. Ober, William B. (1979), *Boswell's Clap and Other Essays: Medical Analyses of Literary Men's Afflictions*, Southern Illinois University Press, Carbondale
4. BPL Ms. Eng. 483 (408)
5. BPL Ms. Eng. 483 (15-60)
6. BPL Ms. Eng. 483 (15-60)
7. BPL Ms. Eng. 483 (2)
8. BPL Ms. Eng. 483 (15-60)
9. BPL Ms. Eng. 483 (15-60)
10. BPL Ms. Eng. 483 (15-60)
11. BPL Ms. Eng. 483 (15-60)
12. BPL Ms. Eng. 483 (15-60)
13. BPL Ms. Eng. 483 (15-60)
14. BPL Ms. Eng. 483 (15-60)
15. BPL Ms. Eng. 483 (15-60)
16. BPL Ms. Eng. 483 (15-60)
17. BPL Ms. Eng. 483 (15-60)
18. BPL Ms. Eng. 483 (15-60)
19. BPL Ms. Eng. 483 (15-60)
20. BPL Ms. Eng. 483 (15-60)
21. BPL Ms. Eng. 483 (15-60)
22. BPL Ms. Eng. 483 (15-60)
23. BPL Ms. Eng. 483 (2)
24. BPL Ms. Eng. 483 (15-60)
25. BPL Ms. Eng. 483 (15-60)
26. BPL Ms. Eng. 483 (15-60)
27. BPL Ms. Eng. 483 (15-60)
28. BPL Ms. Eng. 483 (15-60)
29. BPL Ms. Eng. 483 (15-60)
30. BPL Ms. Eng. 483 (2)
31. BPL Ms. Eng. 483 (2)
32. BPL Ms. Eng. 483 (15-60)
33. BPL Ms. Eng. 483 (61-63)
34. Cranch, John (1799), *Narrative relating to the real embalmed head of Oliver Cromwell, now exhibiting in Mead-Court, in Old Bond-Street*. Printed in London. Mark Noble's copy with extensive annotations.

Chapter 4

London

To know how well-off JC was when he left Axminster in 1787 is difficult, not only because the amount of capital he had was obscure but because to determine equivalence between 18th century and modern Britain in financial terms is generally agreed to be problematic. In addition, for an individual like JC there would have been personal priorities for expenditure, for example records exist of him buying books and going to theatres, then both relatively expensive activities, but in neither London nor Bath did he set up a household and employ servants. Without definite information as to his means it is difficult to know how courageous was his decision to leave Axminster for London. When there he seems to have done only a little further lawyering and to have tried to make some money by painting and writing. However, apart from a few star performers, payment for the creators of artworks of all kinds was poor, although at the point of sale such items were sufficiently expensive to be beyond the means of most citizens[1]. If JC did acquire capital of £400 this would have been equivalent to the average income for a British family for some four or five years. But at a time when the population of Britain totalled approximately 10 million there are estimated to have been no more than ten to fifteen thousand individuals rich enough freely to consume artworks. For the majority, finding five shillings to buy a book or go to the theatre would have been an exceptionally rare or non-existent event. There is little information about JC's expectations concerning his future financial security at the moment when he left Devonshire. He would, in any case, have been unable to predict the economic turbulence, accompanied sometimes by high levels of inflation, which arose at the beginning of the 19th century.

For good or ill his relative financial independence encouraged JC to move to London and thus be at the centre of cultural activities of all kinds and also to be nearer to his great friend, Mrs Feilder who, as detailed in Chapter 3, was at first acting as housekeeper to Lord Romney nearby in Kent and who later also lived in London. It should be added that the metropolis was also a centre for ill health, false friends and spiteful professional rivalries and if JC achieved some notable successes there, disappointments were also numerous.

So, immediately after his adventures in the West Country with the Adams family, JC left Axminster for ever. In a letter[2] to his sister Elizabeth and her husband, James Elworthy at No. 1 Old Broad Street, dated 25th July 1787 he wrote, "I hope to see you within these 3 weeks, and request to have your lodgings reserved for me (if agreeable to you, and they are unengaged) from the 15th August. Probably I shall want them a great part of the winter or so long as you can spare them."

Although he initially stayed at Old Broad Street, and surviving letters with that address exist up to 1790, JC seems not to have permanently settled down in any part of London. However the city seems to have been his principle abode for some twenty years, although while based there he clearly travelled widely within England and even abroad. A 1790 letter[3] to him survives from his friend John Andrews which says, "You are right in supposing that I had not (nor have yet) seen your Flemish Journal" but that and much else seems to be lost. In a letter from 1792 he described himself as "only having lodgings in London" and a note on the back of his painting *Cottage Interior* dated 1793 states that it was painted at Bath. Indeed JC seems to have disappeared from the capital around then for so lengthy a period that a long letter of legal advice he had written was published by William Langworthy, who believed that he was actually dead. This incident is described in greater detail below.

Unless further caches of documents are discovered, our knowledge of him at this time will remain episodic. There are enough suggestions in later correspondence to confirm that he never entirely gave up business of the type for which his training as an attorney suited him and when he finally left London to settle permanently in Bath in around 1810 there was still some tidying-up of these affairs to be done. However, his time in London seems to have been mainly dominated by the 'fine arts' and intellectual pursuits. His attempts to establish himself as a painter are detailed in Chapter 5. He made a number of firm friends and sometimes his assistance to them forms the basis of surviving knowledge of his activities through acknowledgements of his contributions in their published works.

Of London itself he gave this overall impression in a letter[4] written in 1790, of which only his draft exists and the addressee is unknown:

"...The most surprising thing to be seen about London, of a simple, single object, is the shipping between London Bridge and Deptford. This grand aggregate of important objects is really stupendous and who[ever] sees it, either with or without much contemplation, will but lightly esteem the little glittering splendours of the court, the theatres, pantheons, &c. I think the wealth, the power and the splendour of England is much more sensibly discernible in the spectacle just mentioned and even in those tumultuous scenes, the wharfs and commercial streets of London, than in the proud and easy silence of the unpopulated squares and superb vistas of Westminster."

Health

In the same letter he revealed how London was literally getting on his nerves: "...I verily believe that...I could better bear the brunt of a battle (I mean that sort of battle which is composed of gunpowder, and smoke, and helter-skelter and ball and bayonet), than a sudden rap at the door or an unkind word". In fact health problems were a recurrent problem while he was there. For example, he developed tinnitus[5]: "...the noise in my ear, though incessant, has not, 'till now, been violent... the great misery of [it] is that nobody can perceive it, either in its cause or in any material effect, and what can't be seen or somehow or other made an object of sense can neither be cured nor pitied." As already mentioned, his temporary retreat to Bath during the early 1790s was attributed to ill-health. In 1802 when he had evidently been involved in preparations for the celebrations of the Treaty of Amiens[a] he had made himself ill by overwork according to a letter[6] from his sister Mary Willcocks to her son James:

"...I suppose you will have grand illuminations and rejoicing on this joyful treaty being signed. What would I give to see what Brother has done for the occasion. [I] am very sorry to find by your letter that he is so unwell. I

---

[a] Although we don't know details of what JC was doing it is possible to make an informed guess. The treaty was marked by a spectacular official pageant involving fanfares, a proclamation, bands playing, soldiers marching, gun-salutes, bells ringing and the Lord Mayor and other officials joining in a parade. The evening, it was unofficially agreed, was to be marked by 'illuminations' and woe-betide any organization or individual who in the more central parts of London did not have some sort of lighting in his windows. The more affluent arranged to have 'transparencies' prepared and this is what almost certainly engaged JC. Very fashionable at the time these consisted of allegorical paintings on paper or thin cloth which was varnished to render it translucent and then back-lit with lamps or candles. Great numbers of these were produced for this occasion. In fact, the *European Magazine and London Review* devoted seven pages to describing just the most spectacular of the decorations.

hear he had done himself no good by his close study about this business, you must when it is over give us some description of it: give our kind love to him when you have an opportunity."

Towards the end of his time in London, JC occasionally stayed in the house of Michael Bowman in Harley Street and one item of his expenses there which appeared in accounts he drew up later[7], was for "medicines and medical attendances", although there are no details of specific illnesses. Occasionally JC also complained of leg problems[8,9] but this is scarcely surprising in someone who walked incessantly and, indeed, similar complaints were frequent in correspondence of that period and JC seems to have suffered less in this respect than many others.

Politics

Although he will probably never have been able to vote, JC was obviously interested in politics, both English and American. He was an admirer of William Pitt the younger, who was indeed generally popular for being honest, competent and a wonderful orator. One of JC's longest surviving letters[10] was an account of proceedings in the House of Commons and although it is not known to whom it was addressed it can be dated by its subject matter to April 1794. According to his account he attended the House of Commons to hear debate of some private member's bills, presumably for personal business reasons. However, this was the period when some of the greatest speakers of all time were to be heard, although there were obviously also plenty of incompetents and even the greats had their off-days.

"...The Minister for East India affairs spoke[b] [for] two hours. His arrangement, though [it] promised to be simple, was complicated in the very outset, grew more and more confused and, at length, totally lost itself.

In debating the bill for enlisting Frenchmen Mr Fox adopted narrow principles and was positively dull in his arguments. He came off however much better than Sheridan who in misrepresenting and exaggerating what he was to oppose, lost his temper, grew more violent as he became less rational and, too warm to be witty, gave us but one successful sarcasm in the course of a speech that ran full half an hour. How Sheridan got the imputation of a 'squeaker' I can't think – for his voice is manly and his

---

[b] This was Henry Dundas (1742-1811) who controlled pre-Imperial India with what Canning called a system of 'pillage and patronage'.

action not ungraceful. His *tout ensemble* much rather constitutes a 'growler' than a 'squeaker'.

Mr Burke poured forth a declamation against the present tyrannizing powers in France – replete with all that fine pathos, poignant wit, spirit and beauty of diction for which his eloquence has been long distinguished but which (as is often the case with that extraordinary man) had very little relation to the points of debate.

The pleasant, the graceful, the dignified Pitt, a being whose powers, so far transcending everything I had imagined, and realizing perfections that I had not conceived possible in the constitution of human nature, overwhelmed my soul with astonishment and admiration."

JC concluded his account with this charming word-picture:

"...While the house was breaking up, keeping my eye steadily upon the ministerial phalanx, and observing that they all stayed behind while the rest walked off, I determined to stay too, as long as should be practicable. In a few minutes every soul was gone except poor Pilgarlick[c] in the gallery, and a group below of the most curious composition that could interest the eye of a painter. Had I been to paint it the arrangement would have been as follows:- on the further side of the table sat Johnny Ley[d], as grave as an old fashioned mustard pot. The speaker descending from his chair seemed very glad to leave work, to release his wig from the rigid duty of an exact stationary equilibrium and to sit down cheek by jowl with his secretary Sam Dunn, whose attention meanwhile seemed wholly taken up by an ingenious attempt to make a whirligig of a pair of snuffers. Next to him stood 'the greatest man that ever lived in the tide of times'[e] in familiar high giggle with the clerks and understrappers; tossing about both his hat and his head with the utmost vivacity, and very good naturedly indulging his right toe with the liberty of kicking his left heel. Dundas, in the likeness of a parish clerk, beating time with his budget upon the treasury trunk, by way of assisting a critical attempt of Sergeant Colman, to balance the speaker's mace upon his chin. In short if you retain the idea of a vestry meeting, rendered sociable by having gained a lawsuit for the parish, and by the prospect of enjoying a good dinner at the parson's expense, you will have the express image of [the scene]."

---

[c] JC is referring to himself as Pilgarlick i.e. a bald man. J.T. Smith's portrait engraving of JC done in 1795 indicates that he had what would nowadays be called a 'comb-over'.

[d] John Ley was Clerk Assistant to the House of Commons appointed in 1768.

[e] 'the greatest man that ever lived in the tide of times' is a quote from Shakespeare's Julius Caesar being Anthony's remark on seeing the dead Caesar. Presumably here JC is referring to Pitt (William Pitt the Younger).

The addressee of this letter must have been some close confidential friend or relation who knew JC's acquaintances including Simon Bunter and John Andrews but it offers too little internal evidence to say who. In it he also frankly recounts how different political views caused a temporary breach with John Andrews who was not a supporter of Pitt but who was:

> "...the friend of my earliest remembrance – the monitor and comforter of every period of my life. Why harbour any displeasure at the political errors of such a man from any other motives than those of love and esteem? Yet so I fear it is. My sincerity compels me to own that his inflamed and intemperate sentiments respecting public affairs have brought on me the misfortune of being less pleased with him than I have been and still wish and even hope to be. Some asperities have I believe escaped us – a consequence that I feared indeed from the beginning, and therefore from the beginning cautiously endeavoured to avoid. But his last letter forced me to own what he cannot like to hear; and as I cannot retract my opinions, nor expect him to decline the vindication of his, the break must necessarily remain unclosed, unless he will take one end as readily as I will take the other of that veil of mutual forgiveness which I wish should be drawn over the question forever."

Learned Pursuits

London provided much to stimulate JC's lifelong interest in old buildings (see Fig. 12). A great deal of reconstruction was taking place which necessitated recording of antique structures before they were demolished. In addition JC despised the modernisation of old churches the destruction of whose "venerability" he regarded as barbarous[11]. Had he lived into the Victorian age he would have seen such barbarity carried out on an industrial scale. His younger friend John Thomas Smith (1766-1833) shared these attitudes to a high degree. Before he knew JC he had created the profusely illustrated *Antiquities of London and its Environs*, published in 1791 and JC assisted Smith in the creation of his later *magnum opus*, a book of engravings called *Antiquities of Westminster* published in 1807. These volumes earned him the soubriquet *Antiquity Smith*. Smith had thought of becoming an actor and JC's love of theatre combined with their shared interests as artists meant they had a great deal in common. Among friends JC was a witty conversationalist as was Smith so they will have enjoyed each other's company. Later they were to drift apart but there was never a decisive break and in a letter late in his life[12] JC asked to be remembered to Smith who was by then Keeper of Prints at the British Museum. An earlier letter[13] survives in which JC invites Smith to join a

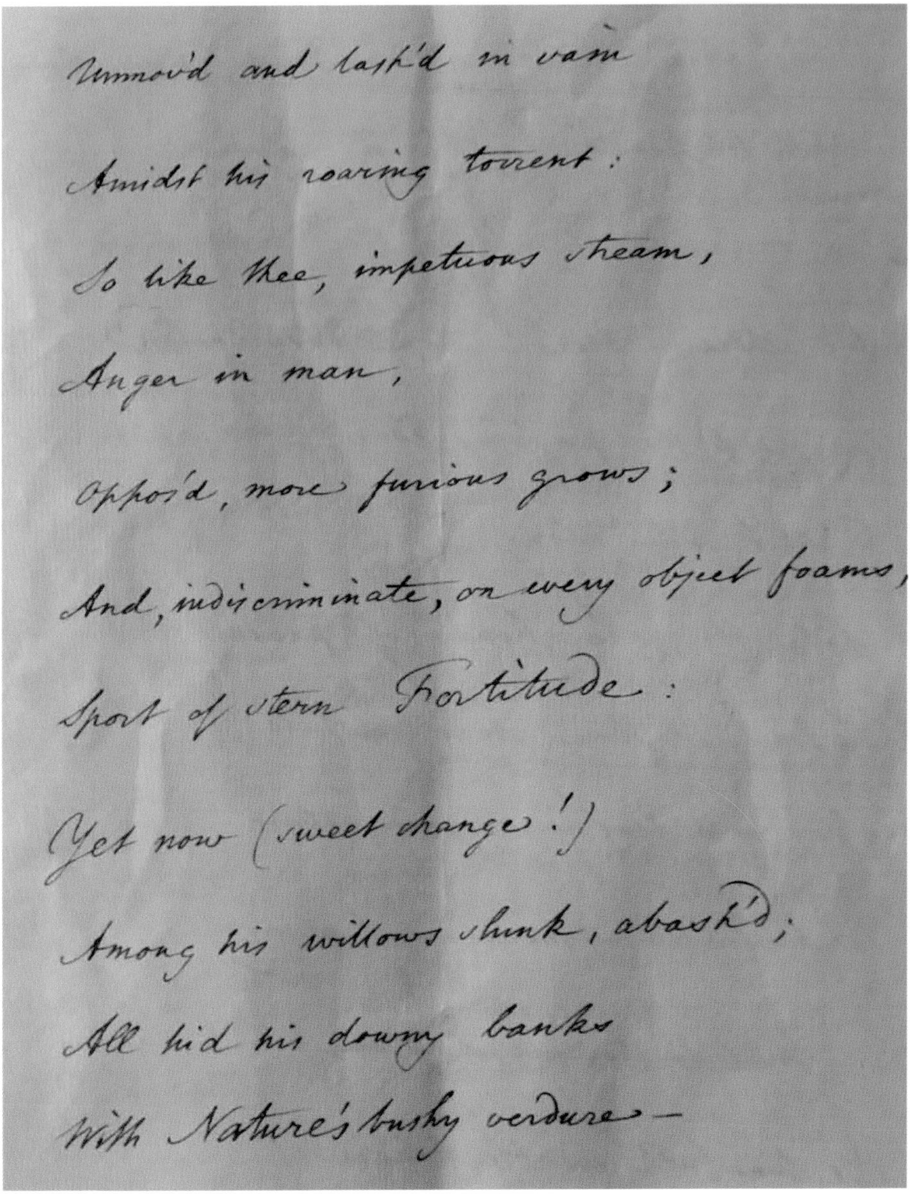

Unmov'd and lash'd in vain

Amidst his roaring torrent:

So like thee, impetuous stream,

Anger in man,

Oppos'd, more furious grows;

And, indiscriminate, on every object foams,

Sport of stern Fortitude:

(Yet now (sweet change!)

Among his willows shrunk, abash'd;

All hid his downy banks

With Nature's bushy verdure —

Fig. 1. A page from *Buckfest Abbey, a descriptive, poetical journal* written by JC when he was 18 years of age. The ruins of the abbey were close to Kingsbridge, Devonshire and thus near JC's childhood home.

Fig. 2. Oak House, Axminster, Devonshire, photographed in 2017. This was home to Simon Bunter, the attorney who made JC his apprentice.

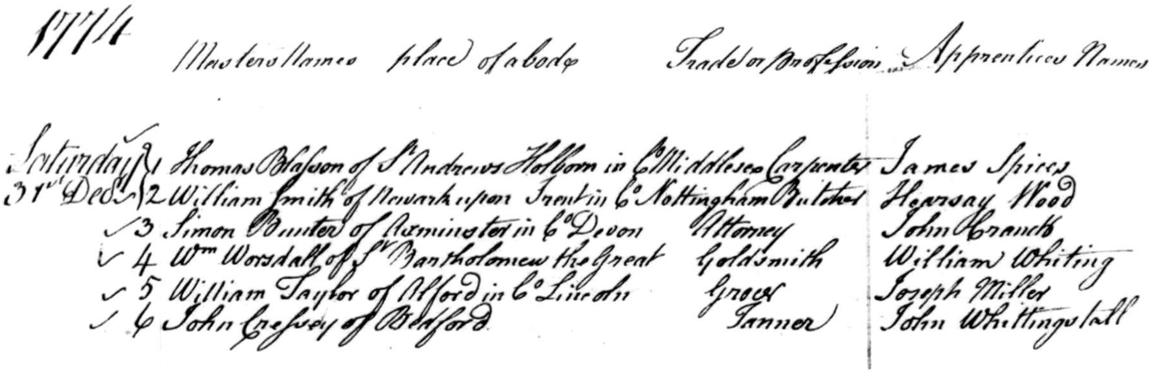

1774	Masters Names	place of abode	Trade or Profession	Apprentices Names
Saturday 31st Decr	1 Thomas Blasson	of St Andrews Holborn in Co Middlesex	Carpenter	James Spires
	2 William Smith	of Newark upon Trent in Co Nottingham	Butcher	Hearsay Wood
	3 Simon Bunter	of Axminster in Co Devon	Attorney	John Cranch
	4 Wm Worsdall	of St Bartholomew the Great	Goldsmith	William Whiting
	5 William Taylor	of Alford in Co Lincoln	Grocer	Joseph Miller
	6 John Cressey	of Bedford	Tanner	John Whittingstall

Fig. 3. The indenture of JC as apprentice to Simon Bunter, extracted from the Record Board of Stamps: Apprenticeship Books, Series IR 1; The National Archives of the United Kingdom, Kew, Surrey. These are registers of the tax received respecting apprentices indentures as required by the law which applied between 1710 and 1811. His entry is No. 3 in the list shown.

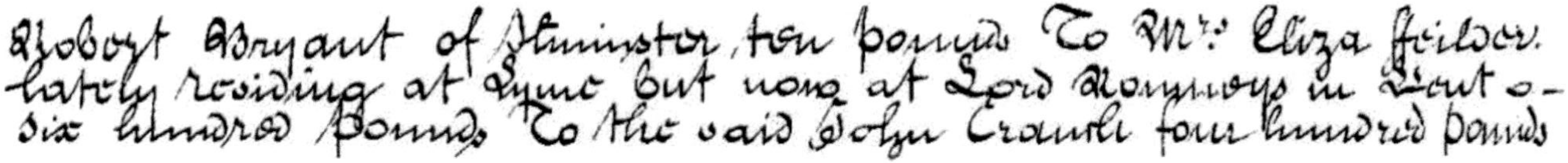

Robert Bryant of Axminster ten pounds To Mrs Eliza Feilder
lately residing at Lyme but now at Lord Romneys in Kent
six hundred Pounds To the said John Cranch four hundred pounds

Fig. 4. Extract from Simon Bunter's will showing that JC's explicit monetary bequest was for £400 and not £2000 as has been suggested elsewhere. In the preceding line is Bunter's bequest of £600 to Eliza Feilder, "lately residing at Lyme but now at Lord Romney's in Kent". (Will copy in the Public Record Office of the UK National Archive)

Fig. 5. Portrait of JC in his 30s. The author believes this to be a self-portrait. It is unsigned as might be expected if JC painted it for someone who knew him well (Painting privately owned; photograph courtesy of Robert D. Mussey Jr.).

Fig. 7. Portrait of Joseph Palmer, JC's uncle by marriage to his aunt Mary. Engraving based on a painting by John Singleton Copley.

Fig. 6. The only known portrait of Richard Cranch, uncle of JC. (original held by the Massachusetts Historical Society).

Fig, 8. Portrait of Hannah Cranch Bond. The only image of one of JC's siblings known to the author (original in the Bond Family Papers in the Collection of Historical Scientific Instruments at Harvard University. © The President and Fellows of Harvard College).

Fig. 9. Portrait of the young William Cranch Bond looking as JC would have known him (from the Bond family papers in the Collection of Historical Scientific Instruments at Harvard University. Image © The President and Fellows of Harvard College).

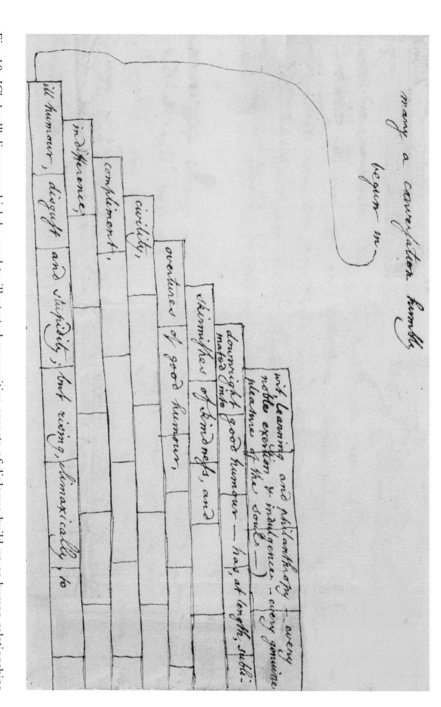

Fig. 10. JC's 'wall' diagram which he used to illustrate how positive aspects of dialogue build up as human relationships develop.

Fig. 11. Escutcheon which JC created to introduce his thesis on Bath's Roman remains. The title page which follows reads: "An Account of Antique Remains found in the city, suburbs & vicinity of BATH since the year 1814; with observations concerning them, and concerning the antiquities in and near Bath generally. By John Cranch, Member of the Bath Library and Philosophical society; member of the American Academy of Arts and Sciences; and fellow of the American Antiquarian Society. Respectfully presented to his brethren, the president and members of the American Antiquarian society. From Bath, 23. Oct. 1818."

Ruins of the Convent of Nuns, Minories, London.

Published for the Proprietors, by W. Clarke, New Bond St. to J. Carpenter, Old Bond St. May 1, 1810.

Fig. 12. Engraving of a nunnery created from a drawing of JC's by B. Storer in his *Antiquarian and Topographical Cabinet* (1810), Vol 7 published in London. The ruins had been demolished before the book was published.

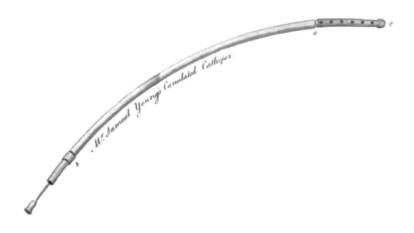

Fig. 13. Engraving created from a drawing by JC of "an important improvement of the female catheter" by Samuel Young, as reported in the Medical and Physical Journal of 1805.

Fig. 14. The Old Queens Head, Islington, as JC would have known it. This building was demolished in 1829 and replaced with the inn of the same name which still stands today.

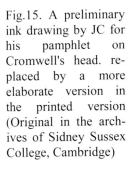

Fig.15. A preliminary ink drawing by JC for his pamphlet on Cromwell's head. replaced by a more elaborate version in the printed version (Original in the archives of Sidney Sussex College, Cambridge)

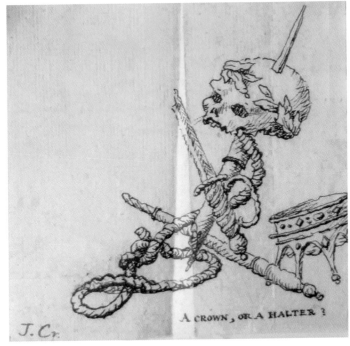

J. Cr.

A CROWN, OR A HALTER ?

Fig 16. The probable head of Oliver Cromwell painted by JC in 1799. Modern photographs of the head show that JCs painting was an accurate representation of the relic (Photograph by Mark Scudder; ©The Master and Fellows of Sidney Sussex College, Cambridge).

Fig. 17. JC's signature in a First Folio edition of Shakespeare's plays (No. 48 in the Folger Shakespeare Library's collection of first folios).

10th April, 1805.

THE SOCIETY for SUPPRESSION of VICE, having sent their usual admonitions to certain persons at Edmonton, who kept their shops open, and publicly employed their men on Sundays; and having, in consequence of the disregard paid to their admonitions, brought several of the offenders to legal punishment, the respectable part of the inhabitants of that neighbourhood were roused to more extensive exertions in the same way; and those exertions appear to have been followed by the most salutary and decisive effects.

The subject having been lately detailed in a letter to the Society, no apology is here offered for recommending the example, as worthy of being followed in every town and village in the kingdom.

By order of the Committee,
JOHN CRANCH for the Secretary

Fig. 18. Advertisement placed by JC on behalf of the Society for Suppression of Vice, in the *Kentish Weekly Post or Canterbury Journal*, Friday 19th April, 1805. Later the same year he was replaced in his role as its representative. (Image © The British Library Board).

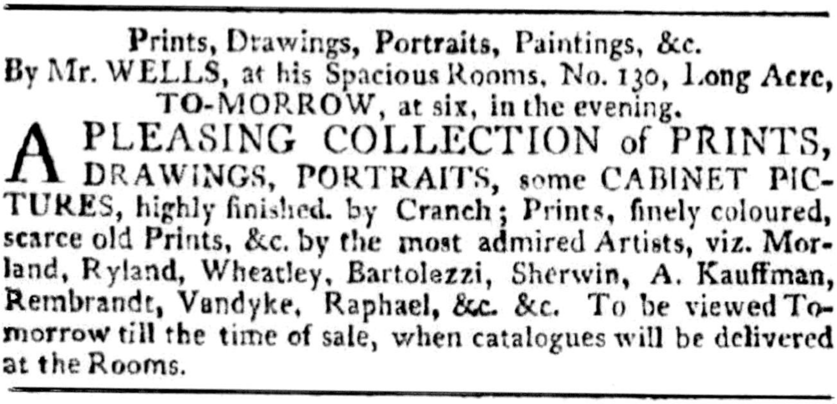

Prints, Drawings, Portraits, Paintings, &c.
By Mr. WELLS, at his Spacious Rooms, No. 130, Long Acre,
TO-MORROW, at six, in the evening.

A PLEASING COLLECTION of PRINTS, DRAWINGS, PORTRAITS, some CABINET PICTURES, highly finished. by Cranch; Prints, finely coloured, scarce old Prints, &c. by the most admired Artists, viz. Morland, Ryland, Wheatley, Bartolezzi, Sherwin, A. Kauffman, Rembrandt, Vandyke, Raphael, &c. &c. To be viewed To-morrow till the time of sale, when catalogues will be delivered at the Rooms.

Fig. 19. Advertisement for a sale of artworks, placed in the *Morning Chronicle* of Tuesday 19th November, 1805.

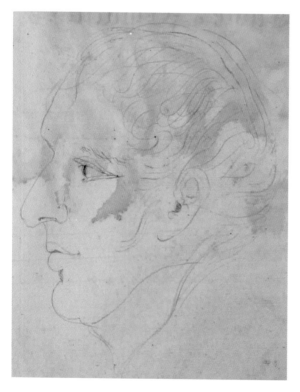

Fig. 20. Sketch found in a ledger originally from Hilary House, Axminster, Devonshire and dating from a period when JC was a clerk there. (Document in Devon Heritage Centre, Exeter).

Fig. 21. *Moonlight Landscape with Hadleigh Church* by John Constable. This was, "painted in the manner or style of Cranch." (Painting privately owned; photograph ©The Gainsborough House Society).

Fig. 22. *Kitchen Interior* painted by JC (1793; © Bristol Art Gallery).

Fig. 23. *Dovecote* painted by JC. (c 1800; Painting privately owned; photograph © Lowell Libson & Jonny Yarker Ltd). The painting is very likely to have been based on the medieval dovecote at Pridhamsleigh Manor near Totnes, Devonshire which survives today as a protected monument. This was close to JC's home when he was a youth and has architectural features similar to those depicted in the painting.

Fig. 24. *Penitents* painted by JC. On the back is written: "Painted at BATH by John Cranch for his friend Abraham Crocker, 1813." (Painting privately owned).

Fig. 25. *Snow Scene with Three Figures*, painted by JC. The man is riding his pony sidesaddle.

Fig. 26. *The Plaisterer* painted by JC, (1806, © Yale Center for British Art, Paul Mellon Collection).

Fig. 27. *Snow Scene with Figure* painted by JC. The building has been described as a chapel but it seems more likely that it is an ancient house-barn built to accommodate animals at ground level and humans above.

Fig. 28. *November 5th Bonfire* painted by JC (1793, privately owned. It shows the burning of effigies of Guy Fawkes and the Pope).

Fig. 29. *View on the Shannon* painted by JC (1792; © Aberdeen City Gallery).

Fig. 30. *Snow Scene* painted by JC (1806; privately owned).

Fig. 31. *Playing with Baby* painted by JC (1795; © Victoria and Albert Museum).

Fig. 32. *The Miser* painted by JC (1791; © Royal Albert Memorial Museum & Art Gallery, Exeter).

Fig. 33. *Carrier's Cart* painted by JC (1796; © Royal Albert Memorial Museum & Art Gallery, Exeter).

Fig. 34. Abraham Crocker (1742-1821). Portrait attr. to Samuel Woodforde (© Frome Heritage Museum, Frome, Somersetshire).

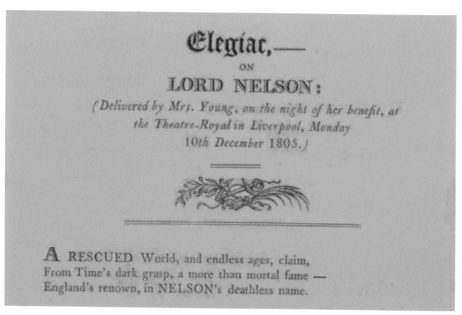

Fig. 35. The title and first part of a 31-line Elegiac on Lord Nelson written by JC for public performance after the Battle of Trafalgar and printed by the Crocker family. His name is printed at the foot of the poem.

VETUSTMROMANARE

AN
ACCOUNT OF
MONUMENTS & REMAINS OF
𝕬𝖓𝖙𝖎𝖊𝖓𝖙 𝕬𝖗𝖙𝖘,
collected in and near the City of
BATH;
more particularly at WALCOT
between the beginning of April
and the end of June 1815; when
they were transferred to the COR-
PORATION, and deposited in this
museum.

By JOHN CRANCH, an inhabit-
ant of Bath, and a member of
the American Academy of arts
and sciences.

Fig. 36. Escutcheon on the front page of the pamphlet JC created for visitors to the first museum in Bath dedicated to Roman remains and which describes his discoveries. Not surprisingly, it shows signs of much handling. (© Bath Record Office Archives & Local Studies).

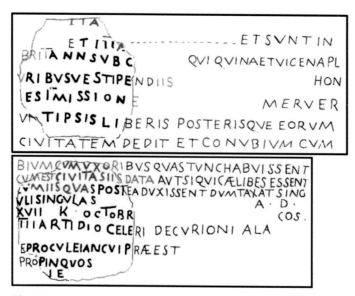

ITA

ET IIIA ....ET SVNT IN
BRITANNSVBC QVI QVINAETVICENAPL
VRIBVSVESTIPENDIIS HON
ESIMISSIONE MERVER
VNTIPSISLIBERIS POSTERISQVE EORVM
CIVITATEM DEDIT ET CONVBIVM CVM

BIVMCVMVXORIBVS QVASTVNCHABVISSENT
CVMESTCIVITASIIS DATA AVTSIQVICÆLIBES ESSENT
VMIISQVASPOSTEADVXISSENT DVMTAXAT SING
VLISINGVLAS A · D ·
XVII K · OCTOBR COS ·
TIIARTIDIOCELERI DECVRIONI ALA
EPROCVLEIANCVIPRÆEST
PROPINQVOS
VE

Fig. 37. Attempted reconstruction by Samuel Lysons of the entire texts from both sides of the fragmentary *Tabula Missionis Honestae* discovered by JC at Walcot in 1815. (See Archaeological Journal of 1877, Vol 34, pp318 and 319).

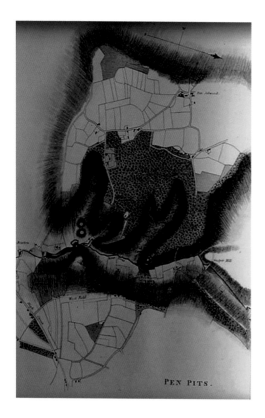

PEN PITS.

Fig. 38. Map of Pen Pits contemporary with JC's pamphlet on the subject. Taken from *The Ancient History of Wiltshire, Volume 1* by Sir Richard Colt Hoare. Published in 1812 by William Miller, London. The dots in the central area of the map each represent a pit and the total number surviving at the beginning of the 19th Century was obviously very considerable.

Fig. 39. Escutcheon forming the frontispiece of JC's pamphlet on Pen Pits. *Aluredus* is the Latin version of the name Alfred. *Edintune* is the ancient name of Edington in Wiltshire, spelt thus in the Domesday book. Edington is generally accepted as the site of the battle at which Alfred the Great's Anglo-Saxon army defeated the Danes led by Guthrum in AD 878.

Fac simili of a fragment of a marine plant found by me in Kingsbridge river, 1799. The stellata had precisely the texture and appearance of burnished gold leaf, while fresh from out of the water, but faded after a day or two. J.Cr.

This specimen (of the Murex stain) is from my own experiment made at the same time – about October 1799, at Thurlston rocks. John Cranch.
See p. 123.

SIR JOSHUA REYNOLDS.

Fig. 40. Extract from a page in Polwhele's *History of Devonshire* showing some of JC's numerous annotations and inserts including the sample of cloth stained with dye from the *Murex* sea snail.

Page 89.

	BURIALS in the Parish of *Walcot* in the County of *Somerset* in the Year 18*21*				
	Name.	Abode.	When buried.	Age.	By whom the Ceremony was performed.
No. 709.	John Cranch	Nelson point	30	70	G. Berry

Fig. 41. Extract from the register of burials at St Swithin's church, Walcot, Bath, showing the record for JC.

party to explore, "the venerable relics of St. Faiths, and... the subterranean chapel at Aldgate." Many copies survive of Smith's portrait engraving of JC which forms the frontispiece of this volume.

JC spent many weeks delving through old documents in the British Museum. If he wrote personal accounts of his researches then on the whole they must be lost or unidentifiable. Much journalism was at that time written anonymously, or signed with a pen name or initials. But even though contemporary biographical accounts of his life suggested that he may even have edited a periodical the author has been unable to find any trace of it. However, he was clearly generous with his time on others' behalf and these efforts were acknowledged in their writings. For example *Antiquities of Westminster* includes the following acknowledgements[14]:

> "...Mr Smith is indebted to his steady friend Mr John Cranch of Kingsbridge in Devonshire for pointing out the subject of this painting (... a representation of the destruction of Job's Children, Job, chap ii, v.11) which had eluded the skill of several persons; he is also under obligations to the same Gentleman for his kindness and assiduity in copying several ancient records in the British Museum contained in this work."

And also:

> "...See it at length in Rymer's *Foedera*, vol vii, p794. For many voluminous extracts from Rymer's *Foedera* and from many difficult MSS in the British Museum, Mr Smith is obliged to ...Mr. Cranch before mentioned."

As suggested before, it is clear that JC knew the Bible intimately and it is also apparent that in reading Rymer's books which were histories of legal and political developments in England dating back to mediaeval times, he was by now able to cope with texts written largely in Latin.

Smith was a good artist and a fine engraver but he was a poor manager and disorganised regarding money. The *Antiquities of Westminster* project took an inordinate amount of time to be completed. Both JC and Smith were distressed at the rapid destruction of old London and by the time the volume appeared Smith recorded that of 246 buildings portrayed 122 had already been demolished. Recognising that new information had come to light during the book's long gestation Smith inserted addenda at the end including letters from those who had gone on with research after their initial involvement. To these JC contributed a series of carefully referenced findings:

"Dear Smith, I take for certain and of obvious course that what relates to Anthony Woodville's bequest of his heart to our Lady of the Pewe (*Nichols, Coll. of Royal Wills, pages 352 and 353, note – and Dug. Bar. II. 233,* there referred to) as well as what relates to the countess of Richmond's donation to the Dean and Canons by her will (*Nichols, ibid. 361*) has been observed and made use of in some part of your work.

That the structure of St. Stephen's chapel had obtained, at least, the highest and most decided approbation, in an age distinguished for architectural refinements and magnificence, is apparent from the will of King Henry VI which particularly and emphatically directs that the stalls and rood-loft of the choir of Eton College, "shall be made in manner and form like the stalls and roode loft in the chapel of St. Stephen at Westminster." (*Ibid.p. 296*).

King Charles II after his restoration gathered some acorns from the Royal Oak at Boscobel and set them in St. James's Park or garden and used to water them himself. *Tour through Great Britain, by a Gentleman, in 4 vol. 12mo. 1753, vol. ii, p379.*

Saint Stephen's Chapel, within the ancient royal Palace of Westminster was built by King Stephen about 1141. *Remarks on London, by W. Stow, 12mo. 1722, p123.*

In the passage out of Westminster Hall into Old Palace Yard, a little beyond the stairs going up to St. Stephen's Chapel, on the left hand, is the house belonging to the ancient family of Cotton wherein is kept a most inestimable library of manuscript volumes, famed both at home and abroad, collected with great expense by Sir Robert Cotton. *Antiq. of London and Westminster, by N. Bailey, (author of the Dictionary) 12mo. 1734 p.241.*

The Gate-house at Westminster is so-called, of two gates, the one out of the College Court towards the north; on the east side thereof was the bishop of London's prison for clerks convict: the other gate adjoining the first, but towards the west, is a gaol or prison for offenders thither committed: these gates were both caused to be built by Walter Warfield, cellarer to the monastery, in the reign of Edward III. *Ibid. p. 242*

At the upper end of Westminster Hall is a marble stone, (perhaps table or bench) of nineteen feet in length, and three feet in breadth, and a marble chair where the Kings of England formerly sat at their coronation dinners and, at other solemn times, the lord chancellors: but now not to be seen, being built over by the Courts of Kings Bench and Chancery. *Ibid. p. 240.* It is to be wished that when the proposed alterations of those places shall commence, every lover of our monarchical antiquities will interest himself in the preservation of these venerable relics; since the same barbarous insensibility that buried them alive will scruple as little to profane or destroy them, when disclosed. JOHN CRANCH"

Part of the reason for quoting JC's contribution at length is to show the fastidiousness of his scholarship; he was no dilettante. His final paragraph reveals his passionate concern to preserve ancient things, long before this became a matter of public policy in the United Kingdom. Although in the 18th and early 19th century he was not entirely alone in his interests, there seems to have been a typically English divide between certain gentlemen amateurs and those like JC and Smith who were prepared to get their hands dirty. The Society of Antiquaries of London was founded in 1707 and granted a royal charter in 1751 but of course neither JC nor Smith became members, which would have required them to pay a substantial subscription. More information about Smith is provided in Chapter 5.

Another friend of JC for whom he did research was the physician and cancer specialist Samuel Young. The late 18th and early 19th century saw the beginning of what would be recognised later as a scientific approach to medicine and the final displacement of fanciful theories such as the *humours* which had held sway since ancient times. Although only relatively superficial solid tumours were recognised as cancer and treated, physicians like Young had some success with application of pressure dressings to the lesions and the use of caustics. Then, as now, a 'literature search' was considered desirable both to prevent rediscovery of existing knowledge and treatments and to give credit to predecessors where it was due and this was where JC contributed, as Young wrote[15]:

> "...A friend of mine, Mr John Cranch, who had been particularly requested by me not to overlook any paper or remark relative to Cancer, during his researches among old writings, at the British Museum, met with the following and gratified me with a copy: viz. *New Discoveries concerning Cancers, addressed to Charles Bernard, Esq. Sergeant-Surgeon and Surgeon in ordinary to Her Majesty Queen Anne By William Beckett, Surgeon, and F.R.S.* It was placed as an advertisement at the back of one of the original numbers of the Spectator. After considerable search, this paper was met with, bound up with others of Mr Beckett's works as published by Curll."

JC was aware of the publication of some of Young's work to which he had contributed. In writing to Philip Crocker[16] in 1805 he referred to his contribution (Fig. 13) to work just being published [17]:

> "...if he sees his friend Sam Young's little essay 'on Cancer' published by Philips, and (perhaps) the <u>next</u> number of the *Medical and Physical Journal*, you may recognize some considerable <u>veins</u> of my handiwork in the <u>former</u>, and in a paper referring to a print from a drawing of mine, of

an important improvement of the female catheter by the aforesaid Young, in the <u>latter</u>."

The story of the publication of one of JC's surviving literary works, *The Œconomy of Testaments*[18] is quite strange but its composition arose from his characteristic generosity in helping a friend whose identity is now lost. This person had sent his own proposed will to JC during 1791 in what was described as 'a parcel' so we can imagine a sheaf of papers containing many well-meaning but ill thought-out proposals. The friend gave JC *carte blanche* to make comments and the result was a 30-page discourse on will-making in general. First came a warning against seeking the assistance in composition from the sort of local wiseacre who once read a book such as *The Complete Parish Officer* or *The Sure Guide to Constables*. He then pointed out that, in practice, if the intention of a will was clear the legal system in England was tolerant of non-lawyerly language:

> "...I should judge it sufficient to employ indifferently, any ingenious man of letters in habits of giving prudent advice – of guarding things from obvious and avoidable difficulties – and (above all) of expressing rational intentions in terms which, at once, *can* be understood and *cannot* be misunderstood."

But most of the text was dedicated to warning of the danger of complicated bequests which relied on trustees for their execution. This seems a little ironic since, as an attorney, he had been trustee for the Bunter and Drake estates but he pointed out that trustees themselves might die and their responsibilities possibly be inherited by less competent or honest individuals. Thus, for example, bequests should only be made to living persons and well-meaning attempts to leave property to unborn descendants should be avoided.

He continues in language which is still entertaining today but which must have made the gorge of many of his fellow attorneys rise:

> "...What would you say of the common attempt to perpetuate *land* in a family? This grand farce, you know, is begun by drawing up writings which import that the land is thereby entailed and appropriated to the family and its posterity, in a certain line of succession, "for ever and evermore". The old gentleman (the father of this folly), assured by an immediate volume of parchment prolixities, difficult to read, and impossible for him (and sometimes indeed for anybody else) to understand, that neither the "young buck", nor many a generation after him, will be able to get rid of the darling family estate, tolerates his gout a

while longer enjoys the "*mentis gratissimus error*"[f] in his easy chair, and finally sleeps with his fathers. Meanwhile, the young one, prepared by his adventures at College, at White's or at Newmarket; drove by duns, cajoled by courtesans, or (which would be the most prevalent of all) whetted up to perverseness by *restraint* – whirls down to the old mansion, takes possession, gets a fresh lawyer, or the old one *fresh fee'd*, and by the counterfarce of a "fine and recovery", demolishes, at one stroke, the whole laborious fabric of the entailment; down comes the timber, and before Old Squaretoes has passed the Styx, the 'family estate' shall be trembling under the eloquence of the "superlative" Mr Christie and his ivory hammer. Is this *caricature*? No; a thousand instances daily convince us that, if a ludicrous, it is yet a faithful portrait of existing truth!"

And then he points out the potential for legal delay to ruin lives:

"...The trustee – (for I have already proved the alarming assertion that it is impossible to know who, or what, that trustee shall be) *refuses* to act; or by absence or legal disability, *cannot* act. What remedy? Chancery! The court of Chancery only (and that perhaps after a long and grievous series of those oppositions, evasions, or chicane practices, which however that tribunal be competent to *surmount*, it cannot, in its nature, prevent) can remedy so disastrous an occurrence. Chancery! – The very word is an electrical shock. Your whole business is struck motionless in an instant; and one whom you think the most deserving of her sex, and whose labours and cares so largely helped to acquire and preserve this imagined source of comforts for retirement and declining years – with an innocent, perhaps a deserving and yet a helpless family, is left, in unavailing astonishment, to *starve* amidst surrounding *plenty!!!*"

And so to its publication. JC had helped William Langworthy in some way with a book entitled *An Attempt to Promote the Commercial Interests of Great Britain* published in 1794. Even though Langworthy was a lawyer his book was primarily about metallurgy and mining. Specifically it was designed to promote a method for protecting iron from corrosion by coating it with tin with a view to creating corrosion-free equipment and fixings for ships. Clearly the two men had not met at this point and the help which JC provided, presumably by letter, is unknown. Mining of metals in Britain which was then mainly carried on in the West Country, was a subject with which JC might well have been familiar.

---

[f] *Mentis gratissimus error* is a most delightful reverie of the mind (i.e. an hallucination as described by Horace). White's was a gentlemens' club in London. Newmarket refers to the racecourse. Christie was the founder of the auction house which still bears his name.

Chapter 4

When *The Œconomy of Testaments* was published it contained the following text written by Langworthy:

> "...The Late Mr John Cranch, a very deserving native of Kingsbridge, whose simplicity of manners, sweetness of disposition, versatility of talents, extensive knowledge and profound judgement, I had flattered myself, as he had honoured me with his notice, would have made him a most valuable acquaintance to me. But on my return from the country in November to my great disappointment and sorrow, I was informed that from a too severe an application to the study of painting and of the preparation of colours, his health was so impaired that, being advised to quit London, he had gone into the West of England, where he shortly afterwards died.
>
> I have been accidentally favoured by some MSS of his, which lay in the hands of one of his acquaintance in town. One of these manuscripts is a letter to a friend who had submitted to his consideration the form and intentions of his will; and, as I think its publication will be of general utility, I have taken upon me the charge of printing and publishing it, under the title of "Reflections on the mischievous consequences generally arising from the usual dispositions of property by will". If Mr Cranch has any relations living in England, I shall be happy to account to them for the profits, if any should arise from the sale of the book. Another of the manuscripts is an irregular poem in blank verse, entitled "Buckfast Abbey" written at the age of eighteen in a very pure style, and possessing many beauties. And the third manuscript is a profound criticism of Dr Johnson's edition of Shakespeare's plays (octavo 1765) and on the play of "The Tempest" and the notes upon it exhibited in that edition. In case I should ever be tempted to collect and publish my own little juvenile scraps of poetry, I will print Mr Cranch's poem with them, and his notes on the Tempest shall not be left to the lovers of Shakespeare."

Both the poem and JC's criticism of Johnson's edition of Shakespeare still survive, the former pasted into the back of JC's copy of Polwhele's *History of Devonshire* as mentioned in Chapter 1 and the latter in the Boston Public Library collection of Cranch papers. By the time Langworthy's own book was published in 1794 he knew JC was still alive so it appeared with the following 'Advertisement' at the front:

> "...The Author is happy to add that Mr Cranch, the gentleman whose death is lamented in a note ... recovered from his illness; and, as it would be attended with much inconvenience to rescind the note, he hopes Mr. Cranch will forgive him for publishing it."

Langworthy's preface to JC's book is itself a nice summary of the work and worth quoting in part:

"...It seems, that the valuable reflections it contains had their origin in a letter addressed by the author to a friend, who had drawn up his will himself in those loose, equivocal, and defective terms, by which the meanings of such instruments are so often brought into dispute, and many an honest man has found a *law-suit* where he only expected a *legacy*."

It appears that the testator had led himself into errors of *principle*. He had made the dispositions even of his *monied* and personal property, so full of contingencies, restrictions, multiple trusts, and other perplexities, that the author, to whose opinion and advice he had in prudence submitted the paper, found it his duty to offer some special and serious argument, to induce his friend to alter and simplify his intentions."

Although its publication had not been intended by JC himself, he was obviously happy that the *Œconomy* had been brought into the public domain and its authorship is mentioned in the text under J.T. Smith's portrait engraving of him. It also attracted the attention of critics. The *Critical Review* was unsympathetic[19], implying that wills not written in legal jargon by a professional would be even more liable to lengthy litigation in the Court of Chancery. The *Gentleman's Magazine* was even sniffier[20], suggesting that "...his editor supports his objections with arguments not always fairly put and with injudicious ridicule of trustees or professional men." Evidently these comments were written by lawyers. It is worth pointing out that JC's loathing for the Court of Chancery anticipated Charles Dickens's similar contempt expressed in his novel *Bleak House* nearly 60 years later.

As mentioned in Chapter 2, Langworthy later emigrated to America and secured a letter of introduction[21,22] from William Smith to John Adams.

Music

Of the fine arts there is least known about JC's interest in music although he is generally acknowledged as having skill in that regard and one of those who attended his funeral was Mr H. Seine, a piano teacher in Bath whose wife was a singer. There is no definite record of JC playing an instrument but in 1804 he inscribed his name on a choral part-work, which survives, so he may well have sung[23].

Evidently he could read a score sufficiently well to appreciate the force of a composition without hearing it played, as evidenced by a letter[24] he wrote in 1787 in which he tells a friend that he has missed a commemorative festival of Handel's music in London:

"...Perhaps I ought not to regret it: there is music of Handel's which I cannot even silently peruse but with much agitation. How should I have withstood it in its aggrandized effect – in all its pomp of expression – in all its plenitude of 'gorgeous eloquence'."

Letters survive from 1787 in which JC corresponded with his American cousin Eliza Cranch about music. He sent her a collection of pieces and complained jocularly when she failed to respond as he wished[25]:

"...And so I am thanked for the 'quantity' of music sent. What a Dutch compliment! Oh, coz, try your hand again, for if you can't extract [more] from the 'quality' as well as 'quantity' of the gift how shall I bear such mortification?...Let me hear then how your spirits kindled at 'The Invocation', how your soul melted at the strange harmonies and pathos of 'the III elegy', sunk, delicious, under the thrilling passages, the delicate fugues, the easy successions, the happy combinations, the ever beauteous incident that distinguishes the canzonet 'Time has not thinn'd my flowing hair' or soared to sublimity and paradise with the 'Vital Spark of Heavenly Flame'[g]; or in the sacred raptures of Haydn!"

She had sent him an 'Indian' poem to set to music but his courage as a composer seems to have failed him and if he ever did create any music it seems not to have survived.

Time has not thinn'd my flowing hair was by William Jackson (1730-1803), and so probably were the pieces he called *The Invocation* and *The III Elegy*. William Jackson was a fellow Devonian from Exeter where he was the cathedral organist and JC was a great admirer of his. Amongst JC's annotations in Polwhele's *History of Devonshire* is a biographical essay of more than one thousand words on Jackson, dated 1812. In it he praised both Jackson's music and his writing. He recorded that he had visited Jackson's house and had seen there his portrait painted by Gainsborough, who was a friend of Jackson. JC also noted that he later expanded this essay and had it printed for private distribution among his friends, although no copy has been found. His concluding remarks read:

"...Posterity too, if I do not over-rate the merits of Jackson, will justly regret the negligence and injustice of the present age if a more ample account of so distinguished an ornament of his country, do not preserve those particulars of his life, which must otherwise be lost to the admirers

---

[g] *The Vital Spark of Heavenly Flame* was by Edward Harwood (1707-1787) with lyrics by Alexander Pope.

of genius and originality of a character as worthy of commemoration as any that (at least) the county of Devon[shire] has in any age produced."

The same might be said of JC himself. Of Jackson the author can report that a fair amount of biographical material has been published about him, some of which has found its way onto the Internet, and much of his exquisite music is available at the time of writing (2018) both as scores and recordings.

The Old Queens Head

From a letter[26] dated 4th April 1800 we know that JC was then residing at 9, Rufferts Row by Islington church. How long he lived there is unknown but it was long enough to be on terms of familiarity with a local inn, *The Old Queen's Head*, depicted in Fig. 14 as he would have known it. Although the building illustrated was demolished in 1829, the brick hostelry which replaced it in 1830 still stands today in Essex Road, Islington. Its timbered Tudor predecessor was much lamented when it was taken down although some of its internal architectural features were preserved in its replacement and can still be seen. Certain traditions attached to the original building, notably, a supposed association with Sir Walter Raleigh which would have appealed to JC as a Devonian. The only firm justification for this appears to be that Queen Elizabeth granted Sir Walter a patent 'to make licences for keeping of taverns and retailing of wines throughout England'. It was suggested that this tavern might have been one of those to which Raleigh granted a licence, and thereafter its name marked the reign in which it happened. However, evidently more significant to JC was another tradition that the Queen's favourite, the Earl of Essex, lived in the house before it became an inn and that she occasionally visited him there.

A portrait of JC in convivial mood can be gained from an event there in 1796. One has to assume that JC and his friends were 'regulars' and that one day they had a party there during which JC presented a large, engraved pewter tankard to the landlord Mr J. Scott. The tankard became something of a landmark in its own right and remained in both the old and new buildings at least until 1839 when Mr J.H. Burn produced ten copies of a handbill recording JC's verse which had been engraved on the tankard. Luckily one of these survives in Oxford University's Bodleian Library and here is the poem:

INSCRIPTION RECORDING A LOCAL TRADITION
ON CRANCH'S FESTIVOUS TANKARD
PRESENTED TO J.SCOT, LANDLORD OF THE OLD QUEEN'S HEAD, ISLINGTON

Here liv'd Elizabeth Tudor, who ('tis said)
Took off her *man's*, yet sav'd her *maiden*-head;
Which those who like *old musty things* to rake in,
Say might be true – for 'twasn't *worth the taking.*
But great queen Bess had nobler things to brag on,
Than the old wig she hung young Essex' peg on –
Or, as I might less bawdily have sung,
Than *any* wig that ever on peg hung:
Bess was the good old mother of her folk;
And, with her sturdy staff of English oak,
Gave, what she'd never *take,* many a *good stroke* –
Stroking so well, indeed her *Spanish* lover,
'Twas thought he'd never more want *doing over.*
And so, God bless old England, head and tail –
(This town, by th'by, has neither one nor t'other.)
And grant the Queen's Head tap may never fail;
But spout, more vig'rously than any other,
As *pure* a virgin stream, and a *little* stronger,
Till I can *drink* no more, or *pay* no longer.

J.C. 1796.

JC while personally being virtuous was capable of amusement at the supposed foibles of our forebears. He lived at the period of transition between Georgian licentiousness and Victorian prudery and several later written descriptions of the verse were laughably sniffy[27,28] and refused to quote it in full. However, early in the 19th century it was appreciated, notably by the poet Charles Lamb (1775-1834) whose biographer Edward Lucas recorded[29], "At the Old Queen's Head he puffed his pipe and quaffed his ale out of the huge tankard presented by a certain festivous Master Cranch of bonifacial aspect and hue, to a former host". Although the tankard may still have been in situ[28] as late as 1868, when the author contacted the current owners of *The Old Queen's Head* in 2018 they unsurprisingly had no knowledge of its whereabouts if indeed it still exists.

Cromwell's Head

The history of a head thought to be that of Oliver Cromwell briefly played an important part in JC's life even though the artist, John Constable, was critical[30] of his neglecting painting to work on it. JC's involvement was actually an ideal vehicle for his combination of antiquarian, artistic and even business skills. His professionalism in researching its provenance and curating an exhibition of it in London during 1799 remains unchallenged by the numerous subsequent investigators of the relic.

Regrettably, in recent books and articles, attention paid to the head has not been matched with similar attention to biographical details of JC and his family. All modern accounts which the author has read contain errors, for example, even getting dates wrong which would have been easy to get right. For this reason a fuller account is given of this subject than a strict account of JC's personal involvement might merit. His artwork for promoting the exhibition of the head has repeatedly been reproduced without acknowledgement even though the pamphlet he wrote entitled *Narrative Relating to the Real Embalmed Head of Oliver Cromwell, Now Exhibiting in Mead-Court, in Old Bond Street, 1799* can still readily be purchased in facsimile today.

So, what follows is a narrative relating to the *real* involvement of JC in the Cromwell head affair. Even at the end of the 18th century, two hundred years after his birth, Cromwell was still a controversial figure with a prominent person such as Joseph Banks (1743 -1820), President of the Royal Society, desiring to be excused from seeing the remains of the, "old villainous republican, the mention of whose very name made his blood boil with indignation"[31]. However, while the exhibition was not a commercial success there was, in fact, no official objection to its taking place. George III was passionate about all things scientific and, if he heard about it at all, would probably have simply been quite interested.

Researches by antiquarians into the authenticity of the head continued into the 20th century but by the time of its interment in 1960, in the chapel of Sidney Sussex College, Cambridge, little doubt remained that, extra-ordinary as it seemed, this was indeed Cromwell's head. Much of JC's work concerned the chain of custody of the head and its inherent physical features. His pamphlet summarised what could then be discovered about its previous owners and discussed what has always been its main claim to be genuine, namely, that it had been embalmed very professionally (known to be the case with Cromwell's corpse but an extremely rare occurrence in England at the time). This had allowed it to survive subsequent mistreatment and retain sufficient features for analysis after well over a century.

Undisputed history[32] tells us that upon restoration of the monarchy, the prominent republicans Cromwell, Ireton and Bradshaw were disinterred in 1661 and their corpses hanged at Tyburn. They were then beheaded and the heads mounted on iron spikes fitted to oak poles and exhibited on top of Westminster Hall where Cromwell's head remained for 25 years until a storm blew it down. It was a controversial object so there is some doubt about who then took it and hid it but before long it was purchased by the Russell family of Cambridgeshire who were thought to be related to the Cromwell family. Eventually it was inherited by one Samuel Russell, a louche and impecunious comic actor, who showed it, in around 1780, to James Cox the sometime proprietor of a famous museum of curiosities. Cox after considerable effort succeeded in buying it and in turn sold it to the three brothers called Hughes who, being strong democrats and this being the period of the French Revolution, determined to exhibit it.

JC would have been in political sympathy with the Hughes brothers given his strong support of the American Revolution and he undertook the work of researching what could be discovered to confirm authenticity of the head and of publicising the subsequent exhibition. This he obviously did at his own expense although he clearly hoped at least to be reimbursed if not rewarded if the exhibition was a commercial success. This was not to be and when it closed JC estimated the value of materials in his possession at £7 and hung onto them as security for the money owed to him by the Hughes but never paid. They included some medals associated with Cromwell and the contract of sale of the head from Russell to Cox. The head itself and JC's wonderful painting of it (Fig. 16) remained at that time with the Hughes brothers.

A high proportion of surviving material about the head is now kept in the archives of Sidney Sussex College, including the painting which is kept in an oak cabinet. One letter from JC to Hughes about their research prior to the exhibition, but dated only 'Tuesd Aftern', is also there:

"...There is a letter from Mr Cox – with information certainly, though still more *about*, than *to*, the necessary Samuel Russell and I fear it would be held incredible that Mr Cox should never have known how R[ussell] came by the article, unless indeed we suppose it to have been obtained surreptitiously which, to be sure, may be natural enough; and, possibly, the passage I have marked A in Mr C[ox]'s letter may be meant distantly to countenance a conjecture of that kind. At all events we must, if possible, find out Russell, and get what we can from him – primarily & principally, his relationship to Mark Noble's Russells; and then, what he chooses to disclose of the history of the descent of the subject. A plausible course of derivation must be made out; and though that derivation in some instances may not have been perfectly consonant to the laws of *meum and tuum*, yet it may equally avail for our purpose, be equally curious and interesting, and so equally to the point of the authenticity of the subject itself, to shew that it got into the hands of some of the former owners by some indirect adventure.

Shall we run down to Walford 2 or 3 days hence and try to smoke a pipe with the old boy upon it? If not, pray write him your best thanks, and attribute his "ready attentions in the matter to that love of Virtue which has ever distinguished him, etc." and press (*fortitu in suavita*) for a speedy account of Russell; that is how to come at him."

The Mark Noble mentioned was the rector of Barming in Kent and an amateur historian who specialised in studying Cromwell[33], as described in Chapter 3.

Other surviving documents at Sidney Sussex College include JC's letter of instruction to the printer concerning the handbill which was distributed to advertise the exhibition of which, apparently, 260 copies were printed. JC's handwritten text for the handbill also survives as does a preliminary ink drawing of his (Fig. 15) which is clearly an early version of the illustration published in the pamphlet.

The three Hughes brothers all died suddenly at relatively young ages and afterwards in 1815 Josiah Henry Wilkinson, a friend of the last to survive, purchased the head from Hughes' daughter. It is substantially thanks to the interest of Wilkinson and his descendants that JC's work can be partially reconstructed because they pursued JC and his heirs, as well as others involved, in order to acquire any materials which would aid their own quest to further establish the head's authenticity. In the summer of 1819 JC, late in his life, was visiting Devonshire from his home which by then was Walcot near Bath in Somersetshire. He met Wilkinson at the house of one Mr W. Clutterbuck in Widecombe. On 13th November he wrote[34]:

"To W. Clutterbuck – to be communicated to Mr Wilkinson about the Cromwell papers. JC

Sir: When I attended Mr Wilkinson at your house in the summer, I did not recollect, or but very imperfectly, the papers in my hands respecting the

Dunbar medals, the head of Oliver Cromwell, and the transactions incident to the exhibition of these curiosities in Bond Street in the year 1799. Having since directed these with other papers to be sent hither from London where they had remained ever since, and having safely received them, I should be glad if Mr Wilkinson were informed of it; but not knowing his address, I am under the necessity of relying on your civility to excuse the liberty I take in requesting you will be so obliging as to inform Mr Wilkinson that these papers appear to me to be important to his purpose; the identical original assignment of the head from Sam Russell to James Cox Esq. and various other documents being among them. The purpose of my keeping them could only have been in the way of pledge for the payment of my particular demand on the proprietors which I recollect to have compounded with Mr Hughes at seven pounds, just before he retired into the country; but I never received a penny of [what] you'll perceive has been due now almost one and twenty years. I have only to add, however, that on receiving that sum, I am now ready to deliver all these papers here in Bath to you in Mr Wilkinson's behalf immediately; but I shall conceive myself justified in not delivering them to any other person, or [under] any other condition. I have the honour to be your obedient humble servant, John Cranch, At Mr Coward's, Nelson Terrace, Walcot"

JC was then a little over one year from his death and the proposed transaction never took place. JC's will left all his possessions to the son of his favourite brother William who was also called John (and is referred to in this chapter as John2). For the sake of completeness and to set the record straight this account will complete the tale of interaction between the Cranches and the Wilkinsons over the Cromwell material which was not concluded until 1898. In 1856, Mr A. Wilkinson was put in touch with the brother of John2 who was called Joseph and who lived in London. Joseph then corresponded with John2 who lived in Devonshire and who still retained much of JC's Cromwell material but evidently not the Cox-Russell contract which had always been regarded as critical to the chain of custody of Cromwell's head. Here are extracts from three surviving letters of Joseph Cranch which can be found in the Sidney Sussex College collection:

"Jan 24, 1856. 1 Chancery Place, Camberwell, New Road, to Mr A. Wilkinson Esq, M.P., Beckenham.

Sir, In reference to the documents concerning the Head of Cromwell, I find my brother in Devonshire had those papers, left by our late uncle John Cranch whose authority for the authenticity of the subject may be safely relied on – a rigid investigator in Antiquarian and Historical researches.

I happen to have a letter from his friend and correspondent about the period of Mr Cranch's connexion with the subject – he writes under date - June 9 1800:

I have also to make acknowledgements for the pamphlet which you sent me. The Head of Cromwell appears to have undergone as strange vicissitudes as the (bronze) head of Sejanus in Ancient Rome as described by Juvenal. Whoever was the author of the narrative, I presume either yourself or J. Smith, I am much obliged by the communication of a curiosity which I never before had an idea of. My faith is however, I must confess a little weakened by the supposition that the real Head of the Protector after having been exposed on the top of Westminster Hall for a quarter of a century must notwithstanding the virtue of the aromatics which would have preserved it simply from putrefaction have suffered so much from haste and injury from the weather as to reduce it almost to a bare skull or at least to have rendered the features undistinguishable – but perhaps I may be mistaken in this notion.

By the above quotation from a worthy country Attorney, I infer the pamphlets contained valuable historical notices on its subject. The Mr Smith there named was a friend of Mr Cranch and was afterward Keeper [of Prints] in the Antiquarian Department of the British Museum.

Whether our correspondent's supposition that the head is now reduced to a bare skull – or that some external ligament & covering still remain I cannot judge not having ever seen it – and I would add that at some convenient opportunity it will be highly gratifying to have a sight of it. Perhaps it is the only deceased Monarch's head that can be seen above ground. I am very respectfully your Obedient Servant, J. Cranch"

"Aug 5, 1856, 1 Chancery Place, Camberwell New Road.
Sir, My brother's letter in reference to the Cromwell MSS places them at my disposal and he adds, "If I find anything more in future I shall put it by for you".

I have now enclosed the receipt for the sum mentioned when I was at your house which I named to my brother – Your cheque for the amount will settle the matter.

I take this opportunity of sending (to accompany the MS) 3 casts from dies in reference to the same subject These I find among my Uncle's papers – one having the Head of Cromwell with the password used by his order at the battle of Dunbar "The Lord of hosts" – the other is supposed to be the interior of the old house of Commons at that particular juncture when the Protector made use of the well-remembered phrase "Take away that bauble". I am sir, yours very respectfully, J. Cranch"

"Aug 14th, 1856 1 Chancery Place, Camberwell New Road to Mr A. Wilkinson Esq, M.P., Beckenham
Sir, I have today received a letter from my brother in Devonshire wherein he says in relation to the MSS of Oliver Cromwell, 'I have again looked

out large maps and papers of Uncle John Cranch's but do not find anything further on the subject – to the best of my recollection one of the MS mentions of a proposition of having the papers with Mr Clutterbuck on Mr Wilkinson's behalf. It is quite possible the frequent transfer from one to another may account for the absence by being lost in the opening frequency of the packet. I now however have the affair in your hands…Make what deductions you think proper. Although I have no hope of finding anything more but in the event of any such coming to hand I would with pleasure present it as forming part of the other documents.

I would suggest in the absence of the shipment from Samuel Russell – to James Cox – it is a satisfactory substitute to evidence that such a document was in being for many years after – and if the paper is lost – the fact itself is thankfully shown in Mr Cranch's letters referring to it – and through that medium the present ownership can be satisfactorily traced to the family of Russell who I think you mentioned were a remaining branch of the kinsmen of Cromwell.

As my brother by his letter places the letters at my disposal and in accordance with your suggestion of 6th inst – that a deduction ought to be made for the absence of the documents referred to – I would propose the sum of five pounds – for the MSS as they are, if it suits with your approbation or otherwise I would leave entirely to your own better judgement as to what would be proper. I return the MS enclosed in your last. Your reply will oblige, Sir, Very respectfully, J. Cranch"

There now follows a letter from Selina Cranch Bond the American, JC's great niece and daughter of William Cranch Bond, who was described in Chapter 2. This has led to various invented stories in the literature on Cromwell's head but which, to a student of JC's family, seem highly implausible. In 1898 Selina was evidently visiting England and the letter dated 28th January was sent from Babbacombe in Devonshire to Horace Wilkinson:

"…The correspondence you have recently had with my cousin Mr J. C. Willcocks of London, will explain my purpose in addressing you. I understand from him that you are willing to pay ten pounds for the assignment (i.e. the document of title) of the Head of Oliver Cromwell from Samuel Russell to James Cox, the date of which paper is April 30th 1787. This amount is quite satisfactory to me as I hope it is to yourself, and I make no delay in transmitting, (by registered letter) the document to your address at Seven Oaks, hoping that it may be received in the same good condition as it now is.

I may add that my attention was first called to this subject by an article in the Boston Herald of 24th November 1895; recollecting then that I had seen amongst family papers some relating to Oliver Cromwell. I looked through those at hand and to my great surprise found the identical document in question. I can only suppose that it was brought to the United States many years ago by Mr J. Cranch, who was my uncle and who resided for some time in my father's family there, and that on his return to England this, with some other similar effects, were left behind. I am very glad now to transfer it to an appropriate place amongst other relics of one of England's greatest men."

Her second paragraph was guesswork. John was a common given name among the extended Cranch family and her recollection of a visit to her family home by a relative of that name could easily have been of someone other than John2, most likely an American relative of the same name. Indeed, John2 was not her uncle but a cousin. What is most important is that her suggestion would make liars of John2 and his brother Joseph in what they said in 1856. The author is sure John2 was not in possession of the Cox-Russell document then, as he stated, and was honest when he said that he would offer it to the Wilkinsons if he came across it. It is also clear that in the 25 years between JC receiving the Cromwell papers in Bath and this correspondence with Wilkinson, the Cromwell papers had been handled by others. Had a member of the Kingsbridge Cranch family visited the United States in the latter half of the 19th century this would have been the subject of endless fascination and gossip which would certainly have been recounted to the author. No such tale existed.

How the Cox-Russell document came to be in the United States must to a small degree remain speculative although several writers about Cromwell's head have uncritically accepted what Selina Cranch Bond said about John2, one even suggesting that he died in the United States. However, a much likelier explanation is that JC gave the document directly to Selina Cranch Bond's father, William Cranch Bond, who certainly met JC after the latter had recovered his cache of Cromwell documents. In his letter of 13th November 1819 JC mentioned the Cox-Russell document specifically as being in his possession at that time. William Cranch Bond was in England for considerable periods and on 18th July 1819 he married his English cousin Selina Cranch at a great family ceremony in Kingsbridge, Devon. So what seems most likely is that JC either gave or lent the Cox-Russell document directly to Bond so that, later, his daughter (named Selina after her mother) would find the document among her father's effects. After its adventures the Cox-Russell contract of 1787 does now lie in Sidney Sussex College archives confirming the chain of custody of Cromwell's head so keenly sought by

JC and the Hughes brothers in 1799. Evidently when they did run Cox to earth he gave it to them.

As mentioned in Chapter 2 William Cranch Bond was a great Anglophile and visited England frequently. As a noted astronomer and first director of the Harvard University Observatory (1845-1859), a substantial collection of his papers have found their way to Harvard University's Collection of Historical Scientific Instruments and, somewhat surprisingly, someone has added to them some of his daughter's correspondence concerning Cromwell's head together with the Boston Herald article of 24th November 1895 which spurred her interest in the first place[35]. Selina Cranch Bond was born in 1831, the year of her mother's death (presumably the two events were connected). She lived to a great age, dying in 1920. She obviously kept in touch with her English relatives as evidenced by her visit to Babbacombe, Devonshire in 1897 when she corresponded with descendants of JC's siblings William A. Cranch and James Willcocks both then residing in London. W.A. Cranch was clearly John2's son whilst James Willcocks was almost certainly the son of John Willcocks who was JC's nephew and the principal mourner at his funeral.

Also in the Sidney Sussex archive is a copy of a letter from Horace Wilkinson dated 9th November 1895 in which he states that JC's painting of Cromwell's head has written on its reverse, "picture of Oliver Cromwell's head by Cranch". According to this letter, the picture seems to have still been in JC's possession when original contact between JC and J.H. Wilkinson occurred in 1819. After the painting was encased in its box the note on the back ceased to be visible.

Shakespeare and the Theatre

JC was a great admirer of Shakespeare and wrote about his work in several surviving documents. In J.T. Smith's portrait of JC he is holding a volume of Shakespeare's works. JC's signature and the date 1807 (Fig. 17) is to be found in one of the surviving first folio editions of the Bard's plays, now designated No. 48 in the Folger Library collection[h]. Some of the pen and ink sketches inserted in this volume have plausibly been

---

[h] The Folger Shakespeare Library is situated on Capitol Hill in Washington, DC, U.S.A. It has the world's largest collection of the printed works of William Shakespeare.

ascribed to him. It is not surprising that JC was attracted to Shakespeare because he was of a type JC particularly admired, the native genius, about which he was to write an essay later in life (see Chapter 6).

Shakespeare's relatively humble origins would be seen by JC as providing a clear uncontaminated wellspring of inspiration and he would have been contemptuous of those who assume that only an aristocrat could have written the plays. One surviving text JC wrote concerned *The Tempest*, a play which had a curious history. Usually it is considered the last play Shakespeare created completely by himself but, after his death, it was not performed again from the text he wrote until the middle of the 18th century. Rather, an adaptation by Dryden and Davenant written in 1667 and various other pastiches were performed regularly well into JC's lifetime, notwithstanding the growing bardolatry of the time. Writing[36] in 1795 about a performance he had seen of the Dryden-Davenant adaptation JC could not contain his contempt for the mangling of Shakespeare's dramatic construction. Modern critics have read all manner of sexual, racial and even colonial politics into *The Tempest* and its adaptations, seeming to lose sight of the fact that 17th century playwrights' main intention was to entertain a varied audience and not to preach at it.

"...the lovers of Shakespeare have been mortified (I had almost said insulted) with a partial burlesque of this play, at Drury Lane theatre, under the title of '*The Tempest*, as altered by Mr Dryden'. It has induced the author... to add a few words here on the general character of *The Tempest*, and on those strange attempts to enlarge and improve the fable of it.

The story adopted by Shakespeare is clear and simple, and the moral important and amiable: the matter and the action silently spread into rich and unexpected varieties which, as they proceed, on the one hand leave anything in the mind unsatisfied, and on the other have a constant and cautious respect to the end. What the final event shall be, the author takes care shall not be prematurely known but, in the meanwhile, strongly interesting the noblest affections of humanity, gives us to anticipate that it will be an important one. All the parts of this play are individually original and grand and the whole together, contemplated with the sobriety due to its dignity, appears to constitute so harmonious, so noble and (after the critics have nibbled their utmost of it) so perfect a dramatic fabric, as was never raised by any other human ability.

The characteristic complexion of *The Tempest* is a grave, solemn morality. It is, in all its parts, strictly conformable and true to that intention and its author could as easily have resolved to introduce Bartholomew fair, or a fight of Johnson and Mendoza, as that unnecessary sophistication with which Mr. Dryden has attempted to impoverish and disgrace it and which a British audience in the proudest area of its taste is capable of suffering to vex the spirit of our ever living bard.

The episode with which, in evil hour, Mr. Dryden was tempted to sully his own fame by deranging and vitiating *The Tempest* is far enough from ridiculous in itself, though short perhaps of its author's usual strength it is … even [an] ingenious amusing interesting [piece]. But it was going the whole length of absurdity to attempt to mix it with the solemn sublimities of *The Tempest*, to the spirit and intentions of which it is absolutely foreign and which there is not a single character or circumstance that is not depreciated by it. The lovely 'child of Nature' Miranda, degenerates almost into a comic flirt; becomes artful and ripe for all the disgusting vulgarities of coquetry and lost to her original dignified simplicity.

Upon the whole, the writer of these observations takes upon him to pronounce, that the scheme and substance of this pretended improvement, is altogether a scandalous invasion of the rights of Shakespeare, derogatory to his Genius [and] a perversion of his design."

There is another very strange association of JC with Shakespeare which concerns the Bard's appearance. In the late 18th century a true likeness of Shakespeare was urgently sought, only for it to be discovered eventually that none with totally convincing provenance existed. That remains true today although one image has long been settled on and every schoolchild by now thinks (s)he knows what the Bard looked like.

A battle raged over various contending portraits and this has been documented elsewhere[37]. However JC became associated with one in particular, the *Felton Shakespeare*, which appears also to have found its way to the Folger collection. The term 'appears' seems appropriate to the author because JC is a contender for having painted it but by his usual standards as an artist the painting in the Folger seems of rather poor quality. However, the editors of *The Literary Gazette and Journal of Belles Lettres* in 1828 categorically said of the Felton portrait[38]:

"…In stating its history, and that it was painted by Cranch we repeated the declaration of one of Cranch's most intimate friends, who knew of the facts as they occurred, and who had often enjoyed a laugh with Cranch at the folly of those who had been deceived."

It seems quite possible that the 'intimate friend' of JC alluded to was J.T. Smith who would have been fully aware of JC's activities at the relevant period. It is inconceivable that JC would have intended seriously to deceive anyone about his revered Shakespeare although it is not impossible that he and Smith colluded to play a joke on the art-buying public. The Folger Library nowadays catalogues the Felton portrait as being an oil painting on a wood panel by an unknown artist dated ca. 1792, but in the 18th century it was taken seriously, by some, as a contemporaneous portrait of the Bard himself.

Those who were intent on deception for financial gain invented quite an elaborate 'back story' about the history of the painting, not least among them the first recorded seller, the *European Museum* which on 31st May 1792 sold it as ostensibly 'the property of an anonymous gentleman' to Mr Samuel Felton of Drayton, Shropshire for 5 guineas. This was probably already more than JC could command for his own acknowledged paintings although, as will be recounted in Chapter 5 he was exhibiting under his own name simultaneously at the *European Museum*.

The painting was sold and resold at ever-increasing prices at auction right into the 20th century. One 18th century acknowledged expert on Shakespeare, who endorsed the Felton portrait as genuine, was George Steevens (1736-1800) who, writing in 1794 observed that the rear of the panel was inscribed, 'Guil. Shakspeare, 1597. R.N. ' When the 'N' of the inscription was found later to be a 'B' it was immediately associated with Richard Burbage, Shakespeare's actor colleague. But when modern techniques including UV light and X-rays were employed by the Folger Library on what is supposedly the Felton portrait, which is in its possession, the inscription could not be found. So had yet another deception occurred between the 1790s and the 20th century acquisition by the Folger collection? It seems inconceivable that this very important element of the supposed provenance of the painting would not have been carefully preserved.

Steevens was, in any case, known to be something of a prankster and it is acknowledged that his imprimatur of the Felton portrait might have been a joke. However, it certainly had material consequences at the time because a print based on the Felton portrait sold by one William Richardson (who had introduced Steevens to the Felton Portrait) made a great deal of money. A letter[39] JC wrote to Steevens, dated 28th May, 1789 survives, so the two might well have known each other. It enclosed a copy of the will of one Thomas Shackspur which JC had unearthed and he enquired whether Steevens thought this could be a relative of the Bard.

That JC had a general liking for the theatre can be deduced from various surviving records. He attended plays and corresponded with an actress. He wrote an elegiac on the death of Nelson which was declaimed by one Mrs Young on the night of her benefit in 1805 at the Theatre Royal at Liverpool and printed for distribution by his friends the Crocker family (see Fig. 35). The theatre enjoyed a tremendous blossoming during JC's life and, among the places he stayed, Bath and Bristol had active playhouses as well as London. There is no doubt that JC attended performances frequently and knew several actors. He wrote an obituary[40] of James Biggs, an actor whom he obviously knew well but who died at the age of only 27. Although Biggs latterly performed at Drury Lane in London he started his career in Bath where JC must have first encountered him. JC's second paragraph takes a swipe at metropolitan condescension to provincial theatre:

> "...The Bath theatre being a provincial one, it seems that the Londoners have usually considered the public taste and judgement of that place as if it were in some sort provincial too; and it seems as if Bath had quietly acquiesced in this notion. Neutral critics, however, considering Bath as a common centre of polite intelligence (the ATHENS of pleasurable science) have contended that the notion is erroneous and that Bath, so far from being inferior to London in the respects alluded to, must necessarily afford a purer and more essential spirit of dramatic criticism than the metropolis which, on this consideration, has been supposed much more likely to be adulterated with mob prejudices and to convey less correct opinions with only the advantage of a *louder* voice."

Of Biggs himself he wrote as follows and one cannot help but see echoes of JC's own qualities and personality in this account of his young friend, an impression strengthened by his signing off with the famous line from Catullus's lament for his younger brother:

> "...His attainments in music were very considerable, both in science and practice and, in respect of literature, the hindrances and disadvantages incident to the employment of his early years operated only to 'spur the sides of his intent', for his knowledge of books as well as of men and things was solid and extensive. And, unless the partialities of friendship mislead his biographer he would soon have interested the public as much in the character of a comic writer as by the genius and abilities of an original actor...His heart was humane and generous, his manners mild and unassuming, his temper cheerful and his conversation... sparkled with pleasant whim and with eccentricities 'that were wont to set the table on a roar'. Hail and farewell! JOHN CRANCH"

Horace Walpole

How well JC knew the much older Horace Walpole must remain a matter for conjecture although, as reported in Chapter 2, he obviously conversed with him sometimes. There is an interesting survival from their acquaintance. To express gratitude for his visit to Strawberry Hill, JC sent Walpole a rare book (William Habington's *Castara* of 1640) on 17th August 1789. Both the book[i] and his covering letter[41] survive:

> "...I have made much inquiry and can neither find any other copy of this book, nor (which still more surprises me) any further account than the book itself furnishes, of so fine and amiable a wit as its author. My present information therefore tempts me to suppose the fame of both to have sunk in that oblivious gulf, which probably overwhelmed so many other (contemporary) men and monuments of genius – which so soon followed the production of *Castara*; and I should not have presumed to request from Mr Walpole the condescension of accepting this book (curious as I think the matter of it) but under a persuasion of its being likewise extremely scarce; or had any less exceptionable mode of expressing my gratitude for the favour of having been permitted to contemplate that sanctuary of curious literature and of the delicate arts at Strawberry Hill. J. Cranch"

At that date, JC was presumably still lodging with his sister Elizabeth Elworthy because his address in the letter is given as 1 Broad Street, London.

The Society for the Suppression of Vice

JC's reason for leaving London permanently was probably a series of disappointments and, once gone, he seems never to have returned. His last attempt to get married (detailed in Chapter 3) will certainly have been one of them but failure to receive an appointment that he was clearly sure of must have been another. In July of 1802 he was already writing[42] to his nephew, James Willcocks, concerning a prospect for gainful employment which was then "merely in a way of preparation" but for which he obviously had high hopes. Although he did not specify what this was, the letter was sent in the same year as the foundation of *The Society for the Suppression of Vice* and later he seems to have been certain of a permanent appointment there. In February of 1805 JC's sister Mary Willcocks wrote[43] to her son John,

---

[i] The volume itself is now in the Dowse Collection of Massachusetts Historical Society.

"...I must now give you some account of your uncle John's good fortune. He is appointed secretary to a Society for the Suppression of Vice. We don't know the particulars of what it is but its income is two hundred a year and may be more, with a handsome house to live in."

This was no mere fancy on JC's part because clearly he was public representative for the society for a while. In a notice published in the *Kentish Weekly Post or Canterbury Journal* on 16th April 1805 (Fig. 18) written from 31 Essex Street in London, headquarters of the society, and signed "JOHN CRANCH pro Sec", he drew attention on behalf of the general committee of the society to a law forbidding "Profane Swearing" and requesting that clergy read the relevant statute in their churches and chapels on each Sunday following quarter day. In the same newspaper on 19th April 1805 JC again, writing a notice on behalf of the society, reported that, despite admonition, certain persons at Edmonton kept their shops open and "publicly employed their men" on Sundays and that the society had therefore "brought several of the offenders to legal punishment". This example was offered, "as worthy of being followed in every town and village in the kingdom."

We cannot be certain of what went wrong but it seems very likely that JC had received a firm promise of continued employment from one faction of the Society but that this was outvoted by another which favoured the appointment as secretary and attorney in 1805 of one George Prichard who went on in that role until 1836 when it was passed to his son. The purpose of the society was to ensure enforcement of the existing laws concerning Sunday observance, obscene publications, disorderly premises etc., but how that was to be achieved and who should be involved was clearly a matter of controversy. Roberts[43] seems to have done as much as is possible to disentangle the personnel and the arguments, given inadequate surviving documentation and the confused politics of the time, but it seems impossible to determine why JC was rejected. He was conventional enough in his personal behavior to pass muster although he was clearly no prude. As an attorney he would also have been qualified for the role since the society used the courts to pursue its purposes, although his distaste for court appearances might have been difficult to overcome. However, he probably would not have passed muster as an enthusiastic communicant of the Church of England and certainly the clergy formed a large part of the membership of the society.

A possible clue as to how JC got involved with the society in the first place lies in one of his obituaries. According to the *Bath Herald* before moving to Bath "...he... turned his attention to literature, and at the request of a gentleman, he conducted as the Editor, a moral and religious weekly paper". No trace of this periodical has been found by the author but it seems possible that JC was already working with one of the founders of the Society for the Suppression of Vice.

By 1810, when JC parted from London, he evidently wanted nothing more to do with the metropolis. He was nearly 60 years of age but either from inclination or necessity he clearly expected to continue working. It seems probable from letters he wrote after moving that some specific project had taken him to Bath but that when it quickly went sour he still declined to leave his favourite city. Apart from career considerations it was a much healthier place to live than London and it also supported the cultured and educated society he loved.

References

1. Hume, Robert B. (2015), *The value of money in eighteenth-century England*: incomes, prices, buying power – and some problems in cultural economics. Huntington Library Quarterly, vol. 77 pp. 373-416
2. BPL Ms. Eng. 483 (2)
3. BPL Ms. Eng. 483 (422)
4. BPL Ms. Eng. 483 (142)
5. BPL Ms. Eng. 483 (140)
6. BPL Ms. Eng. 483 (155-201)
7. BPL Ms. Eng. 483 (64-107)
8. BPL Ms. Eng. 483 (202-19)
9. BPL Ms. Eng. 483 (64-107)
10. BPL Ms. Eng. 483 (142).
11. BPL Ms. Eng. 483 (141)
12. BPL Ms. Eng. 483 (64-107)
13. BPL Ms. Eng. 483 (145)
14. John Thomas Smith (1807), *Antiquities of Westminster*, pp. 154, 174, 257-8. Printed by T. Bensley for J.T. Smith, London
15. Samuel Young (1818), *Cases of Cancer, Part 2, Being Further Reports of Cancerous Cases Successfully Treated By the New Mode of Pressure*, p7, London
16. BPL Ms. Eng. 483 (147)
17. Young, Samuel (1805) Medical and Physical Journal, vol. 14, pp. 490-2
18. Cranch, John (1794), *The Œconomy of Testaments; or, Reflections on the mischievous consequences generally arising from the usual dispositions of*

property by will, published with a Preface by William Langworthy of the Honourable Society of the Inner Temple. Printed by J. Johnson, Bath.

19. *The Critical Review or Annals of Literature* vol. 15 (1796) pp. 458-9. Printed for A. Hamilton, London

20. The Gentleman's Magazine, vol. 65 pt 2 (1795), p760, ed Sylvanus Urban. Printed by John Nichols, London

21. Letter to John Adams from William Stephens Smith (his son-in-law), 21st January 1796, in the possession of the Massachusetts Historical Society

22. Margaret A. Hogan *et al.* (2013) *The Adams Papers,* Adams Family Correspondence, vol. 11, July 1795–February 1797, pp. 160–162, Harvard University Press, Cambridge

23. Greer, David (2016), *Manuscript Inscriptions in Early English Printed Music*, Routledge, London

24. BPL Ms. Eng. 483 (2)

25. BPL Ms. Eng. 483 (139)

26. BPL Ms. Eng. 483 (64-107)

27. Thomas Cromwell (1835), *Walks Through Islington*, p. 237, Sherwood, Gilbert & Piper, London

28. *Notes and Queries* (1868), 4th Series vol. 1, p. 542, London

29. Lucas E.V. (1905), *The Life of Charles Lamb*, vol. 2, p. 118, Methuen & Co, London

30. R.B. Beckett ed. (1964) *John Constable's Correspondence,* Early Friends and Maria Bicknell (Mrs. Constable), , Vol 6, p23, Suffolk Records Society, Ipswich.

31. J.H. Wilkinson and Sir Henry H. Howerth (1911), *The Archaeological Journal,* Vol. 68 pp 233-236 and pp237-251

32. Fitzgibbons, J. (2008), *Cromwell's Head*, The UK National Archives

33. Noble, M. (1787), *Memoirs of the Protectoral House of Cromwell* in 2 Volumes, 3rd edition, London

34. Manuscript in Sidney Sussex College archive

35. William Bond & Son records and Bond family papers, Collection of Historical Scientific Instruments, Harvard University

36. BPL Ms. Eng. 483(2)

37. Schoenbaum, Samuel (1993) *Shakespeare's Lives*, pp209-212, Oxford University Press, Oxford

38. The Literary Gazette and Journal of Belles Lettres, Arts Sciences &c. (1828) p603 London

39. BPL Ms. Eng. 483 (146)

40. *The Monthly Mirror* (1799) Vol 7, pp 237-239

41. BPL Ms. Eng. 483 (64-107)

42. BPL Ms. Eng. 483 (202-219)

43. Roberts, M.J.D. (1983), The Society for the Suppression of Vice and its Early Critics, 1802-1812, The Historical Journal, 26, 159-176

Chapter 5

The Artist

Introduction

It is as a painter that JC is most recognized today but this biography is not intended to provide a detailed analysis of his art. However, several of his pictures are shown in the illustrations (Figs 22-33) and JC's unique style is apparent to any viewer. His natural talent as an artist was recognised from an early age by those around him in Devonshire and during his long life he had considerable success as a painter. The fact that he was entirely self-taught and had developed his own techniques together with clear ideas about appropriate subject matter has led to belated recognition of his qualities in more modern times. As a consequence, examples of his paintings are to be found in a number of prominent institutions including the Yale Centre for British Art, the Louvre, the Victoria and Albert Museum and the Tate Gallery. Bristol and Aberdeen city art galleries have examples and, as might be expected, the principal art institution in Devonshire, the Royal Albert Memorial Museum and Art Gallery in Exeter has a substantial holding.

When JC went to live in London in 1787, although as always he had irons in many fires, he seems to have made a name for himself as a painter. Artists have always been numerous and in competition for attention. The old route to success by securing a rich patron still existed but was an unreliable path to fame or fortune. Besides, JC was financially in-dependent during much of his time in London and he was in any case no sycophant and had impressively strong views on what was appropriate as subject matters for his art. He evidently painted some portraits, particularly of his family, but survivals are few and he probably didn't much enjoy the work. To put this in context, JC's friend J.T. Smith gave voice to an artist's ambivalence about portrait painting in a posthumously published journal[1]. About the year 1789 he wrote:

> "...This year proved more lucrative to me than any preceding, for at this time I professed portrait painting both in oils and crayons but, alas, after using a profusion of carmine and placing an eye straight that was misdirected, before another season my exertions were mildewed by a

decline of orders...It was at [Edmonton]...that I *profiled, three-quartered, full-faced* and *buttoned up* the retired embroidered weavers, their crummy wives and tightly-laced daughters."

Given his friend's amusing cynicism it is not surprising that JC seems to have confined portrait painting mainly to his family although one equestrian portrait by him (*Portrait of Henry Knight of Bath*) appeared at auction in 1977.

JC did paint some landscapes, usually containing human figures, but whilst the location of these scenes is sometimes recognisable (e.g. *View on the Shannon* (Fig. 29) in Aberdeen Art Gallery), others seem to have been invented (e.g. *Monk with a Lantern in a Moonlit Rocky Landscape* in the Louvre). If JC sketched scenery on his various travels, no survivals have been found. However, in the context of his antiquarian work and other practical matters such as his pictures of craftsmen, one would assume that he made preliminary drawings. Sketches were mentioned as some of his property left behind in the garret he rented at Rathbone Place during the later period of his stay in London.

Certainly JC often seems to have relied on his imagination to create art, rather than use models, for example, in his humorous *Monks Merrymaking* which is in the Tate Gallery and for his *Death of Chatterton* which seems to be lost but was admired when painted. He is now best known for his so-called *genre* paintings of ordinary folk going about their usual domestic activities or trades. In this regard he somewhat resembles the Dutch/Flemish artists such as Teniers the Younger whom JC clearly admired, declaring in a letter[2] from 1805 that he sought to be 'the English Teniers'. As social documents many of JC's paintings are remarkable records of everyday life of his time, often including much fascinating domestic detail. The Victoria and Albert Museum in its online discussion of JC's painting, *Playing with Baby* (Fig. 31) makes comparison of his work with other English artists such as Joseph Wright of Derby (1734-1797) and George Morland (1719-1797). JC will certainly have seen Morland's work when he was in London but although he, like Wright, often painted partly-lit or artificially-lit scenes, it seems unlikely that Wright was an influence since his paintings were largely created and sold around Derby, well away from places where JC spent his time.

Although JC occasionally painted on moderately sized canvases he frequently preferred wooden board. Indeed, the thin panels of seasoned wood prepared for use in coach building were a favourite artist's medium in his day. JC clearly took a scientific approach in his technique because the surface and pigments of many surviving paintings are remarkably intact with little craqueleur. Others, having been kept for a long time in unfavourable domestic surroundings, have suffered some damage. A majority of his works were 'cabinet paintings' i.e. small pictures intended for small rooms, and his brushwork was very finely detailed; indeed he was described in one directory[3] as a miniaturist.

He paid considerable attention to the frames for his work, which were often intricate. For example, when preparing to exhibit at the British Institution in 1806 he wrote[4] to his frame-maker:

"...you'll be so good to make a frame for a companion picture to the *Village Pump* which Jem put in when he came last: I hope you have the pattern either in memory, or memorandum. If not, the enclosed when smoothed out is the exact size of the tablet; the members are:

1 - innermost a small hollow
2 - a square of the same dimension
3 - the small water leaf - (these 3 members together making about 1 inch)
4 - a small square raise pretty boldly
5 - the rich leaf &c in a bold hollow
6 - the sticker ribbon a flat side. The breadth of the frame is about 3 full inches as near as I can guess.

But the principle thing is despatch; I understand from Mr. Green that the Institution will be ready for receiving applications in about 8 days, and my letter and 8 pictures are all ready except the frame."

Exhibitions and Catalogues

When trying to establish himself in London JC needed to exhibit his paintings. This was a period when British artists were still unfashionable compared with those from mainland Europe and classical or religious subjects for art were preferred as subject matter. However, a vanguard of admirers of domestic painting and naturalistic subject matter was coming into existence and surviving records of some quite formal exhibitions (see e.g. Fig. 19) suggest that JC had a good reputation amongst them.

In 1791[5] a gallery which specialised in British paintings and called itself *The European Museum* exhibited, "Above four hundred capital pictures" amongst which was specifically mentioned "...*The Death of Chatterton*, the original composition of Mr Cranch, a self-taught artist, lately from Devonshire." The same gallery in 1792 advertised its Grand Spring Exhibition[6,7] of 500 paintings at King Street, St James's Square, stating that, "Whilst the patrons and encouragers of British artists may here select, for less money than what is demanded for copies of foreign paintings, the genuine and original works of the following eminent artists", and listed as well as JC many artists who have enjoyed greater posthumous fame, not least, Sir Joshua Reynolds.

JC's painting of *The Burning of the Albion Mill*, which was hung at The Society of Artists also in 1791, is now apparently lost but, on the whole, exhibition in London gave provenance which has assisted in the survival and continued recognition of JC's work. The *British Institution for Promoting the Fine Arts in the United Kingdom* opened its Pall Mall gallery in 1805 and held exhibitions for living artists which was much appreciated by them as a 'shop window' for their work. JC was no exception and showed a total of eight pictures there in 1807 and 1808. One of them, *The Plaisterer*, (Fig. 26) now in the Yale gallery as mentioned above has even become somewhat of an emblem for the modern plastering trade and is reproduced in some of its advertising material today. It can also be purchased in facsimile and even as a cushion cover. When first exhibited it attracted favourable notice and one critic writing[8] in *The Director* described it as "This beautiful cabinet picture would have been overlooked by an eye less scientific than the purchaser's (Captain Ansley). The colouring is in a quiet cool style and the touch admirable. The scene appears to be a perfect representation of some shattered but picturesque cottage". Another exhibited at the same time and which obviously survives is *A Snow Scene* (Fig. 30) which can be purchased today in reproduction as a poster.

One contemporary catalogue[9] which survives is that for an auction held in June of 1807 for the sale of artworks owned by the late Reverend John Brand. This revealed him to have been an admirer of JC. A total of 188 artworks were sold including paintings, drawings, engravings and busts. Of these only 44 were attributed to named artists and they included a total of five painted by JC. Other artists included Joshua Reynolds, Van Dyck, Canaletto, Holbein, Claude and Morland. The lots of JC's works listed are interesting. Two are loosely described, one as "a *Small Painting*" and another as, "a *Landscape and Cottage* by Cranch, a small pleasing picture", neither of which seems to be known today, but both "*The Smugglers*, a pleasing and well executed Cabinet Painting, by Cranch" and a "Small Cabinet Painting, *The Inside of a Kitchen* by Cranch", have appeared at auction in modern times. Indeed, the latter is now in Bristol Art Gallery and is shown here as Fig. 22. However, of greatest interest in the catalogue is, "*The Death of Chatterton*, painted by Cranch". The suggestion that Sir James Winter-Lake, J.T. Smith's patron, "owns" (sic) the painting has been quoted and requoted right up to the present day. Responsibility for this appears to be widespread but uncritical reproduction of the entry in the *Dictionary of National Biography* of 1888 which in turn quoted the caption to J.T. Smith's engraving of JC. Even when the dictionary was written it was obviously incorrect to claim that the painting belonged to Winter-Lake because he had died in 1807. But if Winter-Lake even during his lifetime owned the picture for a while (which seems likely; see below) he clearly gave or sold the painting to Brand who was a fellow member of the Antiquarian Society and who pre-deceased Winter-Lake by about one year. In the margin of the catalogue are scribbled the names of the purchasers but illegibly in the case of *The Death of Chatterton*.

Perhaps because of its subject matter, JC's painting of Chatterton has been mentioned quite frequently in literature[10] but the author of this biography has found no clue to its current whereabouts despite following-up every lead which has arisen over many years. In this context, JC reportedly[11] wrote the following verse on the back of a painting which, judging by its content, can only have been the Chatterton:

> What steads the shiv'ring artist, Fancy's fires;
> The shadow'd garb -- the visionary bread;
> Condemn'd in cold obscurity to pine,
> Himself unclad, and, "mid the feast, unfed."

JC also figured in the 1809 auction catalogue[12] of artworks which had been owned by Nathaniel Smith, described as printseller and sculptor and who was J.T. Smith's brother. These were described as, "*A small sea piece and a moonlight ditto by Cranch.*" As mentioned above, JC had a penchant for painting night scenes, illuminated by moonlight or the flames of a fire. A final catalogue of pictures has been discovered from JC's lifetime, dating from 1812 and issued by one Mathew Mitchell of London and which included a JC painting *From the Beggar's Opera*, but again its current location is unknown.

Much of JC's painting was done later in life when he lived in Bath and it was an important source of income for him. Presumably to avoid confusion with his American painter cousin of the same name (John Cranch, 1807–1891), JC is in modern auctioneers' catalogues sometimes called "John Cranch of Bath". Although JC clearly visited Bath even when his main residence was London between 1787 and 1810 (his painting *Cottage Interior* is signed and dated "CRANCH 1793 BATH") most of the pictures for which he is known were created in the metropolis. His address given in the British Institution catalogue, mentioned above, was 47 Rathbone Place, London. It seems likely that he contributed to exhibitions of paintings in Bath during his later years but no relevant advertisements or catalogues with mention of JC have been found.

The Artist as his Contemporaries Saw Him

Independent accounts of JC's artistic efforts are limited and not necessarily well-informed. However, William Knight, the son of his first employer in Axminster, is credited as one of the sources for the biographical note on JC in Wilkinson's 1832 manuscript *History of Axminster* and he undoubtedly knew JC personally when young, as recounted in Chapter 1. This is the only known source for some of the following information:

> "…The beauty, rapidity and correctness of his writing were extraordinary and in addition to his severer studies he made considerable progress in music and drawing. His peculiar talent for the last mentioned art was manifested in a circumstance quite consonant with his decisive and original style of thought and action. During the absence of his employer from the office on a winter's day, Cranch amused himself in front of the fire place by executing a design on the panels of a large oaken chimney-piece with the pointed end of a red-hot poker producing an effect by the boldness of style and execution which was universally admired.
>
> …he practiced [painting] under the instruction of Sir Joshua Reynolds who used to say that Cranch was the best critic and possessed the greatest judgment in paintings of any man he ever knew.
>
> …a few of his pictures may be seen at Hilary House, Axminster, the residence of William Knight Esq."

There are numerous surviving examples of JC's handwriting which confirm how good it was, to the great benefit of his biographer. As regards

Joshua Reynolds, JC will certainly have met him because Reynolds was permanently grateful to JC's relative John Cranch of Plympton in Devon, a lawyer and family friend, who helped arrange for Reynolds to train with the successful London painter Thomas Hudson (who was also born in Devon), and to make a trip to Italy. But although Reynolds was President of the Royal Academy when JC went to London it seems that he did not interfere with hanging for the annual exhibition and, certainly, JC's work was never shown there. This is unsurprising because there was huge competition for places and Somerset House was far from an ideal venue with even Associates of the Academy complaining that their paintings were ill-positioned. If JC ever was an assistant in Reynolds' studio it would only have been as one of the many employed with finishing the background and clothing of the master's portraits; hack work with which JC would rapidly have become bored. As already mentioned, JC's own work was unusual in its day and avoided the then-fashionable religious or classically inspired themes which is another reason for lack of interest by the Academy.

It has to be said that although pyrography seems to have been one of JC's talents no surviving example of this work has been found by the author and Hilary House exists no more. A reference discovered in literature to JC's pyrography is somewhat tenuous. At an exhibition in 1873 at the Royal Albert Memorial Museum in Exeter of portraits of Devon and Cornwall worthies a poker-work portrait of Sir Joshua Reynolds in cap and gown was shown[13]. An article[14] the subsequent year in the *Archaeological Journal* described it as, "probably the work of John Cranch an assistant to Sir Joshua Reynolds, born at Kingsbridge, Devon, in 1751. He excelled in 'poker pictures' ". One would think that pokerwork is fairly indestructible unless actively disposed of but its long subsequent unfashionableness probably led to much destruction of examples. It must be said that there is never any mention of this skill in surviving JC writings known to the author and it may only ever have been a 'party trick' of which he was not particularly proud.

The early paintings mentioned as being at Hilary house have not been identified which is a pity since they would have shown his development as an artist. A speculation might be made that two paintings held by the Peabody Essex Museum in America could be early works by JC and if so they were probably painted during his time in Axminster. They are today attributed simply to 'John Cranch' but resemble JC's work more than that of his American cousin of the same name. The subject matter, respectively, *Sailors* and *Tailors* would certainly accord with his future propensity for depicting people engaged in trades of varying kinds. They are somewhat crudely painted in comparison with his later work but that would not be surprising in the early work of a self-taught artist.

A minor work from JC's time in the employ of the Knight family does survive (Fig. 20) and if he cannot be identified for certain as its creator then nor can any other person of his ability be shown to have had access to the office ledger[15] where it was drawn.

Exactly when J.T. Smith and JC became friends is not known although Smith suggested that he sought JC's acquaintance after seeing his art (see below). However, as described in Chapter 4, both were obsessed with ancient buildings, lamenting their destruction and seeking to preserve a record of them and both were artists each, for a while, doing what he could to promote the other's career. Personally, both were knowledgeable, egalitarian in spirit and possessed of considerable wit so one can imagine them enjoying each other's company. In 1795 Smith published the engraving of JC already mentioned as the frontispiece of this book and based on a portrait of JC which he had painted himself. This painting seems to be lost, although Smith claimed that it was in the possession of Sir James Winter-Lake, but specimens of the engraving have found their way into a number of public collections including the Royal Collection and the National Maritime Museum in London. Several copies were distributed to JC's Devonshire relatives one of which, unfortunately now badly foxed, was passed down to the author.

In 1788 Smith had been invited to be drawing master to Winter-Lake's daughter at his country house *The Firs* at Edmonton and he went to live nearby. JC wrote a poem[16] *On retiring to Edmonton* in 1795 which was evidently motivated by one of his visits to Smith. It is dedicated *To Solitude* and the first verse goes:

> Mother of Silence, and calm thought;
> With mental pleasure fraught;
> At whose mysterious 'hest each passion fades –
> Hail to thy sylvan shades!
> From vice and folly, man and mis'ry free;
> I come, dear matron solitude, to thee.

But he starts to think better of keeping to his own company and the last two lines read:

> To dear society ah let me fly!
> And give thy sombre charms to Mis'ry, Guilt and Death.

Certainly while at Edmonton JC formed part of a loose group of cultured friends which has been dignified in modern times with the name of *The Edmonton Circle* for reasons which will become apparent. Smith was to write a vivid encomium[17] of JC in his published work *Remarks on Rural Scenery with Twenty Etchings of Cottages* which was published in July of 1797:

> "...If (to use the language of Mr Walpole) some parts of this work are more accurate than my own ignorance or carelessness would have left them, I must insist upon telling the world that I am indebted for that advantage to my friend Mr Cranch who obligingly condescended to correct what he could not have descended to write.
>
> To this head, of suiting every object to its place and circumstances, I must beg leave to be indulged in referring to a picture of the supposed circumstances of the death of Chatterton*, painted by Mr Cranch under the very uncommon predicament of having taught himself the art of painting in oil after he was thirty six years of age. In the curious and interesting little piece, designed to represent an event, which will be lamented while there is any sense of excellence, or any feeling of pity, in the heart of man, every object and incident is cautiously excluded which bears the least semblance of ease or consolation, or which has least tendency to divert mental pain, while every image of misery is combined to awaken sympathy and point regret. A wretched garret, bare and ragged walls, a patched casement, the beggarly account of empty boxes, scattered fragments of literature, mean and rent garments, the miserable flock bed, the horrid indications of poison – and every symptom of despair! Perhaps the image of youthful genius, hurried on to misery by a proud consciousness of its own powers and claims on the world, and struggling its last under the combined tortures of oppression and the most violent bodily pain, could not have more forcibly or feelingly expressed. It was remarked to me by an ingenious gentleman, that the chilly colouring of this picture was happily appropriate to the sentiments suggested by the subject. I knew nothing of this artist 'till the merit and circumstances of his original essay induced me to seek a friendship which I shall ever hold it an honour to retain.
>
> *In the possession of Sir James Winter-Lake Bart, at his seat at Edmonton who has been pleased to honour it with particular notice."

Smith goes on to be extremely rude about another contemporary depiction of the death of Chatterton which must presumably have been H.

Singleton's painting which was engraved by Edward Orme and dated 1st May, 1794. Whilst JC must have been flattered by the compliments paid to him one cannot help wondering if the criticism of another artist created enemies for him.

It is interesting to reflect on why JC was fascinated by Chatterton as a subject for his painting and the answer may very well lie in the similarity of their background. Chatterton was articled to a Bristol attorney in 1767 but was not treated well, being required to be in the office from 8 in the morning until 8 at night, eat in the kitchen and sleep in the same bed as a servant boy. He in turn did little to learn the law, being more interested in writing verse, and he finally ran away. Although JC was better treated and more dutiful during his legal career, his own feelings of frustration and boredom with uncreative legal drudgery may well have aroused sympathy for his unfortunate contemporary. He may also have found parallels in his own experience of how inhospitable London could be for a creative individual with little access to patronage. However, anyone reading Chatterton's biography[18] with some knowledge of modern psychology will probably suspect, as the author does, that he suffered from bipolar disorder.

JC's Correspondence related to painting

Considering that when JC left Axminster to go to London in 1787 he hoped to establish himself as a painter, his surviving letters from this period have surprisingly little to say about it. Indeed those few already described in previous chapters form a high proportion of what is available.

Writing[19] to his friend Abraham Crocker on 17th April 1787 JC gave a glimpse of his views on construction of a picture. He had obviously been commissioned by Crocker to send an illustration of some poverty-stricken settlement:

> "...This sketch, or scratch, or whatever you can bring yourself to call it, was made upon the place, in a very windy and cloudy time. It comes to you reluctantly, not on account of its imitative imperfections (which were unavoidable) but because the objects, though most originally wretched and even possessed of singularities of misery in the parts, were most un-favourably arranged for a tout ensemble; and could not be grouped with effect, that is, so as to be picturesque in ugliness, any more than in beauty."

In a letter[20] of 31st May 1790 John Andrews wrote from Devonshire to his friend JC in London confirming that he had received a consignment of pictures from him and commenting on their subject matter which included depictions of an old soldier selling newspapers and a man plying a dowsing rod, presumed to be seeking metal ore underground. Of one picture he said: "...You'll be pleased to hear that this piece has much pleased sev[era]l men of taste who have looked at it. I am proud... at finding them struck with the same circumstance as I was, it being particularly happy in the light shining in from the window." As with so many of JC's paintings referred to in correspondence at the time, the whereabouts of these two is at present unknown.

This was the same letter referred to in Chapter 4 which mentioned JC's "Flemish Journal". It seems that around this time JC must have visited Flanders although the author has found no other reference to this journey. JC's predilection for the work of painters from the Low Countries is well known and they may have been the focus of his visit. Of course, territorial boundaries have changed since JC's day and a 'Flemish' journal might be presumed to include what is now the southern part of The Netherlands as well as the northern part of Belgium which now bears the name of Flanders. Additional confirmation that JC's main interest in his visit would have been art is the fact that a Devonian would not conceivably visit that part of the world for its scenery.

For the next 15 years surviving letters contain only rare references to JC painting although he evidently got round to creating a portrait of his nephew, James Willcocks, because his proud mother Mary, wrote[21] to JC in April 1804 saying that he should:

> "...Accept my best love and thanks for the dear portrait which is admired by all that saw it and makes [his] poor old mother as proud as a peacock. But Mary Ann has robbed me of it and hung it up in her room, which I must acknowledge is the best place for it as ours is such a smoky house that I could not hang it up here without spoiling it [and] must be content with visiting it as often as I can."

In his letter[22] of August 1805, already mentioned above, JC wrote to his young friend Philip Crocker:

> "...I am once more (and if it be but in charity to my hobby horse, pray say you are glad to hear it)... returned to painting, determined if my eyes hold out to be the English Teniers yet or perish in endeavouring to be so... My

holdfast is this: Reynolds, docile as a child, improved to the last hour of his practice: the same thing so far is acknowledged of me by others and, what is more to be depended on, I know and feel it myself."

JC's eyes must have held out quite well because he was still painting in 1819. Whether he ever used eyeglasses or other visual aids is unknown but this seems probable since many of his paintings are minutely detailed.

In 1808 JC was reporting to his nephew, James Willcocks[23] that he had painted eight "capital pictures" which one Mr Aspinall had agreed to try and sell for him, but after the unknown crisis in his life in 1810 which left him impoverished, painting became an important part of his livelihood. In November of that year he was fairly sanguine[24], "...I have painted 5 pictures for the exhibition here, that opens in a few days: O for a little bit of good luck now." But by 1811 when he was seeking a loan to tide him over the financial crisis he was expressing a desire[25], "...to save my pictures from the hell of auctioneering". Evidently the auctions of the day would have yielded little and he seems to have avoided this fate for he does not mention the possibility again. In fact that seems to have been a low point and gradually his reputation must have grown locally because in October of 1814 he was reporting[26] to James Willcocks that, "The Princess Elizabeth has bought a picture of me, and I have painted a charming companion to it which I think she must have – it will be shown to her next week."

The last letter[27] discovered about JC's painting comes less than two years before his death. On 14th August 1819, writing to his nephew John Willcocks, he said:

> "...I am profoundly busy in painting, to meet the season... I don't much like to bore my friends with any concern of so insignificant a subject as myself, but this blank corner [of the paper] tempts me to add that I am promised considerable female patronage this winter and that, with this powerful auxiliary, as I certainly paint better, I may possibly fare better than I have in times past."

JC and John Constable

One aspect of JC's life as an artist that is widely acknowledged is his role as mentor to the young John Constable (1776-1837). Constable must have found it inspiring that JC had acquired a professional level of skill and knowledge of painting without formal instruction and it would be typical of the older man to be generous with his time in encouraging and imparting knowledge to the younger when they first became acquainted.

Their meeting occurred in August, 1796 when John Constable, who was still not fully committed to the life of an artist, went to stay with his uncle Thomas Allen, a businessman with antiquarian interests, at his country house at Edmonton. Here he met with a group of friends who shared interests in art, old artefacts and old buildings[28]. Among them were JC, and J.T. Smith. JC must have spent some considerable time with Constable and clearly introduced him to the practical side of painting in oils. In fact, three surviving early paintings by Constable are heavily influenced by Cranch's style. They include *The Chymist, The Alchymist* and *Moonlight Landscape with Hadleigh Church* (Fig. 21). Regarding the latter painting, in a letter to J.T. Smith dated 9th November 1796 Constable stated[29] that, "I have lately painted a small moonlight in the manner or style of Cranch." This Suffolk landscape showing the church spire was shown at an exhibition of naturalistic paintings in 1991 of which further mention is made below[30].

Support for JC's lasting influence comes from the editors of one of the published volumes of Constable's correspondence[31] who wrote, "…to estimate the extent of his influence on Constable we have only to compare his rendering of the still life in a painting such as *Playing with Baby* (Fig. 31) with Constable's treatment of the hardware in the *Boat-building* of 1814, or with many of the details in the *Dedham Mill* of 1820 to see some of the fruits of this short-lived acquaintanceship."

In addition to practical help, JC offered advice on literature about the creation of art thus revealing his own wide reading[31]. He recommended to Constable, in a surviving document dated 30th September 1796, a list of twelve books together with other suggestions:

"Painter's Reading, and hint
or two respecting study:

1. Leonardo da Vinci's treaties on painting:

2. De Pile's —ditto— with the lives of the painters, and the fragment by Rubens:

3 Hogarth's analysis of beauty:

4 Du Fresnoy de arte graphica — (Dryden's prose translation and notes:) — if you like it better in rhyme, Mason's version is spirited and elegant, and has the advantage of some notes by Sir Joshua Reynolds :—

5 Webb's essay on the beauties of painting &c:

6 Algarotti on painting:

7 Abbe du Bos's work on the 3 arts—(l think 3 vols 12°)

8 a small tract by the late Chev. Mengs.

9 —there are many useful hints and helps of study, and many ingenious things to facilitate practice in Gerard Lairesse's book on painting—4°.

10 Richardson (the father) on painting and connoirsseurship—

11 Richardson (the son)—" painter's letters from Italy"

12 Reynold's volume of discourses to the Royal Academy: .— But be cautious it does not bias you against Familiar nature, life and manners which constitute as proper and as genuine a department of imitative art as the sublime or the beautiful:

In literary attainments Roderick Random is, in its kind, as pleasing, and (which is of more importance) as necessary, as the Paradise lost: The "Discourses" are a work of unquestionable genius, and of the highest order of literature; but they go, if I may so express it, to establish an aristocracy in painting: they betray, and I believe have betrayed, many students into a contempt of everything but grandeur and Michael Angelo: the force, and the splendid eloquence, with which the precepts are inculcated, makes us forget, that the truth of Teniers, and the wit and moral purposes of Hogarth, have been, and will forever be, at least as useful, and instil at least as much pleasure, as the mere sublimities of Julio and Raphael: In truth, while these Discourses pretend to greater expanse and com-prehension, I know of none that would hamper and confine the faculties— (I was going to say the blessings—) of our art into a narrower or more inaccessible province:

13 — Poetry and history:

14 The works of great masters (whether in the originals, or in good prints) in order to ascertain by what courses of thought, and by what combinations and contrivances, those works were produced:

15 The works of bad painters may be made highly useful, where truths and falsehoods may be ascertained by comparison with good pictures and with Nature:

16 The most general habitudes of men and things; or Nature, as she is more and less perverted by the social institutions:

17 Nature herself, as divested and distinguished from all accident, and from all the preceding considerations:

18 The art of selecting and combining from the whole that which in exhibition, will best satisfy at once the eye, the imagination and the understanding; or that which will come nearest to this cardinal purpose.

30th Sept. 1796.   John Cranch"

We may assume that this and discussions with JC had considerable influence on Constable since his library came later to contain almost all the volumes listed above and he became a devoted reader about art his whole life. In a letter to J.T. Smith of 27th October 1796 Constable mentioned that he was enjoying reading two volumes that JC had recommended, namely, Leonardo da Vinci's *A Treaties on Painting* (translated into English in 1721) and *An Essay on Painting* by Francesco Algarotti (edition published in 1764)[29]. In his subsequent development as an artist Constable also concurred with JC's belief in the virtue of painting from nature and everyday life. As Michael Kitson has put it[30], "By thus subverting Reynold's idea of the hierarchy of *genres* while not denying his intellectual genius and literary powers, Cranch opened the way to Constable's belief in the equality of all genres and hence to his assertion of the dignity of landscape painting." It has to be said that while JC was prepared to be critical of Reynold's *theory* of art, he had the greatest admiration for him as a painter, as he made particularly clear in a pamphlet he published (see below).

The difficulty Constable had in obtaining recognition from the art world (only being elected to the Royal Academy when he was 52) reflects how pervasive the views were which JC criticised in his comments on Joshua Reynold's *Discourses*. JC had entered the London art world, self-taught, at the age of 36 but Constable when the two of them met was entering much the same world as a man of only 20. In his introduction[32] to a book of Constable's correspondence, R.B. Beckett writes:

> "...The struggle for survival in which he had to join, however unwillingly, left him with a feeling of bitter frustration. 'The field of Waterloo is a field of mercy [compared] to ours' he once wrote... when trying to dissuade a young drawing master from seeking to make a name for himself in London. The metaphor is only a slight exaggeration."

This was, in essence, the same field which JC had entered a decade earlier. Constable in correspondence with J.T. Smith clearly retained friendship and a conscious sense of his debt to JC and mentioned him or sent

157

greetings to be passed on to him in eight letters. In the first[29] on 27th October 1796 he said:

> "...I trust your great good nature will excuse my neglect, in so long delaying to thank you, for the information and advice, you so generously bestow'd on me, and of which I now find the benefit; but in the former, I am likewise oblig'd to your worthy father, and Mr Cranch, to both of whom I desire my particular respects with thanks. I should like to know if Mr C. has sold his Picture of the Alchymists; if he has not I think I could for him, I should be very happy in serving him as much as lay in my power."

However, they do not seem to have been closely in touch. On the 2nd December 1796 in a letter[29] from East Bergholt Constable wrote to Smith:

> "...I expected by what you said to have found some proposals but did not; the next time you call on Mr Cranch you was to put some in your pocket and leave them at Mrs Whaley's (my sister's) at No 15 America Square Minories to be sent the first opportunity directed to me. And now I think on it should like to know how to direct to Mr Cranch. I conclude with best respects to Mrs Smith and your Worthy Father; likewise to Mr Gower and Cranch."

If further correspondence took place directly between Constable and JC, none seems to have survived although they clearly remained aware of each other's existence. On 4th February 1799 in a letter to his childhood friend John Dunthorne[29], Constable wrote,

> "...Smith's friend Cranch has left off painting, at least for the present. His whole time and thoughts are occupied in exhibiting an old, rusty, fusty head, with a spike in it, which he declares to be the real embalmed head of Oliver Cromwell! Where he got it I know not; 'tis to be seen in Bond Street, at half a crown admittance."

This episode of Cromwell's head was discussed in Chapter 4 but Constable's remark shows the lack of sympathy a wholly focussed painter had for a polymath like JC for whom painting always vied for attention with other interests.

JC's pamphlet promoting native artistic genius

Being printed by his friends, the Crocker family, in 1811 at a time when JC was in financial difficulty, it seems probable that his pamphlet[33] *Inducements to promote the Fine Arts of Great Britain...* was intended to generate some income for him as well as promote his own views. An advertisement for it placed in the *Morning Post* of 20th February, 1811, shows that it was distributed by Longman, Hurst, Rees, Orme and Brown in London and Meyler and Son in Bath at the price of two shillings and sixpence. A good number of copies survive today so it probably sold well enough to make him some money. We cannot know whether any of its content was especially calculated to attract likely purchasers but the views expressed seem generally to accord with JC's sincerely held opinions about art and other matters.

He first extols the fine arts generally and pictures and sculpture in particular as important civilising influences on society:

> "…Roused, and allured to attention by the forcible images of truth which these pleasing vehicles exhibit, the soul unconsciously receives their lively impressions; those impressions alone become a security against the rankness of error and of vice and… gradually convert the wilderness mind into a wholesome garden in whose soil virtue makes her strongest shoots."

He then appeals for their patronage to extend beyond London:

> "…these elegant and (now) necessary arts, should no longer be confined to a glutted metropolis; but… they should be planted in every apt soil, cherished by every hand, and be extant wherever the means and occasions of exercising them exist."

The example he chooses for the transcendent qualities of art seems surprising to modern eyes for it is depictions of naval and military engagements which:

> "…scarcely suffer us to imagine the existence of such things as color or pencils, they thunder us into silent admiration, sweep the whole vocabulary of connoisseuring cant off the decks and, taking instant and irresistible possession of the heart, bid it to rouse to deeds of glory, melt with humane sentiment or glow with the ardours of determined patriotism!"

Patriotism pervades this document, written at a time when Britain was constantly at war. This was certainly JC's heartfelt feeling since a large part of the text is devoted to countering the prejudice against British art:

> "…there exists among us, an extravagant and unaccountable prejudice – a function (let us venture to call it) in favour of foreign names and foreign productions; aggravated by an affected depreciation, and almost contempt, of our own."

Whilst acknowledging the qualities of Italian art in particular JC praises the foundation of the Royal Academy and extols the qualities of various British artists considering them equal or superior to their foreign counterparts. He particularly praises Reynolds and Hogarth, drawing special attention to the fact that Reynolds had created masterpieces in several genres before he became almost exclusively a portrait painter.

"…Whether, indeed, in our zeal for raising a school of PAINTERS, we have hitherto sufficiently attended to the more important object of selecting and fostering GENIUS, may, in future, be worth some serious consideration; but that we have genius, nothing which has the least resemblance to evidence, or to argument, can controvert. The most sublime efforts of Italy (and, gratefully be it confessed, sublime many of them are) have never, in ratio of excellence, exceeded the sentiment and pathos of REYNOLD'S *Ugolino*, or the grandeur of his *Hercules*. The utmost faculties of even our own engravers, have not been able to transmit the subtle piquancies of his *Allegory of Pleasure*, or of his *Infant Academy* (though but the mere amusements of his pencil) – nor is it possible that the intelligence and varieties of his portraits can have been more than counterbalanced by the justly-boasted colourings of TITIAN. It has been suggested that REYNOLDS was not competent to historical painting. The strongest argument that has been offered for this notion is that he rarely practiced it. But his *Ugolino*, his *Death of Cardinal Beaufort*, and the few other historicals that he did paint, render it much more probable that the true reason was [that] Portrait could not spare him."

JC's general view on the painter's craft is best summed up in the following passage:

"…Correct drawing or rich colouring, or both, no more constitute a good picture, than large dimensions, or splendid frames… while we ack-nowledge the foundation of our attainments to have been first laid in Italy, as Italy had laid hers in the antique, we have had, withal, the merit of avoiding all her ostentations and extravagances, and that, while we have gratefully adopted and improved upon her real and permanent excellence, we have disdained and revolted from those artificial and false effects which, being unknown to Nature, are impossible and absurd in themselves."

As previously mentioned, the career of Constable sums up how right JC was. For a quarter of a century the Royal Academy did not recognise his genius enough to elect him a member while others lacking his spark but 'correct' in their technique and subject matter were allowed to join.

Some modern opinions of John Cranch as painter

Arnold Wilson, formerly director of the Bristol City Art Gallery, wrote an article[34] in the magazine *Country Life* which lists several of JC's paintings in English collections and compares his work to that of George Morland and George Smith but says:

> "...The simple psychological play and expression in Cranch's paintings are very much his own manner, and in this respect his work is highly idiosyncratic. For the general form of rustic *genre*, however, we have an obvious precedent in earlier Dutch paintings with their attention to domestic interior detail. Dutch painting was, of course, especially popular in England, and there would be no lack of opportunity for Cranch to see examples in private collections. His interior scenes are, however, particularly fresh with first-hand observations of country life. The little rack for saw, hammer and chisels, for example, in *Playing with Baby* is a typically alive fragment, and there is no sense of second-hand repetition or the use of studio props in his wealth of detail. One notices, too, the various pieces of cottage furniture or the useful references to trades."

JC received deserved attention in the 1991 exhibition *From Gainsborough to Constable: The emergence of naturalism in British landscape painting 1750-1810*[30]. This concentrated on his influence on the young Constable but also showed one of his own pictures labelled *Peasants Burning Guy Fawkes* of 1793 (Fig. 28) and another *The Carrier's Cart* of 1796 (Fig. 33) as well as Constable's moonlight landscape painted consciously in JC's style, referred to above. In the catalogue's text by Felicity Owen, JC's paintings are described as being, "...as rare as they are attractive." In passing, one might note that Devonshire farmworkers would have not have recognized or accepted the term 'peasant' and in the illustrations section of this volume the painting is given a likelier title. They also wouldn't have been amused by art critics' usual designation of countryfolk as 'rustics', either.

The 2015 catalogue of auctioneer Lowell Libson introducing JC's painting *The Dovecote* (Fig. 23) in 2015 stated:

> "...This charming interior view of a dovecote is by John Cranch, a little known but fascinating painter who is best remembered for his contact with the young John Constable. The lamp-lit interior shows Cranch's interest in Dutch painters, such as Teniers, and his fascination with the activities of rural life. Cranch's naturalism and interest in subjects beyond the normal range of academic history painting had an important early impact on the young John Constable."

In the modern era some 'naïve' painters have achieved astonishing popularity but it would perhaps be overly optimistic to hope that their forebear, JC, will ever get similar attention. Probably, the recognition that an artist without formal training may reveal natural genius and, with his self-devised technique, convey this powerfully to the viewer has possibly been recognised too late for JC to receive the attention he deserves from the art world. Quite possibly a good many of his paintings survive in private collections and yet others will have been destroyed. As an artist, JC lacked flamboyance and he did not have a definite habit in the way he signed his paintings, so failure to recognise his work is always a danger.

References

1. Smith, John Thomas (1845), *A Book for a Rainy Day or Recollections of the Events of the Last Sixty-Six Years*, Richard Bentley, London
2. BPL Ms. Eng. 483 (147)
3. Annals of the Fine Arts for 1819 (1820), vol. 4, Sherwood, Neely and Jones, London.
4. BPL Ms. Eng. 483 (148)
5. *Morning Post and Daily Advertiser*, 26th October 1791 (issue 5774) advertisement
6. *Public Advertiser* 16th May 1792 (issue 10854) advertisement
7. *Morning Herald*, 20th April 1792 (issue 4099) advertisement
8. *The Director* (1807) vol. 2. Printed by William Savage for the proprietors, London, p.125.
9. Auction June 23rd 1807. Property of the Late Rev John Brand, Fellow and Secretary of the Antiquarian Society. Mr Stewart, 194 Piccadilly, London. Original catalogue in Getty Research Institute, Los Angeles.
10. For example, William L. Pressly (2007) *The Artist as Original Genius* p. 168, University of Delaware Press, Newark
11. Quoted in *The Monthly Mirror* (1803), vol. 16, p. 203
12. Auction notice by Mr Dodd of St Martin's Lane, London, April 26th, 1809
13. Catalogue of an Exhibition of Portraits of Departed Worthies Connected with the Counties of Devon and Cornwall on loan to the Royal Albert Memorial Museum, Exeter, July and August 1873. Exhibit 56: pyrographic portrait of Sir Joshua Reynolds
14. Scharf, G. (1874) *Observations on some of the principal portraits of Devonshire worthies* (including some from Cornwall, exhibited during the Archaeological Institute Congress at Exeter, 1873). The Archaeological Journal 31, 3-28
15. Devon Heritage Centre Cat No 49/26/5/17
16. BPL Ms. Eng. 483 (2)
17. Smith, John Thomas (1797), *Remarks on rural scenery : with twenty etchings of cottages, from nature : and some observations and precepts relative to the picturesque,* published by Nathaniel Smith and JT Smith, London, pp. 24-25
18. Gregory, G. (1789), *The Life of Thomas Chatterton, with criticism on his genius and writings, and a concise view of the controversy concerning Rowley's poems.* Printed for G. Kearsley, London.
19. BPL Eng. Ms. 483 (2)

20. BPL Eng. Ms. 483 (422)

21. BPL Eng. Ms. 483 (155-201)

22. BPL Eng. Ms. 483 (147)

23. BPL Eng. Ms. 483 (64-107)

24. BPL Eng. Ms. 483 (64-107)

25. BPL Eng. Ms. 483 (424)

26. BPL Eng. Ms. 483 (64-107)

27. BPL Eng. Ms. 483 (3-14)

28. Cormack, Malcolm (1986), *Constable*, Phaidon, Oxford

29. Beckett, R.B. ed. (1964), *John Constable's Correspondence,* vol. 2 Early Friends and Maria Bicknell (Mrs Constable), pp. 5 -7 and 23, Suffolk Records Society, Ipswich

30. Various authors (1991) *From Gainsborough to Constable, The emergence of naturalism in British landscape painting 1750-1810*, pp. 13 and 42, The Boydell Press, Woodbridge

31. Parris, Leslie *et al.* eds (1975), *John Constable: Further Documents & Correspondence*, pp. 199-202, The Tate Gallery, London and the Suffolk Records Society, Ipswich.

32. Beckett, R.B. ed. (1966), *John Constable's Correspondence, v4 Patrons, Dealers and Fellow Artists*, p. 3, Suffolk Records Society, Ipswich.

33. Cranch, John (1811) *Inducements to promote the Fine Arts of Great Britain by exciting Native Genius to independent Effort and original Designations*, Printed by the Crockers, Frome.

34. Wilson, Arnold (1972) *Eccentric Painter of the Rustic Genre*, Country Life vol. 152 (issue No. 3929) pp. 906-908, IPC Magazines, London.

Chapter 5

Chapter 6

Bath

JC had made visits to Bath from the time when he was a young man living in Axminster and long regarded it as his favourite city. When he left London permanently in about 1810 it must have seemed the obvious place to settle since much of its beautiful architecture and cultured ambience had already developed during the 18th and early 19th centuries. It was quite close to his relatives and acquaintances in the West Country and it was also a much healthier place to live than the capital. Surviving correspondence suggests that his visits became more frequent from 1806 onwards but when he was nearly 60 he made the decisive move to the city and afterwards seems never to have returned to London. Again, it is difficult to piece together a continuous account of his doings but a substantial amount is known about his last years. Specifically, he seems to have lodged most of the time in Walcot, a parish which was originally a separate village to the North East of Bath but had already effectively become a suburb of the city by the time JC lived there. There is plenty of evidence to show that JC was very active during the last decade of his life and his letters contain little indication of ill-health. However, not long after the move to Bath it became apparent that he was in financial difficulty although this may well have been through no fault of his own. He recovered without getting into official trouble over debt and until his death seems to have made a modest living. Despite his evident generosity to others earlier in his life there is no evidence that he ever sought financial help from anyone apart from seeking the return of money he had lent to others. As he wrote himself to his nephew[1], when his finances were at their lowest ebb, "…Be assured, and convinced I have done all in my power [to recover financially], consistently with modesty and that honourable integrity which I never will, nor can violate". There is plenty of evidence to show that he retained his energy, intellectual powers and wide-ranging interests until the end of his life and that these enabled him to support himself financially after the brief crisis in his affairs.

Money matters

Until he left Axminster in 1787 JC never regarded himself as affluent but clearly when he went to London he had a degree of financial independence. As was made clear in earlier chapters, claims made in several other written accounts of JC regarding the source of his funds simply do not add up. However, his own correspondence attributes a definite but unquantifiable role as his 'benefactress' to Eliza Feilder and it also seems likely that some of his activities made money when he lived in London; certainly he is known to have sold some paintings when he was there. It seems unlikely that he left the capital because of a perceived shortage of funds. He was, as far as he knew, free of debt and had made some loans which he expected to be repaid. It also seems clear that when he moved permanently to Bath he had some employment arranged but that this quickly proved untenable owing to a clash of personalities. Possibly, JC had even invested capital in this enterprise and, if so, it must quickly have been lost. Thus, not long after he had settled in the city he ran out of cash.

Although, later, he considered a return to lawyering in the form of conveyancing real estate, the law had evidently moved on and he was no longer qualified and could not practically become so. Thus his money-making depended on his cultural activities. He found a local market for his paintings (and they are still occasionally surfacing in West Country auctions to this day). He also occasionally made some money with his writing, in which regard having the friendship of the Crocker family of printers will have assisted. Finally, he acquired large quantities of Roman artefacts from his surroundings in Bath and, although this was always for his own intellectual interest, he evidently sold some privately, and latterly the bulk of his collection was acquired by Bath Corporation and formed the basis of the first museum of Roman remains there. He seems never to have lacked the few shillings necessary to pay workmen engaged in building work to set aside Roman materials for him.

The greatest resource for discovering JC's financial affairs during his time in Bath is his correspondence with his nephew, James Willcocks. In fact, were it not for JC's excellent relationship with his sister, Mary, who as previously mentioned, had married James Willcocks senior, very little of JC's correspondence would have survived to the present day. Her daughter, also called Mary, was married to a Mr Moginie with whom later both Mary senior and her son John would live in London. It appears to have been the Moginie family which preserved much of the Cranch correspondence which was later acquired by Boston Public Library. JC had known his nephews James and John Willcocks well when he was living in London and assisted in establishing their careers. He had arranged[2] for James Willcocks to attend the charitable Bluecoat School in Frome, Somersetshire, run by his friend Abraham Crocker. It is not fanciful to say that he treated the Willcocks boys like the sons he himself never had.

After JC left London he relied on James to handle ongoing business affairs and the latter wrote from a solicitor's premises in Lincoln's Inn so presumably had found employment in the law of some kind. Surviving correspondence starts with a highly positive letter[3] from JC on 3rd July 1810. Initially everything in Bath was going well for him including business activities but by 11th September of the same year he was complaining[4]

> "… I am, for the present, very much disappointed in my expectations here. Instead of an open, kindly hearted friend, I find a sullen, austere man, that I can make nothing of, but that he appears to be the same to others and so I have but 'neighbour's fare'."

As soon as 10th October he was writing[5],

> "…Thank God, after infinite vexations and anxieties that have almost killed me, I yesterday quitted Mr W. and all his concerns, I trust, for ever. The whole adventure turned out one of the most mortifying, disgusting and distressing that ever occurred to me or (I think) to any man. I am got back to painting, have got a few comforters and well-wishers round me and am far from despairing that I may yet gain a quiet livelihood by innocent and useful labour, which is now the limit of my wishes in this world."

There seems to be no way of knowing exactly what this failed project had been although JC had complained[6] that Mr W. "affects to undervalue the talents [he] perceives to be progressive, is afraid to cherish, and yet cannot do without". It is hard to know which of JC's talents was being undervalued. His painting could be seen as progressive in its day and his support of independent America showed that as an author or editor he might sometimes be controversial. He had obviously continued with business activities to some degree even if he had abandoned formal lawyering. If he had committed money to some joint project with Mr W.

this might explain the financial embarrassments which ensued so soon after.

In May of 1811 commenced the affair of JC's loans to Mr Bowman. Surviving references to their prior association are scant but in 1799, as previously mentioned, a Mr Michael Bowman was alternate executor to JC in Eliza Feilder's will. In 1803 Mary Willcocks had said in a letter to her son that JC and Mr Bowman had been, "Attempting the doors of the East India House", seemingly a reference to an effort to resolve some financial affair of a joint client. Evidently the two had been associates in business and in later correspondence it becomes clear that JC had even lodged in London with Bowman from time to time and loaned him money. In the cheerful letter[2] of 3rd July 1810 JC suggested that James Willcocks apply to Bowman for an account of JC's journey to Bath. His letter of 24th May, 1811 is generally a little more optimistic about his prospects in Bath but he reported having written four times to Bowman about a loan without reply. He was also concerned that James should take over JC's role as agent for a Mrs Dyson for whom JC had acted as attorney in London. However, the perilous state of his finances at that time was revealed when he wrote[7] that he had to move to cheaper accommodation: "…'Tis true I give but a guinea a week for good board and lodging but this, in my present circumstances, is too much for me and must be relinquished". One of JC's letters to Bowman survives[8]. On 1st May 1811 he had written to him:

"Dear Bowman, Having written 3 successive letters to you, each of them (more anxiously than the last) entreating the favour of an answer (for a single line would have obviated the question), I write this to complain, for the first time in my life, that you do not use me kindly – since I certainly have given no cause of offence. All you have to say is that you will or will not, can or cannot, oblige me with a loan of twenty pounds; the uncertainty of your determination on this point is very injurious to me. Had you wrote duly I should instantly have quitted my present board and lodging (of a guinea a week!) and not have ran 4 guineas in debt; and it might also have enabled me to have sold my pictures creditably: for I am not offered a place to work and lodge *gratis* and, as I should then have nothing to provide but bread for myself, and as I am in sufficient good health, almost any labour would have earned me 7 shillings a week, which is con-siderably more than enough to keep me from starving and is therefore all I want. But having hitherto lived creditably in my present lodgings, I cannot creditably quit them until I have paid what I owe, though it is but little. 'Tis true the twenty would enable me to save my pictures from the hell of auctioneering and leave me not only clear of all difficulties, but absolutely independent and without a single anxiety but to pursue labours that eventually must be crowned with success. But I know very well, my friends may not be able to oblige me with so great a sum and my ultimate – only – cause of complaint is that I am not told so at once; that I am not put out of doubt... that I am thus tortured and injured by unaccountable silence and uncertainty. Pray, dear Bowman, forgive these reflexions, especially since they are the last that will ever escape the lips or the pen of your ever obliged, faithful servant, Cranch"

The following month JC's position became clearer[9]. He had come to Bath with expectations of some remunerative occupation but had found only what he described as a "ruinous connection... [a] sad and ever-to-be regretted folly [that] never will or can be renewed". Now he was in financial distress and in consequence itemised to James Willcocks loans he had made in London which he now wished he could call in. He had lent his friend J.T. Smith about £38 but he evidently knew of Smith's financial incontinence and expressed doubt about any result there; ultimately Smith died not leaving a penny, even for his wife[a]. A doctor G., who owed him £34, he was reluctant to press more than he already had because he had been a real friend who he judged to be an honest man who would pay if he could. This left Bowman as his most substantial debtor who he thought owed him more than £100. But to JC's great chagrin Bowman had already failed to pay out to honour a debt incurred originally by JC to his old Axminster acquaintance John Seymour[b], now in America. Bowman had

---

[a] The artist John Constable was less forgiving than JC and in 1832 threatened to take J.T. Smith to court over a loan of £30: "...for one does not like to be lied out of one's money and understanding." See p383 of Becket, R.B. ed. (1966) John Constable's Correspondence Vol. 4, Suffolk Records Society.

[b] John Seymour was born in in 1738 and was an acquaintance of JC in Axminster. He emigrated to America with his family in 1784 in the same ship as William Bond, JC's brother-in-law. Seymour was a master furniture maker, a business in which he was joined by his son Thomas. Initially situated in Maine he moved to Boston in 1793, the year after the Bond family also moved there. Greatly admired as craftsmen, the Seymours were not very successful financially, largely due to factors out of their control such as the embargo on English goods imposed by Thomas Jefferson in 1807-9 which created a local recession in Boston and also the War of 1812. By the time John Seymour was pursuing this debt with JC he was semi-retired and increasingly indigent until finally he entered an almshouse in 1816, the year in which the debt was finally paid. It is not known how the debt arose and may even have dated from JC's days in Axminster. See: Mussey, Robert D. Jr. (2003) *The Furniture Masterworks of John and Thomas Seymour*, The Peabody Essex Museum, Salem

undertaken in writing to assume and discharge this debt and, "if he has suffered that bill to return to America dishonoured, I am ruined and my heart will burst".

It became increasingly clear as time went on that Bowman was bankrupt and ultimately JC only recovered a small fraction of what he was owed. For now JC was so poor[10] that he could not even return to the capital: "Discouraged by my disappointments hitherto in this place, I might endeavour to make up my mind to return to London, as you kindly advise, but even this I cannot now do without twenty pounds – ten pounds to clear my way, and to save some of the best of my pictures from the miserable fate of an *auction* – a measure which, however, must be resorted to, unhappy as it is, if no other occurs within a short time". However, JC attracted solid friendships throughout his life so in the same letter he could write:

> "…Mr. William Ashley, a respectable tradesman, an umbrella maker who keeps an extensive toy shop in this city, has zealously taken me by the hand; has voluntarily advanced me seven pounds for immediate exigencies; encourages me much to persevere in the hope that times will mend. [He] is endeavouring to sell some pictures for me; offers me his little garden house of two small rooms gratis to live and work in [and] wishes me to take possession of it immediately, as my own. In short, is so friendly attached to me that I know not how to relinquish, at once, a place I so much love and two or three friends, who so evidently appear to [have] regard [for] me. It seems [like] tearing up a plant that has just begun to take root."

James Willcocks obviously contacted Bowman with alacrity because three days later, on 5th June, JC was again writing[11] to James to acknowledge the "disaster in H[arley] Street", and express relief that his esteem for Bowman need not be diminished since clearly some *force majeure* had caused it. Bowman had, "for these many years, been friendly, good and kind to me; and I must be a villain if I suffered any construction of inevitable disappointment, to detract from certain and approved merit". He was going to write to America about his inability to settle his debt to Seymour and intended immediately to reduce his own expenditure. On 14th June 1811 a letter gave more details of what Bowman owed him. JC had promissory notes from Bowman dated 1802 and totalling £500. These loans had been made to Bowman so he could support a Mrs James who expected, but had not received, remittances from India – possibly the reason for the reference above to East India House. James Willcocks had extracted a promise from Bowman to repay £30 which JC described as "nothing".

As soon as 19th June, 1811, JC proposed[12] an accounting which blended a generous interpretation of what Bowman owed with realism about what he might recover. With interest, the original £500 should have become £775 but after subtracting monies paid by Bowman to JC on other occasions the total was reduced to £276 and 8 shillings. But now JC was "willing and desirous" to make an allowance of £160 for lodging in Bowman's house plus medicines and medical attendances for which Bowman had refused to take money at the time, which brought the amount owed to £161 and 8 shillings. JC now again raised the idea of getting a licence to practice conveyancing. He had clearly never completely abandoned business which took advantage of his skills acquired as a lawyer but, being in need, he wanted to return to 'bread and butter' legal work.

James Willcocks then went into the Bowman accounts in detail and concluded that the sum actually owed to JC was £75. During the next year instalments totalling £64 made their way to Bath and that was the end of the matter. The Bowman affair showed that JC was trusting in money matters and perhaps a little lackadaisical as long as he felt well-off enough not to worry about every last penny. However, incidental remarks to James revealed much more about his personality. There is plenty of evidence for the validity of his statement[13] that, "the mainspring of my existence – (the power of serving my friends and relieving distress) is for the present broken". For example, his letters reveal that he often sent presents of money to relatives in his younger days. Elsewhere[14] he generally bemoans the state of the world: "in these disastrous times, everything, methinks, is monstrous. Nothing seems at all like what it once was". Was this the common complaint of people as they aged or was the economic state of the country particularly bad? Another passage[15] reads: "…nothing going on here but eclipses, blazing stars and bankruptcies. One rogue here, who appears to have deserved ten hangings for stealing bank notes in breach of his trust at the post office, is (luckily) to be hanged for an incidental forgery."

Apparently the times really were bad, but in thanking his nephew for one letter[16] he says that, "... it assures me of your steady attentions to me at a time when vulgar attachments most commonly fall off – the time of need". In other words as the modern song says, "Nobody knows you when you're down and out". That was never entirely true for JC because a few loyal friends and relatives always stuck by him but his was a rather hand-to-mouth existence for the last ten years of his life. Insofar as external factors affected JC's fortune it can be said that the period between 1807 and 1814 saw trade wars amongst Britain, France and America[17]. Although Britain suffered the least of the three, indirectly these created an unstable economic environment which included an export-led boom from 1808 to 1810 which abruptly ended in the summer of 1810 with commercial failures and merchant bankruptcies. It seems entirely possible that Bowman was caught up in these.

On 16th October 1813 JC wrote[18] to James Willcocks about several business matters and concluded, "...Accept my best thanks for your kindness respecting the legal qualifications for practice; which being impracticable to me, I shall now think no more of". So his idea of conveyancing had come to nothing and indeed that seemed to mark the end of his lawyering days. As the legal profession became more organised during the late 18th century it became the target for taxation and from 1804 both attorneys and conveyancers had to pay an annual licence fee to the government and this was increased again in 1815[19]. Whether JC would have had to pay additional costs to re-establish himself as either attorney or conveyancer is difficult to say but it seems likely that lack of money caused him to abandon the idea.

A sad coda to JC's relationship with his nephew James Willcocks arose when the latter became chronically ill and died young. In his last days James came to Bath where JC sought out lodgings for him and helped to care for him. So many illnesses were untreatable then that it is not clear what ailed James, for multiple symptoms were described in letters as his health declined. A letter[20] of 9th August 1819 from JC indicates that recovery was then still hoped for:

"...The little cottage where I am just removed to has really some advantageous and delightful points and forms so striking a contrast with anything about London and so much more so with 'Cross Street Hatton Garden' [where James was evidently then living] that I already anticipate the pleasing hope of resigning it to you the moment you arrive. In the meantime my good humoured little gossip of a landlady, and I, mean to exert our utmost diligence in rendering it as tenable and convenient as we can. I gave her the short of your story and at once interested her in your favour. 'Tis astonishing, after so long a series (near 10 years) of apparent apathy and insensibility to your poor old uncle's situation, character and merits (pardon the little flash of vanity) to see how many <u>able</u> friends have, all at once, as it were, sprung up round him – seeming to vie with one another in comforting and assisting him. Much of these advantages I shall, of course, now hope to see transferred to <u>you</u>. In one word, then, <u>come away</u>, my dear fellow! And doubt not, that, 'by hook or by crook' – in some place, and by some friendly or lucky instrumentalities or other, we shall be able to get a wholesome quiet place and good milk for you – with (I hope) plenty of good ripe fruit into the bargain."

In the event James declined to displace his uncle and other lodgings were found for him very close to where JC lived, but he steadily declined and on 22nd October 1819 JC wrote[21] to his sister Mary Willcocks to tell her that James had died that morning:

"...from considering that the difficulties and vicissitudes of this wearisome pilgrimage are from your long observation and experience so well known to you, I hope and trust you are prepared to hear that our dear relative, gradually and almost imperceptibly, 'fell asleep in the Lord', at about the hour of nine this morning...He spoke with great effort, yet his mind was strong...This wonderful lamp shone brightly to the end. He was among good and kind friends."

The Crockers

Although mention has been made in previous chapters of the Crocker family, it became especially important to JC when he lived in Bath and thus was close to Frome where the family was based, so it seems appropriate to give a fuller account of this relationship here. From a small amount of JC's surviving correspondence from his Axminster days it is clear that he became acquainted with Abraham Crocker (1742-1821) (Fig. 34) early in life. Both were friends of John Andrews of Modbury in Devonshire whom, as mentioned above, JC had known from childhood. While JC was in Axminster, Abraham was a teacher in nearby Ilminster but he became Master of the charitable Bluecoat School at Frome in 1783 remaining in that position until 1815. However of considerable importance to JC was the fact that the family also became printers and booksellers.

The earliest two letters[22,23] discovered from JC to Abraham date from 1787, the year that JC left Axminster for London, but their chatty, familiar tone and subject-matter of shared interests and acquaintances confirm that they had already known each other for some while. In his letter of 19th April of that year JC has obviously enclosed a drawing made at Abraham's request of some poverty-stricken settlement as mentioned in Chapter 5. He also referred to the death of Edmund Rack in February of that year whom both obviously knew. Rack, as well as being a well-known Quaker was the compiler of comprehensive topographical notes on Somerset[24], later incorporated into a history of that county. Crocker had cooperated with him, being described by Rack as "an able mathematician and surveyor". Much of the subject matter including old churches and Roman antiquities were interests that clearly JC and Crocker had in common[25].

In 1790 JC submitted Abraham's essay *The Art of Making and Managing Cyder* to the American Academy of Arts and Sciences of which JC had recently been made a Fellow and JCs letter[26] to John Adams concerning this was quoted in Chapter 2. Of Abraham's four sons, John, and James seem to have concentrated on the bookselling and printing enterprises while Philip and Edmund, both highly skilled draughtsmen, occupied themselves in creative occupations. Edmund Crocker obviously acquired his father's surveying skills because he created maps for the first Ordnance Survey of Britain and the British Library houses much of his work.

Philip (1779-1841) was employed for his drawing skills as an illustrator for Sir Richard Colt Hoare's *History of Ancient Wiltshire*[27] and evidently impressed Hoare personally since he appointed him steward of his Stourhead estate, a post Crocker held for 30 years. The Hoare family were wealthy bankers who had owned Stourhead since 1717 and progressively turned it into the exquisite estate which survives to this day under the protection of the National Trust. In a letter[28] to his friend Mrs Feilder, JC described 'sublime Stourhead' as one of his favourite haunts. JC must have known Philip since he was a boy but their shared interest in antiquities and their artistic skills seem to have made them especially close later on. For example, in 1799 a note[29] from Philip, then visiting Devonshire, implores JC to take care of his health and get out of London:

"...The centre of the City of London, cannot be a fit place for you at present: the constant breathing of the air of your room which is impregnated with the phlogistic particles of oil, turpentine and varnishes made of bodies more phlogisticated than these are, must be too much for one whose whole soul has been exerting itself for a long time past. Come hither, come hither immediately."

The letter from JC of August 1805 quoted in Chapter 3 showed just how close the two were in its discussion of Philip's disappointment in love. It also bemoaned the fact that JC seemed to have lost touch with Abraham Crocker. This can only have been temporary because evidently when JC was living in Bath he frequently visited Frome. In 1813 he gifted his painting *Penitents* (Fig. 24) to Abraham with its inscription on the back, "Painted at BATH by John Cranch for his friend Abraham Crocker, 1813". In writing[30] to James Willcocks in January 1815 he was able to say:

"...I perceive that my influence in this town and at Frome increases considerably; and if I could serve Mr M[oginie], by any way promoting his trading interests in either neighbourhood, he may freely command me – Dick Willoughby, the top grocer at Frome, whose sister Jem [James] Crocker married, is my intimate acquaintance.

We drank your health at Frome New Year's day – when we <u>all</u> met at Innox hill cottage and 'smoked the calumet of peace'. Phil [Philip Crocker] came from Stourhead on purpose to meet me. Edmund has just now finished another of the statistical maps. Sir Richard Hoare has asserted it to be the best that has yet been produced by the hands of man. I am of the same opinion!"

In June of 1815 Philip Crocker came to Bath to view JC's antiquarian collection bringing news[31] that Hoare meant to call on him to praise his works. In August of the same year, in a letter[32] to James Willcocks, JC said he was expecting a visit from his American nephew William Cranch Bond to be introduced, "on reasons of business as well as friendship" to the Crockers.

The Crocker's printing business was of great importance to JC because the family printed several of his later works. Exactly when this business got under way is moot but the Frome museum website suggests 1783 as a starting date. It was obviously busy by 1797 when apparently books, pamphlets and posters were in production. It is worth noting that Abraham's treatise on cider, mentioned above, when published in England in 1799 was actually printed by R. Cruttwell in Bath although in

December of the same year JC's brother William reported in a letter[33] to JC that he had received a consignment of almanacs from Abraham and would try to sell them. Printers at the time were the nearest thing to the modern publisher and will have developed contacts with booksellers, but presumably the Crockers took some time to develop those. As far as can be discovered, the oldest surviving document written by JC which the Crockers printed was his Elegiac (Fig. 35) of 1805 on the death of Admiral Horatio Nelson at the Battle of Trafalgar which was mentioned in Chapter 4. The next surviving document is JC's pamphlet *Inducements to Promote the Fine Arts in Great Britain...* printed in 1811 and discussed in Chapter 5. However, in terms of JC's life the most important document the Crockers printed for him was probably the pamphlet *A Brief Enquiry Concerning Pen Pits* which was published[34] in 1820 just a year before he died and which is discussed in detail below.

The Antiquary

JC's interests extended widely in the fine arts but his interest in antiquities had priority over all others except painting. As in many other intellectual areas, interest in antiquarianism grew during the 18th and early 19th centuries. The dominant factor in JC's involvement was regret at the loss of old things and his sense that what replaced them was not necessarily better. This informed his need to preserve at least a record of the past and, where possible, the ancient artefacts themselves. Whether cooperating with J.T. Smith in preserving a record of old London buildings, examining ancient Devonshire burial sites before they were quarried for road stone or paying Bath labourers to hand him Roman materials they found when carrying out excavations for building work, these themes were constant for him. In fact, JC's admiring letter[35] about Smith which was published in the *Gentleman's Magazine* could as well have been describing his own motivation to preserve old things:

> "...Without fortune and without assistance, at the age of twenty years he projected his original design of preserving by drawing and engravings every vestige of antiquity that he should find susceptible of it within the metropolis and its environs. In the execution of this project by timely and vigilant attentions, by unwearied application of his talents as a draughtsman and engraver, frequently amidst mortifying refusals and hindrances, and sometimes not without personal danger; in short by the same combination of zeal and ability which actuated Hollar and Vertue, he has rescued from oblivion for posterity a faithful portrait of almost every

antiquity in and about the metropolis that has remained in existence within the last twenty years."

JC's was a very practical approach where theory came after painstaking examination of material remains. This seems an obvious approach to the modern mind but, as with much else in English life of the time, public institutions were dominated by a monied and largely dilettante group of people. The London Society of Antiquaries had been founded in 1707 and granted a royal charter in 1751 but there was never a suggestion that JC would have joined. However, he was elected to membership of the transatlantic equivalent, *The American Antiquarian Society*, on 15th April 1818 and wrote one of his three surviving essays on the Roman remains at Bath for its members as mentioned in Chapter 2. There is no specific record of how his election took place because no relevant correspondence survives. His uncle Richard Cranch had died in 1811 but Richard's son William (JC's first cousin) was a member of the society, elected in 1813. A single record of JC receiving a report of an American archaeological discovery in 1817 exists as was also mentioned in Chapter 2, so it can be inferred that transatlantic correspondence about this shared interest in fact continued until late in JC's life, albeit little record has been found.

It was in Bath that JC made his most memorable antiquarian contribution, but some earlier work is described here to show how JC was a pioneer of what would now be called rescue archaeology. This example was undertaken near Kingsbridge on 21st October 1799 by a party which, as well as JC, included his brother-in-law James Willcocks senior, his nephew James Willcocks junior and his brother William. The numerous prehistoric Devonshire burials marked by barrows were a magnet in the 18th century for labourers, employed to repair roads, because they often contained dressed stone. It is an alarming thought that, as a result, much of Devon's archaeology lies to this day buried deep under its highways. If expeditions such as JC's occasionally discovered burial goods such as pottery or weapons, on this occasion the grave contained only bones and charcoal. However, careful measurements and descriptions of the barrow were recorded by JC. These notes found their way to Abraham Hawkins of Kingsbridge who was gathering material for Polwhele's *History of Devonshire*. Being dissatisfied with the extent to which his material was used, Hawkins decided to publish his own volume about Kingsbridge and Salcombe, as recorded in Chapter 1.

Chapter 6

The Roman ruins of Pompeii and Herculaneum had been known about before JC was born[36] and systematic excavations there started in 1738. Although Britain was known to have been under Roman occupation for four centuries nothing remotely comparable to those domestic remains had been discovered here. For much of the 18th century, interest in Roman Britain mainly concentrated on military aspects of the occupation of which there are indeed notable relics, especially in the north, including the structure known nowadays as *Hadrian's Wall*. Towards the end of the 18th century interest increased in Romano-British domestic architecture and tesselated pavements, in particular, became tourist attractions.

The position of Bath on the Roman network of roads was known for certain and a few Roman buildings had been discovered in the area before JC took up residence. Antiquarian interest there, as in most places, was left to a few enthusiastic locals and initially attracted little attention from the Society of Antiquaries. A history of Bath[37] by John Wood, republished as late as 1765 made almost no mention of the Roman period. Discoveries in 1790 including 70 inscribed stones, a gorgon's head and pieces of the Temple of Minerva were communicated to the Society of Antiquaries and another history of Bath by Richard Warner published in 1801 gave a more thorough account of the city as a Roman centre albeit with the then fashionable bias of bewailing the military destruction of native Britons and their subsequent seduction by Roman luxury. Cobbling together the minimal accounts by Roman authors and the modest archaeological discoveries to date Warner concluded that *Aquae Solis* (i.e. Roman Bath spelt as then was usual) was a place of some significance which had contained numerous baths and temples.

It was against this background of official concentration on the grand sweep of history and monumental architectural remains that JC worked, finding fascination mostly in small items such as pieces of broken pottery and coins. The value of such items in discerning how people lived is now taken for granted and nothing fascinates a modern archaeologist more than an ancient rubbish tip, but the high valuation placed on analysis of domestic life was just beginning at the start of the 19th century. This was just in time for JC during his lifetime to find his work valued and for his collection of artefacts to form the important component of the first museum in Bath dedicated to the Roman period, as already mentioned.

JC wrote three substantial surviving essays concerning his own discoveries and more generally about Roman Bath. The first of these was his account of his presentation to the *Bath Literary and Philosophical Society* which was published in the *Bath and Cheltenham Gazette* on 12th November 1815. In his first paragraph his admiration for Roman civilisation becomes clear. He considered that such remains of pre-Roman Britain as had been discovered at that time confirmed Caesar's assessment of its barbarity whereas the Romans were "magnificent people". If attempts to rehabilitate the ancient Britons were already well underway, JC did not intend to join in. He reveals his own extensive study of literature concerning ancient Bath by saying no writer, "had at all improved upon the old ground and, for want of real matter, even Mr Wood has liberally supplied his ancient department with hypotheses many of which are undoubtedly among the most incoherent that could have infested a sober mind".

JC's kinder assessment was reserved for Mr Warner's *History, Guide and Illustrations*, "which indeed have left nothing in obscurity that learning and intelligence exerted upon the extant evidence could be brought to elucidate". JC goes on to give a very brief account of the circumstances in which his own collection was made in Walcot where he lived. He then summarised his discoveries, the most numerous of which were thousands of fragments of Samian pottery. In Roman times Somersetshire was an important source of metals and it seems likely that pottery from Samos and surrounding parts of Greece would have provided an inbound cargo for ships carrying metal away. No doubt some pottery items were containers for imported commodities such as wine and olive oil but the fact that much was highly decorated and appropriately shaped suggested that utensils were being brought in as well. JC was well aware that he was dealing with broken items which had been discarded and which could only be appreciated by "…something behind the eye…it will suffice that if but *exuviae* and rubbish they are ROMAN". Hundreds of the shards were, "…profusely, yet tastefully enriched with infinite varieties of ornament impressed *relievo*, representing altars, gods, goddesses, genii, heroes, soldiers, nymphs, satyrs, armour, historical and poetic incidents and allusions, lions, horses and other quadrupeds, eagles, ravens, swans and other birds, fishes, tritons and sea monsters, gladiators and combats, hunting of the stag, hare, wild boar etc., etc.".

When JC started his collection his efforts meant nothing to officialdom. How little can be appreciated by one account of his efforts in a short-lived periodical[38] of the time called *Omnium Gatherum*. He was virtually alone in recognising the potential when, one day in 1814, he saw foundations being dug in Bridewell Lane:

"...Mr. CRANCH, of Bath, who has both a taste for, and a competent knowledge of, Roman Antiquities, had observed the commencement of the labourers' operations and conceiving it very likely that they would come to Roman remains, in the progress of their work endeavoured by promises of reward, to secure them from injury, should any be discovered. The workmen promising attention to his request, proceeded in their business. In a short time they had nearly reached the level of the Roman city, and some imperial coins, and Roman bricks, which were turned up, indicated a rich harvest of antiquities below. Unfortunately, however, Mr. CRANCH was obliged to be absent from the spot for a day; and on returning to it on the succeeding one, he had the mortification to find that a Tesselated Pavement, which had been cleared by the workmen while he was away, was, to the extent of two square yards, completely destroyed."

Much more productive was a second intervention by JC in building works recorded[39] in the *Annual Register* which described memorable cultural happenings during 1815:

"...The curiosity of antiquaries has been very much excited by the discovery of many Roman remains, lately turned up by the labourers employed in erecting a malt-house on the premises of Messrs. Sainsbury and Acres, in Walcot-street, Bath. They consist of fragments of Roman British pottery; of various descriptions of differently-coloured glass vessels; of domestic and culinary earthenware utensils; together with several coins; a tintinnabulum, collected together by Mr John Cranch of Queen-street, who with an activity and perseverance highly meritorious, attended the labourers during the progress of their excavations, secured most of the articles worthy [of] preservation; and has since assorted and arranged them with much judgement and discrimination, for the inspection of the curious."

JC would show his collection to friends who were interested, for example, one of them[40] recorded:

"... the Grecian potters had a mode of impressing characters and figures upon their most finished productions at Samos, particularly their *lavatoria, sudatoria*, vases, and other curious pieces of fine Samian ware as we have seen many beautiful specimens so impressed in the large collection of our friend Mr John Cranch of Bath."

The desirability of providing activities for cultured visitors to Bath was eventually officially recognised and the above-mentioned museum of Roman antiquities was started by the Corporation quite soon after JC had made his discoveries. The second detailed description of his Walcot finds was written specifically by JC for the museum and if little credit is given in modern Bath to its pioneer antiquarians, this document titled *Antient Arts*, at least, has been preserved (Fig. 36). In his extensive introductory remarks he again extols Roman civilisation as contrasted with native British culture of the time:

> "...All the authentic Roman historians (and among them, the most consummate general of his time [Julius Caesar]) have recorded the barbarous characteristics of the British islanders, at the period of their subjugation (footnote: See Caesar's commentaries), and every relic of them that has been rescued from oblivion, (footnote: See Cunnington's Wiltshire collections of antient British relics at Heytesbury) confirms the justice of the imputation – an imputation which, therefore, can (at least) never be extenuated by the fashionable folly of contesting it."

The sentimental attachment to the supposed wonders of ancient British civilisation, based on little evidence, continues to the present day. JC probably earned as little affection then for his disavowal of wishful thinking about antique Britain as he would now. The latter part of this account listed eight categories of objects in the collection he had sold to Bath Corporation including architectural remains, pottery, coins and glass. Probably the most historically interesting item which he had discovered in Walcot did not find its way to the museum and this was a substantial fragment of a rare *Tabula Honestæ Missionis* (Fig. 37) which was described[41] in the official publication of the Antiquarian Society, *Archaeologia*, at the time and described in detail in a later volume[42] on Roman Bath titled *Aquae Solis*. It was a copper tablet given to a veteran foreign soldier to reward his loyal service with a grant of Roman citizenship and this Bath example closely resembled two others found at Malpas and Sydenham in England whose inscriptions were complete enough to be identified as decrees of the Emperor Trajan. Both accounts record it as having been in the possession of JC but it had later passed into the hands of other private collectors and was lost sight of.

Before describing JC's third account of Roman Bath it is worth reviewing how life as an antiquary interacted with his day-to-day existence, since relevant correspondence survives. To put this in context, as already described, JC was a relatively poor man throughout his time in Bath. His desire to preserve old artefacts was so strong that he spent money to do so even when he had little. In the absence of any major public support for museums at the time it was often private individuals who preserved antiquities but this often amounted to no more than putting them in cabinets of 'curios' with subsequent loss of provenance, e.g. gold coins would be all put together irrespective of their origins. JC was conscious of this but he had no choice but to sell most of his collection in order to live. An undated letter[43] to his nephew James Willcocks from November 1815 records the newspaper article mentioned above:

> "...A paper of mine, upon Bath antiquities, appeared in the *Bath & Cheltenham Gazette* of Tuesday last... The Editors appeared to be amply pleased both with my work and with the moderation of my charge, which they paid handsomely. I certainly gain confidence and ground, that way; and I hope it may, by and by, be a source of some auxiliary advantage... the excavation in Westgate Street has since enabled me to add considerably to my collection of relics of antient Roman arts, at the expense of about 4s."

A fuller account of finances related to his collection came in a letter[44] to Willcocks dated 14th June 1815:

> "...The collection of Roman antiquities alluded to in my last, has since been so materially enlarged, and has excited so much public curiosity that our Corporation has held a common hall expressly upon the matter of my memorial; and, consequently to their deliberations at that meeting, a committee of 5 or 6 principal members appointed for the purpose, have this day examined and expressed their full approbation both of the collection and the collector and of the project he has submitted to their consideration, of establishing a Museum of the local and vicinal Antiquities of Bath... I think I may now venture to say it has excited, what I wished and meant to excite; something still better than curiosity – an interest in, and a regard for the subject altogether, in the *patres conscripti* and inhabitants of this town in general.

> Unfortunately, Mr Mayor's brother (archdeacon Phillott) dying last night, I fear that the points of etiquette will prevent the report of this committee from being taken into consideration so promptly as could be wished: there does not however seem to be any doubt of the result, viz. that my proposal for the Corporation to take the collection at £40, will be accepted and the money paid down immediately upon the passing the resolution that will of course be formed upon the committee's report. Had the exigence of my circumstances permitted me to pause and look about for a more advantageous market, I can perceive no reason to doubt that I could have found one, and more than one, ...by dividing the collection into handsome

lots, and disposing of them to amateurs by private contracts or by bringing the British Museum into competition with the local interests and honour of the city. However, as these alternatives were impracticable (in the existing circumstances) I shall be satisfied to close on the terms now under consideration and, perhaps, the zeal and liberal spirit I have shewn for the town may upon the whole, lead to consequences equally beneficial in the end.

For the last fortnight, my garret has been a levee room! – to which more honours have found their way than to that of King Theodore of Corsica[c] when he affected regal state at the Poulterer's in St. Martin's lane (something like this, I believe, was the fact; but I have forgot the particulars).

All the antiquaries within hail have sanctioned me cordially except Sir Richard Hoare who sends word by Phil Crocker (who came round by Bath on purpose) that he means to call upon me today or tomorrow, from his campaign in North Wiltshire. I could not find the paragraph alluded to in my last, in time, but now here it is enclosed[d]. It was a useful and perhaps important testimonial at the time but the collection has been, as I said, so materially enriched since and is altogether of a description and character so extraordinary (perhaps unique) that if the Duchess of Portland's celebrated vase was thought not dear at 3000 guineas, this surprising assemblage of domestic reliques of the antient classical ages, though consisting of 500 fragments [compared] to one entire subject could scarcely be thought dearer at 300. I have not time to add more particulars. Perhaps some day a printed pamphlet may be made of it."

The excitement continued and on 20th June 1815 JC could report[45] to James Willcocks that:

"...The town clerk himself came this morning to request me to meet the committee on my Antiquities, at the Guildhall. The Mayor made me sit down by him and, in the most gentlemanly way in the world, communicated the resolution of the Corporation to purchase my collection on the terms I had offered and we all went cordially together to see the architectural remains deposited in Bath Street and to consult on a new arrangement. This no doubt will all be left to me: I am to give in a project upon it tomorrow and you may one day or other hear of a *Bath Museum*."

---

[c] Theodore Neuhoff (1694-1756) was a German adventurer who at the head of Corsican rebels assisted in briefly wresting Corsica from Genoese control and was crowned king. After the Genoese regained control he sought assistance in England to oppose them but was imprisoned for debt in London. On his eventual release he was supported for the rest of his life by Horace Walpole and other friends.

[d] Presumably a published appreciation of his discoveries, which has not been found.

But in his letter[46] of 28th December, 1815 to James Willcocks, JC is expressing desperation for:

> "…something, anything, from Bowman or Smith if only £2 or £3 which would enable me to hold out until either a favourable resolution of the Museum trustees furnished some ground of assurance, or its rejection of the subject altogether enabled me to pursue my alternative course of endeavouring to dispose of the collection, in pound and two pound parcels. The short of the present state of the matter is that there are 500 articles; and that a hundred pounds has been mentioned as the price. Should my proposal to the Brit[ish] Museum be favourably noticed, I may visit London; but there is too much of felicity in such a notion, for so unlucky a fellow as I am to entertain it for a moment. I know, and could demonstrate, that the Trustees will do wrong if they desert me, but that is nothing to the purpose."

Eventually the wheels of local government must have turned because Bath got its museum and JC must presumably have got his money since his Walcot collection was included. The 1819 volume *Walks Through Bath* included[47] the following passage:

> "…Upon leaving the Freemasons' Hall, cross Stall-Street and proceed through the Colonnade in Bath-Street, on the left of which, at the bottom, and near to the Cross Bath, is a neat little building, containing the "BATH ANTIQUITIES." To the lovers of research an hour or two may be fully employed in examining the various relics of ancient times which have been preserved and collected together and deposited in this building, erected at the expense of the Corporation; and which might be said not only to have filled up a vacant niche, but has given a sort of finish to the Colonnade and Cross Bath. It is open at all times of the day to public inspection, the remuneration depending entirely on the liberality of the visitor... Here is also a thin quarto manuscript, written by John Cranch, a native of Bath, respecting the Walcot Collection; which collection, it appears, has been presented by the above person to the Corporation of Bath."

The building which housed the collection is still standing in 2018 although it is no longer a museum.

JC's last account of Roman antiquities in Bath dated 23rd October 1818 was, "Respectfully presented to his brethren, the president and members of the American Antiquarian Society", shortly after his election to that organisation and it described discoveries in and around Bath since 1814. As mentioned in Chapter 2, he created a magnificent frontispiece for his essay, shown as Fig. 11. This depicts an eagle with a broken wing surmounting a damaged shield, no doubt symbolising both the current state of most Roman antiquities found in Bath but also the imperfect knowledge of the pre-Roman and Roman periods to which he had drawn attention in his writings. Again he prefaced his discussion of the actual remains with complimentary remarks about Roman civilisation, as shown by Roman artefacts, in contrast with the barbarity of prior inhabitants and of those who came after. He conceded that during Roman times some Britons may have become skilled artisans in the Roman manner. However, he acknowledged how scant are surviving Roman writings about 'Britannia' and that native British writers up to JC's own time had little factual information to offer. It is clear that JC had read everything available about Bath's history. Here is a sample from his pamphlet to illustrate his widely-informed, opinionated and witty style:

> "...Inigo Jones himself, who first ventured to insinuate classic architecture, did not live long enough to convert the public mind from dullness and deformity, and when the Earl of Bedford would consent to have only a plain, 'barn-like' fabric for Covent Garden church could only promise his lordship (what Covent Garden church undoubtedly proved to be) the handsomest 'barn' in Christendom! Upon the whole, with respect to antient Bath (except some particular disquisition by Governor Pownall and Mr Lysons[e]) the only clear and comprehensive lights we have, are derived from Mr Warner's History, Guide, and Illustrations."

Thomas Pownall (1763-1819) may have been mentioned here by JC as a nod towards his American audience. Pownall was a sometime British governor of Massachusetts who was highly sympathetic to the American revolution and also a noted antiquary. JC goes on to describe the general lack anywhere of texts dealing with pottery such as the extensive finds he had made in Walcot. This area of Bath had been a rich source of Roman remains and JC speculated that its name might be derived from the Latin: "...*Vallis*, a vale and *costa*, a coast or side; and therefore that Vallicosta, signifying the vale side, afterwards orally contracted to Valcost and from thence easily deviating into Walcot". He describes how at the end of May, 1815, assuming excavation had ceased, he presented "a short memorial on the subject to the Corporation of Bath, in consequence of which, all that he

---

[e] Samuel Lysons (1763-1819) was an engraver and antiquary and was Director of the *Society of Antiquaries* from 1798 to 1809. With his brother he created *Magna Britannia, Being a Concise Topographical Account of the Several Counties of Great Britain*, This appeared in in a number of volumes between 1806 and 1822 but the work was cut short by Samuel's death in 1819.

had then collected to the amount of about two thousand articles, was liberally purchased by them and deposited with the preserved remains of the great Temple and with other local and vicinal antique remains, in their room by the hot bath". He indicated that his collecting went on until at least November of 1815 but his text describing his pottery discoveries is similar to that in his *Antient Arts* document but now he himself described the *Tabula Honestæ Missionis* and Lyson's role in its investigation (Fig. 37) as well as indulging in some self-praise:

> "…Having been honoured with the notice of the Society of Antiquaries of London, collectively, as well as by many of the best-informed British antiquaries and amateurs individually (among whom, may be mentioned the historians of antient Wiltshire, and of Bath; the author[48] of *Naenia Brittanica*, and the indefatigable Mr Lysons) the general authenticity and interest of these collections may be presumed to have passed the ordeal of antiquarial investigation. To Mr Lysons, however, the proprietor is further and more particularly indebted, for his having ingeniously connected and obviated a fragment inscription on a brass plate [it is inscribed on both sides, in transverse directions] as a *Tabula honestae missionis*, or certificate of privileges granted to a Roman soldier. It does not appear that more than five or six of these curious relics have yet been discovered in Britain; and Mr Lysons has illustrated them as of the time of the emperor Trajan, by whose name and authority (indeed) most of them are distinguished. It is remarkable that though some few articles of these numerous collections can be referred only to the later and degraded periods of the empire, no one feature of Gothic, Danish, Saxon, Norman, or antient English origin, has been detected among them; and that the original glossy texture and colour of the fragments of Samian, or red coral vessels (which the author of *Naenia Brittanica* observes were 'transported by the Roman government to its colonies, by occasional supplies') are absolutely and unalterably perfect."

An extensive afterword then gives an account of recent further discoveries of British and Roman remains in the area around Bath and discusses the speculation by the Reverend John Skinner of Camerton in Somerset that his settlement may have been the site of Roman *Camulodunum*. JC also mentions the proposal that the town of Colchester was *Camulodunum* which modern archaeological discovery has decisively proved to be correct.

Were early 19th century antiquaries more inclined to unjustified speculation than modern ones? Science always involves hypotheses which may or may not later be supported by facts. The author would contend that JC was always perfectly well aware of the difference between what was proved and what was a provisional guess. His last published antiquarian writing appeared in 1820 not long before his death, as mentioned above, and was certainly speculative but it was intended to offer an alternative theory of the function of the prehistoric *Pen Pits* in Wiltshire (Fig. 38). The guess then current, namely, that they were quarries for quern stones is still quoted in modern times as though it were fact. The British *Ancient Monuments* website in fact calls them 'Pen Pits quern quarries' although positive evidence for this function was absent[49] throughout recorded history.

A later battle over the purpose of Pen Pits between antiquarians occurred in 1878, when members of *Somersetshire Archaeological and Natural History Society*, made a field excursion which included a visit to Pen Pits (Fig. 38) near the village of Penselwood[50]. The site consisted of a very large number of pits spread over several hundred acres. The place had been the focus of antiquarian interest since the beginning of the century when Sir Richard Hoare, owner of nearby Stourhead and creator of *The History of Wiltshire* had investigated the place and offered two alternative theories, namely, that the pits might be quarries or that they might have been intended for human habitation. So it is not surprising that JC, who knew Sir Richard and Stourhead and its steward, Philip Crocker very well, should find the problem of interest. And the dispute in 1878 was identical to the one discussed by JC sixty years before: were the pits stone quarries or the remains of dwellings? One Thomas Kerslake made the case in 1878 that they were the remains of a pre-Roman city while Augustus Henry Lane Fox Pitt-Rivers, the future British Inspector of Ancient Monuments was in favour of the quarry theory. At least the involvement of Pitt-Rivers stopped further encroachments by agriculture on the area of the pits and and some of them survive today.

JC's document itself is prefaced with another grand engraving of an escutcheon, celebrating King Alfred the Great (Fig. 39). It goes on to offer argument that because the pits are round and regular in construction this militates against the quarry theory. However, JC acknowledges the lack of expected detritus of prolonged human occupation. He favours instead the idea that it was a place of sanctuary, briefly occupied by populations of refugees from Scandinavian raiders at the period when King Alfred was fighting for the very existence of Wessex. JC envisaged that the fighting men of Devonshire, Wiltshire and Hampshire brought their families there, preparatory to the military campaign which lead up to Alfred's decisive victory over the Danes at nearby Edington. JC points out that Alfred was no stranger to massive military engineering works and also that the site would have been ideal for such a purpose, being well-drained with a forest protecting it on one side and the River Stour on the other. His thesis is perfectly reasonable but the history of science is littered with instances where one theory is preferred to another based on its adoption by a person with influence like Pitt-Rivers. It is gratifying that JC's thesis can still be purchased in the form of a paper facsimile two centuries after it was written. JC sent notes[51] to his nephew John Willcocks in London during January of 1820 concerning his pamphlet, the first enclosing the list of subscribers who had each undertaken to pay 5 shillings for a copy. On the 18th January he wrote:

> "My dear John, The other side will shew what I've been about for 3 or 4 weeks past. Should Mr Cox, or any old friends in town, be disposed to favour me by subscribing – (every little will help) – I shall be obliged. Only 150 copies are to be printed; and indeed nearly a hundred are already subscribed for, here and hereabout only. Upon the whole, the thing is likely to answer very well. I have wrote to Jack Smith, presuming him to be still stationary as Keeper of the Prints, at the British Museum and have here enclosed the letter; wishing, of all things that, if you could make an opportunity, you would call upon him personally, present my kind remembrances, and enquiries after him and his family. If such an opportunity do not offer, forward it by the twopenny post. I've just been writing to Kingsbridge too (on the same score); haven't heard from thence since I last wrote to you."

> The enclosed subscription paper, when you return it, will, of course, tell me what copies to send to you, if any; and Smith I suppose I shall of course hear from. But be sure tell me how you all are, and how you get on. Your Affectionate uncle, John Cranch"

In another he supplied his text for promoting the work, writing that, "It is a curious topic; but impracticable for me to say more of it here than that I think the subscribers will not be disappointed of amusement and satisfaction."

> "...Pen pits, concerning which, no rational hypothesis has hitherto been formed, are an immensely-extended arrangement of excavated pits, near Stourhead, the celebrated residence and pleasure grounds of Sir Richard Hoare, in Wiltshire; and the jut of my argument is to manifest them to have been the work *of Alfred the Great*, in a sudden and dreadful emergency, when his people and dominions (of the West Saxon

Monarchy) were hard pushed by fire and sword and desolation, by the ferocious Danes."

Finally, at the end of the month he sent John Willcocks twelve copies of the pamphlet, eight of which had been subscribed already and four which he hoped Willcocks or other friends would be able to sell for him. Now, all the original 150 copies had been distributed except for four he kept for himself, but he was having another 30 printed,

> "...so let me know if any of your friends want one. If [J.T.] Smith wants any, he should notify me immediately, though he probably has his own business to attend to."

Sydney Garden

Loosely attached at the end of one copy of JC's pamphlet, *Inducement to promote the fine arts...*, is the manuscript of an amusing poem he wrote entitled, *Wrote at Sydney Garden on reading the notice against defacing the trees, &c.* The document is now held by the Bath Local Studies unit and is quoted here in full. It is another demonstration that, while JC was no prude, he found gross behaviour distasteful.

Sydney Garden was a commercial pleasure ground laid out in Bath between 1792 and 1794 and it still exists today as a municipal park. Modelled originally on the famous Vauxhall Gardens in London it was a popular place of polite entertainment as well as the setting for the less savoury activities alluded to by JC. New attractions were still being added during JC's time in Bath and the venue remained successful commercially until well into the 19th century.

> Loveliest of that imaginary train
> Which poets give to guard the grave and fount;
> Thou, nymph, whose unseen steps,
> Through these fair haunts, in breathless silence fleet;
> I hear thy gentler 'plainings,
> And of more pathetic impress far
> Than yon familiar oracle's –
> I hear; and only execrate the cause.

> Ah, what avails
> That guided by thy hand,
> Here Beauty strikes; and Taste
> With sweet amenity, corrects;
> If yet, with spurs unhack'd,
> And ears that should be cropp'd

Each recreant knight, and barbarous coxcomb rude,
Thy classic bowers, in paltry spite, deform;
Or (worse) with nauseous hints of *cockney* love
(Still grosser evidence of absent wit) pollute.

O decent nymph
Thy chaste, thy own regrets,
Teach me to feel:
And if, in evil hour – myself and thee forgot –
I e'er profane these shades
With ribaldry obscene, or nonsense vile;
Pour on my head Conviction dire,
And torturing Ridicule, and lasting Shame!

May I never more relish, deprav'd in my fancy,
Bath; Beauty or Wit; or the humour of Anstey:
May I never get over the Styx, for my sin;
But, pursued by some pun from the vengeance of Quin,
Be drown'd on the voyage; and Beau Nash pop me in!

    J. Cr.

The last verse alludes to famous Bath characters, all obviously dead by the time JC was writing. Richard (Beau) Nash (1674-1761) was a dandy, gambler and long-term Master of Ceremonies at polite events in Bath. Although he promoted decorous behaviour he was no snob, unlike many visitors to Bath, which may be why JC jocularly anticipated his help for reprobates. Christopher Anstey (1724-1805), another long-term Bath resident, was best known for his gently satirical poem, *The New Bath Guide*, published in 1766. James Quin (1693-1766) was a successful actor and bon vivant who retired to Bath, which he described as, "a fine slope to the grave". His reputation for quips and puns was celebrated in a book, *Quin's Jests*, also published in 1766.

Polwhele

It is fair to assume that when he was in financial difficulties during his time in Bath, JC was forced to sell his copy of the large *History of Devonshire* by Richard Polwhele[52]. This three volume work in a single binding must subsequently have fallen into sympathetic hands because JC's numerous notes and additions still appear to be intact after two centuries (Fig. 40) and the whole book remains in extremely good condition in private ownership. At some point in the not-too-distant past it has been rebound to a high standard in quarter leather. For certain elements of JC's life and work, already mentioned elsewhere in this biography, it is the only source known to the author. The extent of JC's knowledge on a wide variety of subjects is clear from the scope covered by his written remarks. Most comments are related to Polwhele's descriptions of Devonshire which JC probably knew more intimately than the author himself. Both were extremely interested in the etymology of place names and JC frequently disputed Polwhele's theories in this regard.

Richard Polwhele (1760-1838) was a Cornish clergyman who was responsible for creating histories of Cornwall and Devonshire. In Devonshire, educated individuals from a variety of walks of life wrote contributions and communicated them to Polwhele but, although he is today credited with sole authorship, the resulting three volumes are uneven as though to an extent cobbled together from the work of others. Perhaps this failure to achieve uniform style is not surprising since the entire work comprises nearly nine hundred folio pages.

In a letter[53] to his friend John Andrews dated 5th February 1807 JC had announced his intention to purchase a copy of the book and presumably then did so promptly. But when his copy reappeared to view at auction in 2013 it was apparent that JC's extensive annotations and insertions had continued over a considerable period up to 1812. Preparatory to disposing of the book he inscribed the following on an end-paper:

"...Something of an apology may be proper for my having inserted, among the illustrations, some few topics that do not strictly belong to Devonshire. Wherever such occur, the reader is requested to observe that most of these extras were put in, either as having, in some respect or other an affinity to this history (as for instance the views in Cornwall) or occasional comparative illustrations (as for instance Stonehenge, and some druidical or British remains in Berkshire and Surrey). They happened not to be wanted by me for any other purpose; at all events can do no harm, or may easily be removed and excluded in any future, stricter arrangement. John Cranch April 1812"

JC pasted in no fewer than 110 engravings of Devonshire scenes by Samuel Prout (1783-1852). These are accomplished early works by a young Devonshire artist who later became famous for his watercolours of architectural subjects and was appointed as *Painter in Water-Colours in Ordinary* to King George IV in 1829 and afterwards to Queen Victoria. Prout was an outstanding example of the 'native genius' whom JC sought to encourage. JC also attached a sample of cloth stained with the natural dye extracted from the Murex sea snail (Fig. 40) which he obtained at Thurlstone Rocks, near Kingsbridge, in 1799. Its colour, essentially the same as the Tyrian Purple of antiquity, is still vivid more than 200 years later. He inserted it together with a note critical of an erroneous statement by Polwhele that the dye could be extracted from limpets:

> "...I believe and have long understood, that the common limpet does not yield the dye here alluded to – which (by the way also) is not so properly a "purple" as a crimson. The creature that I know does produce it is a small murex which has a brownish-white shell and is less in size than the common winkle. The natural process of this dye is curious. The matter is contained in an exceedingly minute vessel on the back (not of the shell but of the worm itself contained in the shell). It is extracted on a pin's point and, in the form of a whitish-yellow mucus is then wiped off upon a piece of fine clean linen. It gradually becomes green as it dries, and soon after fixes in a bright medium crimson which cannot, at least by any of the ordinary processes, be washed out, and even seems to grow more brilliant than before. It is therefore in the ordinary sense of the expressions, indelible, and permanent."

Unsurprisingly for an artist, natural pigments must have been one of JC's interests because there is also a sample of cuttlefish ink. Also inserted is a drawing of a heavy brass celt sent in 1802 to JC by his brother William who evidently shared JC's antiquarian interests. Another is of an extraordinarily decorated cross found in the roof of Kingsbridge church in 1810 bearing symbols including a bird on a pillar, a heart, a spear, arrows and a ladder – perhaps of masonic significance rather than strictly Christian.

Like John Aubrey before him, JC was wont to add colourful stories about famous people in his biographical notes. For example, his account of Ashburton-born John Dunning (1731-1783), who was Solicitor General and First Baron Ashburton, included the following:

> "...To complete his physical disadvantages, the person of Mr Dunning was uncommonly thick and squab and his head...somewhat broader than it was long. It would, doubtless, have been censurable and even cruel to call such a figure 'ridiculous' if he had not himself not only been wholly unconscious of it, but seriously thought himself a handsome man. Going over to Potsdam to a grand review of his army by Frederick the Great, he is said to have equipped himself as a Prussian hussar and, mounted on a black stallion, to have attracted a most peculiar attention from the royal [individual] and his generals who are said to have 'quizzed him, without mercy'. I had the honour of seeing both the hussar and the horse at Dartmouth, just after their return.

When by dint of indefatigable labour, he had acquired the means of luxury, he is said to have indulged it with peculiar ardour. His retirement at Putney Heath became a temple of solid sensuality and high voluptuousness. Every guest was engaged, not only to a distinct apartment for the night, but with this extraordinary appendage of hospitality – a fine girl was found between every pair of sheets!"

Death and Obituaries

John Cranch died on 24th January 1821 and his end appears to have come quite suddenly as recorded in his obituary in *The Bath Journal* of 29th January 1821, which was already partly quoted in Chapter 1:

"Died Jan. 24, aged 70, Mr John Cranch, many years a resident of this city and native of Kingsbridge, Devonshire, Fellow of the American Society of Arts and Sciences, painter of an unique picture of the Death of Chatterton, author of the Oeconomy of Testaments etc. ...and many years conductor of a London Paper.

Until within a few days of his demise, his usual fortitude and vivacity of manners had not left him, when the great bulwark of his mind went down with his talents in the common convulsions of death. As the fatal hour approached, which he seemed to have a predestination of, his time had been spent in the general arrangement of his collections of antiquities, as if preparatory for a long tour. Mr Cranch in the nobler sentiments of mental ornament was manly and vigorous, although his manners possessed the fascinating innocence of a child. As an artist, many of his paintings are well known in this city, and particularly amongst his friends, by whom they are now held as most valuable trophies to his memory. Mr C. was in great repute as an antiquary of the first abilities, arising from a rich fund of literary information and deep research into ancient and curious history, of which he was an unwearied pursuer. His classical hours were chiefly employed in deciphering ancient records, abstruse passages, and difficult writings; in which few could equal, and none excel him."

If there was any predisposing factor for his demise just then, only the death of his favourite brother, William, the previous October comes to mind as something which might have deeply affected him. However, 70 years would have been regarded at that time as a very good lifespan, particularly as JC had no immediate family to support his old age. The various contemporary obituaries published in Bath papers and elsewhere, even allowing for reluctance to speak ill of the dead, were very kind. As already mentioned, for some facts about his life these are the only source found, for example the *Bath Herald* of 27th January 1821:

"...On Wednesday evening died, Mr John Cranch, a native of Kingsbridge, Devon. In his early days he practised the law; but having a strong predilection for the polite arts, and a comfortable independence, he quitted the former pursuits and settled himself in the Metropolis, where he had an opportunity of indulging himself in the study of painting. His unbounded liberality at length materially injured his circumstances. Mr C. next turned his attention to literature, and at the request of a gentleman, he conducted as the editor, a moral and religious weekly paper; but here not being more successful, he became a resident in this his favourite city, where he has long indulged himself in the researches of the antiquary and contributed in no small degree to the development and collecting of that vestige of Roman remains, in which this place and its vicinity so richly abounds."

As stated elsewhere, no trace of the newspaper which JC edited has been found although it would not be unusual for an editor of the time to operate anonymously or under a pseudonym.

One charming published poetic memorial to JC was pasted into Davidson's manuscript history of Axminster[54]. This is ironic since Davidson's own notes on JC, derived from people who knew him little or not at all, contained some unpleasant fictions. Insofar as they knew anything about JC their narrow minds concentrated on his giving up his practice as a lawyer and then imagined a decay they believed inevitable if someone abandoned such a 'respectable' profession. The poem, written by someone signing himself "H" and with "Devonshire, 8th March 1821" appended, is given here in full:

"TO THE MEMORY OF JOHN CRANCH

Cranch! in thy varying course, through life's long stage,
Truth's path thy thoughts seemed wholly to engage:
Each latent fact by thee with care was sought,
And ancient usage to attention brought.

Though Law awhile employed thy active pow'rs;
Though forced 'mid Folly's feuds to pass thy hours;
Though doomed to wait the call in Dulness' court:
Still Honour always gave thy cause support.

When competence at length allowed thy mind
To quit the school for subtilty designed:
The bounds of deep research thy genius burst,
And Antiquaries ranked thee 'mong the first.

The pen, the pencil; – shade, light, verse or prose:
Whate're thy object, – excellence arose;

Such charms were ever o'er the subject thrown:
The graces fondly claimed thee for their own.

When sixty years and nine thy glass had run,
And seventy had its full career begun:
Death on a sudden sped his dart's dread flight,
And sent thee hence to realms of glorious light.

Gone, honest Cranch – yes, gone. – Thy life now closed
With confidence on virtuous deeds reposed;
And while, succeeding ages glide away,
Remembrance of thy spotless worth shall stay.

A list[55] of just a dozen 'gentlemen' who attended JC's funeral survives although it is impossible to believe that other acquaintances of his were not also present. The chief mourner was JC's nephew John Willcocks and Edmund represented the Crocker family. JC had made a will[56] although his scant possessions would not have required probate. It was written in August 1819 at Nelson Terrace, Walcot, and, as mentioned in Chapter 4, JC left all his possessions to his nephew John Cranch, son of his brother William. It is quoted here in full as being typical of the man in his concern for others:

> "What little property I have being uncertain or of uncertain value, and those views and intentions which, in earlier life and in better times, I have entertained, being, in just measure now frustrated or become impracticable, all that I think I can properly do is to will, and accordingly I do will, as follows. Subject to the due payment of my just debts, if any (for I am not aware of any) I give, devise, and bequeath all I have in the world, to my nephew John Cranch, of Kingsbridge, son of my beloved brother William Cranch, and to the heirs, executors, administrators & assigns of my said nephew for his and their own proper use and benefit and disposal for ever: and I appoint my said nephew John Cranch to be the sole executor of this my will beseeching those many other friends, deservedly dear to me, to whom I am so variously obliged, to believe that the disposition hereby made, is the necessary & inevitable result of a serious consideration of my duty; and considering they will not, on this or any other consideration, infer that I was unmindful of the many & great kindnesses they have done, and wished to have done, in my behalf. John Cranch"

His funeral took place on 30th January 1821 and he was buried in the graveyard of St Swithin's Anglican church in Walcot as recorded in the parish register (Fig. 41), the ceremony being conducted by one Reverend G. Barry. His demise was the subject of an entry in an 1826 volume[57] of biographical sketches of 230 significant British individuals who had died since 1820. This gives an indication of his prominence in his day; a remarkable level of achievement for a man born with scarcely any material advantages in life and who had received negligible formal education. JC in fact epitomised the old phrase "to pull oneself up by one's own bootstraps" or, in his case, by his shoestrings.

References

1. BPL Ms. Eng. 483 (64-107)
2. BPL Ms. Eng. 483 (155-201)
3. BPL Ms. Eng. 483 (64-107)
4. BPL Ms. Eng. 483 (64-107)
5. BPL Ms. Eng. 483 (64-107)
6. BPL Ms. Eng. 483 (64-107)
7. BPL Ms. Eng. 483 (64-107)
8. BPL Ms. Eng. 483 (424)
9. BPL Ms. Eng. 483 (64-107)
10. BPL Ms. Eng. 483 (64-107)
11. BPL Ms. Eng. 483 (64-107)
12. BPL Ms. Eng. 483 (64-107)
13. BPL Ms. Eng. 483 (64-107)
14. BPL Ms. Eng. 483 (64-107)
15. BPL Ms. Eng. 483 (64-107)
16. BPL Ms. Eng. 483 (64-107)
17. O'Rourke, Kevin H. (2007) *War and welfare: Britain, France, and the United States 1807–14*, Oxford Economic Papers 59, pp. i8–i30
18. BPL Ms. Eng. 483 (64-107))
19. Robson, R, (1959) *The Attorney in 18th century England*, Cambridge University Press, Cambridge
20. BPL Ms. Eng. 483 (64-107)
21. BPL Ms. Eng. 483 (3-14)
22. BPL Ms. Eng. 483 (2)
23. BPL Ms. Eng. 483 (2)
24. John Collinson (1791) *The History and Antiquities of the County of Somerset*: Collected From Authentick Records, And An Actual Survey Made By The Late Mr. Edmund Rack. Printed by R. Crutwell, Bath
25. Somerset Archive Catalogue EDMUND RACK'S TOPOGRAPHICAL NOTES ON THE COUNTY OF SOMERSET, 1780-1787. Somerset Heritage Centre.
26. Letterbook of the American Academy of Arts and Sciences
27. Hoare, Sir Richard Colt, *The Ancient History of Wiltshire*, 2 vols published by William Miller (South Wiltshire, 1812) and Lackington, Hughes, Mavor and Jones (North Wiltshire, 1819)
28. BPL Ms. Eng. 483 (15-60)
29. BPL Ms. Eng. 483 (422)

30. BPL Ms. Eng. 483 (64-107

31. BPL Ms. Eng. 483 (64-107)

32. BPL Ms. Eng. 483 (64-107)

33. BPL Ms. Eng. 483 (382)

34. BPL Ms. Eng. 483 (3-14)

35. *The Gentlemans' Magazine and Historical Chronicle for the year 1801*, vol. 90, part 2

36. Sweet, Rosemary (2004), *Antiquaries: The Discovery of the Past in Eighteenth Century Britain*, Hambledon & London, London and New York

37. Warner, Richard (1801), *The History of Bath*. Printed by R. Cruttwell, Bath

38. *The Omnium-gatherum*: or, Bath, Bristol, and Cheltenham literary repository. Edited by R. Warner and R. Cruttwell and published every fortnight. Printed and sold by Richard Crutwell at Bath. Copy in the Bodleian library undated, but inscribed in 1819 as a gift of the authors. The references to JC occur in a 'letter to the editor' by ARCHAEUS in Issue No. 1. dated 20th August 1814, pp. 25-35, Indexed as "Roman Antiquities near Bath"

39. The New Annual Register or General Repository of History, Politics and Literature for the Year 1815 (1816) pp. 61-62. Printed for William Stockdale, Piccadilly, London

40. Lake Williams, J.F. (1820), *An Historical Account of Inventions and Discoveries in those Arts and Sciences which are of Utility or Ornament to Man,* vol. 2, p. 111, published by T. and J. Allman, London

41. *Archaeologia* vol. 18 p. 438. Communication to the Society by Samuel Lysons on 7 December 1815 introducing a facsimile of the inscription of the *Tabula honestæ missionis...* "in the possession of Mr John Cranch".

42. Scarth, H.M. (1864), *Aquæ Solis or Notices of Roman Bath*, pp. 36-37, Simpkin, Marshall & Co, London

43. BPL Ms. Eng. 483 (64-107)

44. BPL Ms. Eng. 483 (64-107)

45. BPL Ms. Eng. 483 (64-107)

46. BPL Ms. Eng. 483 (64-107)

47. Egan, P. (1819) *Walks Through Bath,* pp. 121-123, published by Meyler and Son, Bath

48. Douglas, James (1793), *Nænia Britannica* Or, A Sepulchral History of Great Britain; from the Earliest Period to Its General Conversion to Christianity. Printed by John Nichols, London

49. https://ancientmonuments.uk/102935-pen-pits-quern-quarries-north-of-combe-bottom-zeals#.WzDjJ9JkiUk

50. Rethinking Pitt-Rivers: analysing the activities of a nineteenth-century collector: http://web.prm.ox.ac.uk/rpr/index.php/article-index/12-articles/792-the-dispute-over-pen-pits/

51. BPL Ms. Eng. 483 (3-14)

52. Polwhele, Richard, (1797-1806), *The History of Devonshire*, First Edition in three volumes in a single binding. Printed by Trewman and Son 1797-1806, Exeter. John Cranch's copy with extensive annotations and pasted insertions, currently in private ownership

53. BPL Ms. Eng 483 (149)

54. Printed poem inserted in the manuscript *A History of the Town and Parish of Axminster in the County of Devon* by James Davidson (1832), kept in the Devon Heritage Centre, Exeter
55. BPL Ms. Eng. 483 (151)
56. BPL Ms. Eng. 483 (152)
57. Miller, William (1826), *Biographical sketches of British characters recently deceased:* commencing with the accession of George the Fourth: comprising two hundred and thirty subjects, chronologically arranged from the periods of their death: with a list of their engraved portraits. Henry Colburn, Colnaghi, Son, and Co and J.A. Molteno, London

Key to individuals with the same name in the Index and their relationship to JC.

Index